STUDIES IN
SEVENTEENTH-CENTURY
FRENCH LITERATURE

STUDIES IN
SEVENTEENTH-CENTURY
FRENCH LITERATURE

Presented to Morris Bishop

EDITED BY
JEAN-JACQUES DEMOREST

Anchor Books
Doubleday & Company, Inc.
Garden City, New York

Studies in Seventeenth-Century French Literature was originally published by Cornell University Press. The Anchor edition is published by arrangement with Cornell University Press.

Anchor edition: 1966

On est tout étonné et ravi,
car on s'attendait de voir un auteur,
et on trouve un homme.

To Morris Bishop, *honnête homme* and rare example of the gentleman-scholar, this volume is offered as a most cordial expression of admiration and respect.

Friends, students, and contributors are privileged to honor the sound elegance of his scholarship, to recognize the fruitful devotion that he has always shown to Cornell, and to hail the earnest charm of his demeanor and style.

CONTENTS

CONTENTS

STUDIES IN
SEVENTEENTH-CENTURY
FRENCH LITERATURE

COMMON-SENSE REMARKS
ON THE FRENCH BAROQUE

By Henri Peyre

Nationalism is the chief culprit, or the readiest scapegoat, for many of the evils which befall our century. Yet, even in the study of literature, art, and philosophy, it lingers in the coolest and wisest minds among us. Our predecessors, from Ranke to Fustel de Coulanges and Gustave Lanson, had cherished the lofty ideal of recording and explaining the past "as it actually happened." They magnanimously aimed at fulfilling the ideal of the Latin historian (who had not eschewed bitter partisanship himself in his annals of Roman emperors), writing "sine ira et studio."

Their goal remains a noble one for us, but also an impossible one where literature is concerned; for literature calls every facet of our personality into play: the sensual man, the man of feeling, the man of passion as well as the creature of reason; the religious, the social, the patriotic being in us. We should obstinately strive for the elimination of our prejudices, but not lose all warmth and life thereby. A Frenchman who has long lived and taught in another country and has often insisted upon viewing literature from a comparative point of view owes it to his audience to see his national heritage as others see it and to divest himself from the haughty and narrow approach to French classicism which once was that of Brunetière and of his followers. He can no longer subscribe, without ridiculing himself, to the notion that France's manifest destiny was to impersonate the classical ideal and either to transmit it to other less-favored

nations or to be envied and misunderstood by them. Nevertheless, his resistance to some of the strange interpretations
of French classicism lately offered elsewhere remains invin-
cible. Is it not a scholar's duty to learn from those who differ
from him, to submit humbly to facts, that is, to texts, to question his own traditional assumptions, but not altogether to
obliterate his own personality or that of his country? The notion of a national temper, undefinable as it is, withstands, in
anthropology, sociology, and history, all the attempts to
eliminate it. There is likewise a national temper or style in
literature and in art. The most universal writer, it has often
been remarked, is often also the most national and the most
local. The most helpful critic may well be he who does not
forsake the inside and intimate knowledge which he may,
from his childhood on, have gained of his own literary past.

For thirty or forty years now a number of foreign students
of the French seventeenth century have assailed French cultural isolationism and tried to persuade Parisians that they
once had not remained immune from the baroque; indeed
that they should be proud of having counted baroque artists
and writers among their classical ones, and that Corneille,
Descartes, Pascal, and Racine himself were in fact baroque
in not a few of their features. The words "classical" and
"baroque" have become well nigh interchangeable under the
pen of many critics and historians of Vivaldi, Bach, Poussin,
Mansard, Lenôtre, La Fontaine, La Rochefoucauld. French
scholars, at first bewildered by an onslaught of their baroquist
friends from Spain, Switzerland, Germany, and America,
half reluctantly came to concede that their obstinate pride
in the purity of their classicism might have been too arrogant.
They even concluded that they might rejoice in those trea-
sures brought to them by present-giving Greeks and that
France could now boast of having had the equivalent of an
Elizabethan drama, as Raymond Lebègue contended, of a
metaphysical poetry, as Alan Boase tried to prove to them,
of a baroque style from Montaigne and D'Aubigné to Pascal, of baroque churches and palaces, and even of a baroque
approximation of Michelangelo in Pierre Puget. Critics re-
sorted to the concept of baroque when dealing with the once

sacrosanct French seventeenth century. Several attempts, none of them conspicuously successful yet, were made to draw up an anthology of French baroque poets. But the concessions thus made by the French, chiefly during and just after World War II when their traditional conviction of their cultural uniqueness had been shaken, were in truth half-hearted. Most of them, the present writer included, would seem to agree today that far too much has been made of the French baroque in literature and to wonder how essential or useful that new category is. This is no stubbornness or misplaced cultural nationalism, but plain pedestrian common sense. Common sense is all that the modest clarification here attempted wishes to evince, in a realm where clarity does not often obtain, along with some distrust of prevailing fashions in intellectual matters. Some truth, if Bacon may here be paraphrased, may well emerge more triumphantly from error than from confusion.

All broad terms designating a style, a mood, a period are crudely unsatisfactory, "baroque" neither less nor more than "classical," "romantic," or "symbolist." Yet "baroque" has lately been broadened in several languages to cover everything at a certain age, including the history of that age. Historians are chiefly responsible for such an extensive use of the word: Carl J. Friedrich in *The Age of the Baroque, 1610–1660*,[1] and, to a lesser extent and with less panbaroquist imperialism, Victor Tapié in *Baroque et Classicisme*.[2] They thus claim for the word "baroque" a universality which was never granted to its rivals; for no historian would entitle the history of Europe between 1880 and 1900 "The Age of Symbolism," and few would blandly characterize as "romantic" the era of Napoleon, of George III in England, of Prussia in 1810–1830, of Austria under Metternich, or of Russia under Alexander I. Yet it is highly questionable whether the baroque ever permeated the sensibility, the manners, the ideals, of an age as much as the romantic revolt did.

[1] New York: Harper and Brothers, 1952.
[2] Paris: Plon, 1957.

The French, moreover, find it hard to be reconciled to a style or to a mood which goes by a name which, to them, invincibly suggests queerness, faulty irregularity, imperfection, and indeed a sort of ugliness which does not even imply that Satanic monstrosity which, to Sade and his successors down to the Surrealists, could appear as a novel form of beauty. Faintly they associate with the word the notion of something rugged, lacking in smooth polish, of a wart injuring the harmony of a pearl or of a face, which is supposed to have been implied by the Spanish adjective *barrueco* in the language of the jewelers. Such an association should be broken and perhaps will be some day; but it has not yet been. On the contrary, the words "classical" and "classic" gain prestige from the connection with antiquity, with models worthy of study in the classroom, from the profound respect paid to French moralists and dramatists of the seventeenth century by the unanimous testimony of present-day writers, be they Péguy, Proust, Gide, Valéry, Mauriac; or Anouilh, Aragon, Camus, and Ponge. In other lands a serious writer using the word "classical" must first defend it against the connotations of frigid and academic imitation and of artificiality. So did Heinrich Wölfflin in opening his volume, *Die klassische Kunst*, in 1898, a study of the Italian Renaissance: "The word 'classical' awakens a refrigerating sensation in us." It has taken many a decade for British critics to agree that classical French literature is not a servile literature bowing to a king, to Boileau's rules, or to the Alexandrian imitation of antiquity.

If the term is confusing, so is the chronology; yet extending such a broad and vague adjective or noun to an indeterminate and varying number of years (from thirty to two hundred, when the baroque age in music, for example, is made to cover everything from Monteverdi to Mozart), applying it to the late Renaissance or to postclassical times, even to romanticism, failing to distinguish it with any rigor from Gongorism, Marinism, *préciosité*, metaphysical, rococo, defies reason and prudence. The art historian who drew attention to one such category, style, or mannerism, Walter

Friedländer, rightly warned us in his small and valuable volume, *Mannerism and Anti-Mannerism in Italian Painting*:[3]

> It would be best if all these terms such as Gothic, Renaissance, Mannerism, Baroque, Classicism and so forth, which were apparently willfully promulgated and defined, were only used when they meant something very definite and circumscribed. In any case a period should always be limited to one or two generations, and not used to include completely different trends under a common denominator like "The Art of the Baroque."

It might be granted that a few elements, such as Wölfflin defined in his famous categories in his important work *Kunstgeschichtliche Grundbegriffe* (1915), are to be found in architecture, in sculpture, perhaps in painting, and more doubtfully still in literature in several countries of Europe between 1560 and 1640. But the proportion in which these elements blended with others, modifying them or being absorbed by them, is the determining factor and a very hard one to define. Of the five or six countries concerned, France, next to Britain, is the one which resisted, toned down, or transformed these baroque elements most conspicuously. Why do most of the great talents of a certain era seem to align themselves behind a few common trends, as the classical writers of France did in 1660–1685, the *philosophes* a century later when no writer, among the thousands who attempted it, succeeded in defending religion with any brilliance, or as the romantic rebels did later against a host of unromantic opponents, is a mystery which we cannot pierce. Some historical factors may have contributed to it, such as the development of the middle class and of urban life in France in 1640 and after; but such explanations are, at best, only approximative.

If there is any validity in the hindsight with which modern historians endeavor to discern which way the "wave of the future" beat in the seventeenth century, it appears from their

[3] New York: Columbia University Press, 1957.

recent works that classicism, far from being obsessed with antiquity, was turned toward the science, the philosophy, the civilization, which later triumphed. Professor Tapié, a historian, opposes the crushing of the middle class, of its realism and common sense and curiosity for positive science, which took place in the countries where the baroque flourished (Spain, Portugal, Italy) and where death, saintliness, and mysticism haunted poets and artists, to the bourgeois society which, temporarily vanquished with the Fronde, staged a comeback under Colbert and provided classicism with its public. Cities developed, while a more agrarian civilization lingered in the "baroque" peninsulas. Professor John Nef, in his *Industry and Government in France and England, 1540–1640*,[4] stressed the revolutionary character of the civilization which grew up in the seventeenth century in the countries where the baroque proved the weakest and classicism, in one form or another, the strongest: England, Holland, and France. Professor Pierre Francastel, an art historian who has always tried not to divorce art from the economic, social, and political conditions of the countries where it grew, while offering a few reservations to Nef's thesis, agreed that "in the intellectual realm, the development of classicism appears as the creative and revolutionary fact, turned toward the future, . . . the definition of a new conception of the relations between man and the world," while the baroque, concerned with the relations between man and the divine, seems rather like a belated survival.[5] The most conspicuous triumph of the baroque was indeed to take place in the countries of Europe whose decline began in the seventeenth century and in the Americas where the religious orders carried baroque art and exaggerated it. Elsewhere classicism, rather than baroquism, proved dynamic and aggressive, and ushered in the modern age.

The sixteenth century in Italy opened with gloomy events which spelled the decline of a splendid flowering: the sack

---

[4] Ithaca, N.Y.: Cornell University Press, 1957.
[5] "Civilisation baroque et civilisation classique," *Fourth Conference of the Council of Europe* (Royaumont, The Council, 1956), p. 19.

of Rome in 1527, which struck the Eternal City like an act of celestial wrath, the foundation of the Index two years later with its hunting out of original thought, and the introduction of the Spanish Inquisition in 1543. The Council of Trent followed between 1545 and 1563 and, in Italy at least, baroque art could be viewed as an aftermath of the Counter Reformation, whereas in France three at least of the most representative baroque poets, Agrippa d'Aubigné, Du Bartas, and Jean de Sponde were, on the contrary, Protestants. Pietro da Cortona, Bernini, and Borromini, born respectively in 1596, 1598, and 1599, and perhaps Algardi, born in 1602, could be looked upon as the chief baroque artists. Michelangelo, who died in 1564, has lately been crowned as the master of mannerism: an art of restlessness and of imaginative distortion, stretching the limbs, varying the length of the head, finding a new and strange rhythmical beauty in dissonances and dissymmetry. He and Pontormo, Rosso, Parmigiano, and Caravaggio have thus been ravished from the baroque annexionists.

Whatever the usefulness of such categories may be, the Italian baroque was definitely a development of the Renaissance and corresponded to an age of misfortune in political life and of national humiliation during which individuals sought refuge in ecstatic saintliness or in heroic tension. It was an end rather than a vigorous beginning, and no rich Italian classicism followed it up. Hence the grieved reluctance with which lovers of Italian civilization like Burckhardt or Italians like Croce have viewed the notion of an Italian baroque, when they have not altogether dismissed it, as Croce did.

In Spain, similarly, in painting and in literature, the Golden Age, with whatever baroque or mannerist elements existed in Góngora, Quevedo, El Greco, and Calderón, entered upon its tarnished decline as classicism asserted itself in France, pilfering many a jewel from Lope de Vega, Alarcón or Mateo Alemán. In England, a case could be made (not without much juggling with words) for a good deal of baroquism in late Elizabethan drama; but the insertion of such a concept, alien to English literary history and even to

English art,[6] would hardly clarify matters. In poetry, Crashaw alone, and perhaps Fulke Greville, could be forced under a baroque label. Those whom Dryden first, then Dr. Johnson, termed the "metaphysicals," have little in common with the baroque features defined in Wölfflin's bible of that art, or with the luxuriance, the living disorder, the heroic tension, the unleashing of imagination, praised by the admirers of the baroque in Italy, Spain, and Portugal or in central European architecture. Donne, Cowley, and Marvell are on the contrary noticeable for their wit tempering or interrupting emotion, their learned imagery, their subtlety in arguing, their pursuit of difficulty. T. S. Eliot, in a famous essay on these poets, contended that they had shrewdly understood the need for poetry to be difficult at the dawn of a complex modern age of questioning and of universal doubt, just as our modern poets must. "The poet must become more and more comprehensive, more allusive, more indirect in order to force, to dislocate if necessary, language into his meaning." If baroque stands for fluid and dynamic emotion against the control of too conscious an intellect, as Eugenio d'Ors and those who subscribe to his fanciful paradoxes like to maintain, English metaphysical poetry was, if anything, antibaroque. So would appear to be Maurice Scève, whom his recent admirers have wished to magnify into a French metaphysical. Little is gained from transposing such categories from one literature into another: Scève has a few, but only a few, elements of a major poet and can only lose, as Jean de Sponde does, when read from beginning to end or when compared to such masterpieces as Donne's first "Anniversary," his "Ecstasy," his "Relique" or Marvell's "To his coy Mistress."[7]

[6] Inigo Jones alone lived during what was, in other countries, the baroque age (1573–1662). Christopher Wren and Vanbrugh, who was thirty-two years younger than Wren, worked late in the seventeenth and early in the eighteenth centuries; they died in 1723 and 1726.

[7] Professor Alan Boase first proposed the name of "French metaphysicals" for Scève and other poets of the Renaissance. He, more recently and prudently, clarified his views in "Poètes anglais et français de l'époque baroque," *Revue des sciences humaines*

Such a brief survey of other countries is not sketched here
in order to strengthen the French in their conviction of their
uniqueness, but because the history of culture can only gain
in seizing the originality of each country and in differentiating the cultures it observes, instead of imposing upon them
the conformity of *passe partout* categories. A few features characterize the baroque attempts and achievement in
France: (a) French baroque, or what may tentatively go
by that name, came, not after a classical age and as a decline
from it, as Henri Focillon had appeared to surmise in a passage from *La Vie des formes* of which far too much, we believe, has been made, but before classicism. (b) It did not
have behind it such a superb and luxuriant flowering as the
Renaissance had enjoyed in Italy: the French Renaissance
was less sure of itself, less lasting, more foreign especially in
painting (Da Vinci, Clouet, Rosso, Primaticcio), more permeated with medieval elements (Gothic, flamboyant, the art
of the Grands Rhétoriqueurs, medieval scholasticism as Gil-
son showed, medieval *fabliaux* and tales, and so forth). But
that French Renaissance, incomparably less creative than the
Italian one, was less of a twilight and more of a glorious
dawn. It already foreshadowed classicism. (c) The reign of
Louis XIII, under which the greatest of the *irréguliers* (or
grotesques or "attardés et égarés," in Lanson's involuntarily
amusing phrase), Théophile, Saint-Amant, and Tristan L'Hermite wrote, was an age of turbulence, of disorderly vitality,
individualism, and heroic tension. But forces working for
order, unity, restraint, for the curbing of bellicose and an-
archistic tensions and the acceptance of the rule of Richelieu,
were equally active and they ultimately triumphed. They
already had asserted themselves under Henry IV, when La
Ceppède, Chastenet, Du Perron, Bertaut, D'Aubigné, Sponde,
and other French baroque poets wrote. (d) France thus
and then seemed to sense that just as much, if not more,
vitality and constructive energy were required to agree as

(Lille), LV–LVI (July–Dec., 1949), 155–184. Odette de
Mourgues has precise and very helpful chapters on this and allied
subjects in her book *Metaphysical, Baroque and Précieux Poetry*
(Oxford: Clarendon Press, 1953).

to disagree, to strive for political security and unity as to give free rein to the individual seeking his own private salvation. Besides, if such a generalization may be ventured, there was, during the religious wars, and there has remained ever since, a strain of Protestantism (later, of Jansenism) in the French character. The eldest daughter of the Church took much from those very Huguenots whom it defeated. There is an earnest moral concern in French humanists, even later in the French eroticists of the eighteenth century, which sets them apart from the Italian humanists. The austerity which is present in Romanesque art and in present-day existentialism, the fervor for the portrayal of inner life and for economy of means which marks the Avignon *Pietà* and the paintings of Jean Fouquet reasserted themselves in the seventeenth century with La Tour, Philippe de Champaigne, the Corneille who evolved from *L'Illusion comique* toward *Polyeucte*, the moralists, Molière himself. Two noble words, which often and involuntarily occur under the pen of a French writer, *lucidité* and *pudeur* symbolize the French distaste for the baroque. Théophile entertained the contemporaries of Louis XIII, and so did many of the satirical and jocular libertine poets, Saint-Amant brilliantly weaving his variations on the melon and Tristan in his charmingly voluptuous *Promenoir des deux amants*. But a deep-seated diffidence of the art which aims at surprising and at dazzling its audience by luxuriance and virtuosity regularly asserts itself in France. The charge of rhetoric usurping the place of poetry, often flung against the French, has always appeared to us an unjust cliché. It is the rhetoric, probably inseparable from the exalted and unrestrained tension, of D'Aubigné, Du Bartas, and even of those other occasionally baroque poets, Corneille and Victor Hugo, which has long kept French critics from recognizing their originality. English critics have not objected so strongly to the enormous and sumptuous rhetoric of Marlowe, Shakespeare, or Milton.

Wölfflin's categories, once regarded as valid for art, cannot without artificiality be transposed to fit literature; even in art criticism they have been superseded today. Many of us entertain grave doubts as to the validity of a purely stylistical study of art or of literature. Is style more than a solution given by the artist to immediate and technical problems? Does it embody, or translate, a vision of the world? Our own answer is unambiguously "no." Wölfflin himself most wisely shunned all ambitious generalizations on form, which have since proliferated in art criticism and invested form with a magical prestige. His penetrating remarks on the linear versus the pictorial, a closed form versus an open form, absolute or relative clearness of objects presented, stable versus unstable balance, when applied to dramatists and prose writers of the classical age seem to us to become groundless. "Bleiben Sie einfach," Burckhardt warned Wölfflin after reading his very first book, *Renaissance und Barock*. Wölfflin did retain a simplicity and a freedom from hazardous sophistry which his ill-advised successors who carried his views into literature have too often lightheartedly relinquished.

A more fruitful approach would seem to lie in a humble examination of the texts, inspired by a previous hypothesis and looking for baroque elements in French literature,[8] but observing also all that restricts, qualifies, and modifies French baroque and heralds classicism. Professor Imbrie Buffum has done so in his volume, *Studies in the Baroque from Montaigne to Rotrou*.[9] So have several distinguished Swiss scholars, the most recent and the most original being Jean Rousset, in *La Littérature de l'âge baroque en France: Circé et le Paon*[10] and in his essay in Volume II of the *Encyclopédie de la Pléiade*.

The awareness of duration is one of the features stressed by Jean Rousset, and the joyful acceptance of change, the amused contemplation of clouds, fountains, waves, and bubbles. Water would thus be the favorite element of baroque artists, as, for different and very flimsy reasons, the horse is proclaimed a baroque animal. Once such a principle has been laid down, not Jean Rousset himself but some of his fanatical

[8] For Wölfflin well says in his great work: "Men have always seen things as they wanted to see them."
[9] New Haven, Conn.: Yale University Press, 1957.
[10] Paris: Corti, 1954.

and distorting followers sit watching for a horse to appear
in a French tragedy, for water to be mentioned by Racine
(harbors, seas, sails, are among the key motives in *Mithridate*
and *Phèdre*) and exclaim: "Here is the baroque!" But
Montaigne, and Ronsard, and Virgil, and Heraclitus before
them had been aware of change as being the essence of life
and a source of mournful regret, as Bergson and Proust later
will be. The classical writers knew that the world outside and
their own feelings were in an incessantly fluid state, but they
thought that art and philosophy had as a function the ar-
resting of that flux, the investing of appearances with the
hidden solidity which their shifting play half conceals, the
search for the One behind the Many which "change and
pass."

Changing is living, and it means also creeping gradually
toward death. The theme of death, which Huizinga saw as
omnipresent during the waning of the Middle Ages, was
far from absent in Republican and Imperial Rome. It pervades Ronsard's and Shakespeare's poetry, Montaigne's thinking, and seventeenth-century French poetry and tragedy,
naturally enough, and Pascal, and Bossuet. What a splendid
case could be made for Bossuet as a "baroque" writer, if only
our contemporaries would return to the reading of that complex and immense writer! Again, in France, the classical
writers inherited the theme, or the commonplace, of death
from the "baroque" poets of 1580–1620, but they easily
eclipsed them through greater intensity and more poignancy:
the treatment of the theme in several of La Fontaine's *Fables*, in Pascal, and later in the great sacred orators, in Mme
de Sévigné and in Saint-Simon, related to attitudes to death
in the careers of Rancé and other great converts who, like
Saint Paul, felt its sting and bowed to its victory, might well
repay a study. The fascination with death and the revulsion
from it leading to creation were not the monopoly of the
baroque age—or of modern "baroques" like Rilke and
Malraux.

One of the baroque features is taken to be the contrast
between appearance and reality, lying or posturing under
diverse masks and the inner sincerity of the tormented self,

becoming and forgetting oneself in the roles played during ballets and ceremonies but, on the other hand, being or facing one's own naked inner self once the transient intoxication with the masked ball is over. Baroque or not, the perception of that contrast between ostentatiousness and simplicity, the social and the inner self, forced itself upon the early seventeenth century, after the joyful attempt of the Renaissance to launch men to the conquest of the world outside. It is one of the themes of *Hamlet* as it is one of *Don Quixote;* Montaigne had already pondered over it and perhaps impressed the poetical reflections of Prospero on "the baseless fabric of this vision." A new philosophy had put all in doubt for Donne, but also for the contemporaries of Charron and Descartes and Galileo. But while the baroque authors whom Jean Rousset quotes were content with expressing their baffled bewilderment ("Je parais en effet ce que je ne suis pas," says D'Ouville), while there was superficial delight in the *trompe l'oeil* of façades, of court ballets, of operas with naïvely intricate machinery, of portrayals of liars by Alarcón and Tirso de Molina, imitated by Corneille and Molière, the French classical writers soon asserted their own vocation. That vocation was one of striving for sincerity and of lifting all the social masks, of denouncing *divertissement,* and of exploring the inner individual in his aloneness, severed from the social pastimes of the *Ile enchantée,* of Vau le Vicomte, or of Versailles. *Dom Juan, Tartuffe, Le Misanthrope,* La Rochefoucauld's *Maximes,* La Fontaine's *Fables,* Pascal's and Bossuet's most vehement passages—all denounce ostentation and hypocrisy, the acceptation of appearances, and bring man back to his own essential truth.

Common sense about the baroque, did our title ambitiously promise? One is soberly reminded of the doggerel about the master of Balliol College humming to himself: "What I know is knowledge; what I know not, is not knowledge." Is common sense what a Frenchman considers that he eminently possesses and, with munificence, extends to others as *la chose du monde la mieux partagée?* Let him however summarize his uninspired and moderate views, rejoicing that they do not differ much from what he considers as the most balanced treatments of the subject done outside France—by Marcel Raymond,[11] Vaclev Cerny,[12] and Franco Simone.[13]

The partisans of the baroque have flattered French literature, which their predecessors long considered as frigid and academic, by extending to it the title of "baroque," which, for them, implies fluid vitality, aggressive vigor, motion and tension, the exuberance of youth. We are grateful to them. They have reinforced the trend of French students of classicism who, very remote from Brunetière's and Faguet's exclusivism, have insisted on the unruly mettle, on the experimental and rebellious features of their writers of 1600–1650. Instead of envisaging all that preceded 1660 as a preparation for French classicism, good only to be immolated to the Great Age, we now relish Théophile, Racan, Maynard, Tristan L'Hermite, in their own right as original poets. We encourage our successors to devote monographs to *L'Astrée* or to *Clélie*, novels of genuine psychological depth, to Corneille's early comedies, or to Rotrou.

The baroquists have done us an even greater service by bringing attention to the poetry of the "years of transition," 1580–1620, which had been ridiculously neglected. Their zeal of neophytes has endowed them with the courage required to read and reread D'Aubigné, La Ceppède, Jean de Sponde, and a number of other poets who, we fear, will disappoint later less enthusiastic students who might attempt to peruse them otherwise than in anthologies. But the domain of the French literary "usable past" has, thanks to the baroque, been vastly enlarged.

Finally, they have forced the French, always prone to some isolationism in the study of their literature and convinced that, like the lion in the fable, they do a signal honor

[11] "Du baroquisme et de la littérature en France aux XVIe et XVIIe siècles," in *La Profondeur et le rythme* (Paris: Arthaud, n.d.).

[12] "Le Baroque et la littérature française," *Critique*, CIX and CX (June and July, 1956).

[13] "Per la definizione di un barocco francese," *Rivista di letteratura moderne*, XVII (July–Sept., 1954).

to the foreign lambs which they devour, to reread the French works of 1580–1650 in the light of European movements, replacing them in supranational trends and also in the light of the fine arts.

It may be readily agreed that many of the features defined by modern aestheticians as baroque were noticeable in France also, and that they have much charm even there: in the poetry of the night and of the darker recesses of the soul, in the playful fantasy of many a drama and novel. The fact nevertheless remains that almost all the examples of baroque imagery and baroque conceit ingeniously collected by Jean Rousset had to come from very minor and deservedly obscure authors, and that very few of these images seem to have been endowed with the evocative power of Donne's or Marvell's imagery, or of Baudelaire's, or even of Cowley's. The relationship which they suggest between two apparently remote objects seldom strikes as true, convincing, and inevitable. When baroque features are, not without straining the terms, discovered in some of the *Pensées* or in *Mithridate* (declared baroque by Gerhard Rohlfs in *Archiv für das Studium der neueren Sprachen*, vol. LVI, 1936, because it is marked with the elaborate majesty of the court of the Sun King), they are very few and far between, as they are in Georges de la Tour or in Poussin. "My natural inclination," wrote the latter, "forces me to seek well-ordered objects, to flee confusion, which is as contrary and hostile to me as light is to darkness." Everything always coexists, and forces of the past, through a time lag frequent in the history of culture, persisted through 1660–1685, while trends pointing toward the future and to the disruption of the classical order were also appearing (libertine poets, Furetière's *Roman bourgeois*, 1666, *Letters from a Portuguese Nun*, 1669). But the French classical era was one of toning down the baroque elements inherited from the earlier decades (the process of *klassische Dämpfung* felicitously defined by Leo Spitzer). Effects of surprise and of shock were eschewed. Exuberance was restrained. Saturation was avoided. The potentiality of motion was suggested, rather than its rendering through tension directed to several poles. Curves and

spirals were controlled. The world within, with its deeper
turmoil of passions vainly fought by reason, was preferred to
the world without. French classicism, in painting and especially in literature, was *un baroque dompté* and great because it tamed but never totally stifled a latent and aggressive chaos. Its equilibrium was ever frail and endangered by
an influx of life, but it was achieved for twenty or twenty-five
golden years.

Even more rash challenges to common sense have sprung
from some baroquist imperialists. Some have claimed that the
French were baroque, not only throughout their classical age
and, later, through the rococo period, but most conspicuously
during their romanticism. Indeed, if baroque elements in style
or in sensibility are first posited in an abstract definition,
they can subsequently be discerned in Victor Hugo's dramas
and in Balzac's novels. But so can they be in Zola, and even
more glaringly in Proust. A whole string of dissertations on
these writers, and many others (Claudel especially and
Bernanos) as "baroque" may some day be undertaken, in
defiance of all sane method. The able anonymous critic who
reviewed Jean Rousset's book at length in the *Times Literary
Supplement* of February 12, 1954, submitted that the
crowning achievement of French baroque might be seen in
Baudelaire's "A une Madone" (and indeed elsewhere in the
imagery of *Les Fleurs du Mal*) or in Jules Laforgue, or even
in Impressionist painting. Impressionism and symbolism
would thus be viewed as completing, two centuries and a
half late, the broadening of French sensibility which had
been attempted only half successfully by the baroque era of
1600–1640. We refuse to take such speculations too seriously. A passionate search for sincerity, rather than delight
in ostentatiousness and in the wearing of masks, characterized
French romanticism.

Implicit behind the claims of those scholars who have attempted to see in the baroque a constant, periodically recur-
ring in art and literature (now foreshadowing a classical
synthesis, now inheriting its legacy), is the assumption that
a certain view of the world and a certain philosophy inform
all the manifestations of a given age. We believe no assump-

tion to be more gratuitous. It was responsible for seeing Cartesianism as everywhere present behind Corneille, Poussin, Boileau, Lully, and Racine; Bergsonism as mysteriously inspiring Mallarmé, Debussy, Rodin, Cézanne, Ravel, Proust, Claudel, nay, Valéry himself. It is comforting for the rational mind to imagine that there is a unity behind all the cultural manifestations of an age, but no contemporary has ever been aware of such a unity or of such an omnipresent philosophy. On the contrary, all contemporaries have always complained of the confusion and the chaos prevailing around them. A questionnaire addressed to the thousand best minds now active in five countries, asking them what the prevailing *Zeitgeist* is around them (baroque, neoclassical, neoromantic, surrealist, existentialist, atomistic, eroticist, and so forth) would surely provide only one kind of near unanimity, as it would have at any time in the past: the unanimous lament that all today is transition, chaos, decadence, and that all unity, all common spirit making for a coherent culture and for a style, is irretrievably lost. Do we not, we, posterity, forgetting contradictions and that everything always coexisted, comfortably pin a label upon a past era, attribute to it a *Zeitgeist*, once the dead no longer can protest against our pigeonholing their remains into some conformity?

All the arts do not flower equally in the same era. There was hardly any music in Italy in the late fifteenth century, in the Low Countries in the seventeenth, while painting reached its zenith. Through a surprising coincidence, many of the brightest stars of the baroque firmament in music, Vivaldi, Telemann, Rameau, Durante, Handel, J. S. Bach, and D. Scarlatti, were born between 1680 and 1685, at a time when the baroque in the other arts had long spent its force. Was the spirit of their age favorable to baroque trends in music alone, while the other arts were going through a neoclassical or a rococo phase?[14] The concept of a unitary and mysterious *Zeitgeist* would hardly stand a close scrutiny, if one submitted it to it. The smaller talents of an age, those in fact whom the notion of the baroque in France fits most

[14] The best book on baroque music is by Suzanne Clercx, *Le Baroque et la musique: Essai d'esthétique musicale* (Brussels: Librairie Encyclopédique, 1948).

aptly, might be brought into it; but not the truly great ones
who, then as always hardly recognized by their contemporaries, stood against the spirit of the age and bequeathed to
posterity the criteria by which their age was ultimately to
be appraised. Most artists express their era and their en-
vironment only by resisting them and thus transcending their
Zeitgeist, "looking before and after and pining for what is
not," substituting a different world for the actual one which
oppresses them.

In our view, the net positive result of many elaborate and
conscientious efforts to detect the baroque elements in the
French writers traditionally called "classical," and presumably still to be called "classical" in the future, has proved
disproportionate to the labor sustained. The most commenda-
ble of such studies recently published is Philip Butler's three-
hundred-page monograph on *Classicisme et baroque dans
l'oeuvre de Racine;*[15] it underlines survivals of what may be
termed baroque sensibility in Andromaque's or in Bérénice's
evocations of nights of terror or of pomp, in Nero's celebrated
narrative of the poetical night in which Junie struck his sadis-
tic fancy, in *Mithridate's* decorum. It stresses, as many admirers of classicism had done, all that is Machiavellian in
Racine's political figures and the fundamental irrationalism
of his tragedy—indeed, of all tragedy. It does so with guarded
attention to nuances, and Racine's classicism remains intact
after that scrutiny, but felt as more alive than Anglo-Saxon
or Swiss commentators used to acknowledge. Our appreciation of French classicism, and our belief that it continues to
deserve that appellation to which praise is attached, emerge
victoriously from the challenge and the wild assertions of the
more extreme baroquists. A certain naturalness, which covers
and tones down passion, excess, exaltation of feelings, and
even impulses of the senses, is probably the rarest and the
greatest of all virtues to be attained by literature and art.
More than anyone else in their century, more than any
Frenchmen before or since, the French classicists of 1660–
1685 achieved that conquest of *le naturel*.

[15] Paris: Nizet, 1959.

MALHERBE
AND HIS INFLUENCE

By Philip A. Wadsworth

The problem of Malherbe—which literary historians have never really faced—is one of influence. His worth as a poet cannot be placed very high. He composed about 125 poems and fragments, enough to fill one volume, and would himself have acknowledged no more than sixty of them as worthy of being preserved. Today he is remembered for a half-dozen odes and a few shorter pieces, and in these above all for certain isolated, resounding stanzas and magically perfect lines. Seldom if ever has such an unproductive artist, who in fact cherished his own sterility, done so much to nurture the generations that followed him. Boileau's famous tribute, *Enfin Malherbe vint . . .*, which astounds us today, did not even have the merit of originality. The idea had been clearly formulated before in a letter by Guez de Balzac, and Boileau could have found a similar opinion among many of his own contemporaries. By 1674, the time of *L'Art poétique*, the Pléiade had been generally forgotten, or was looked upon with distaste, and Malherbe was heralded as the creator of French poetry. But what gave him this reputation among classical writers and what was the nature of his influence upon them?

Everyone knows how Malherbe went about his mission of taming the Muses: his tardy arrival in Paris at the age of fifty, his labors as a writer of official verse for the royal family, his cruel commentary on the works of Desportes, his daily lessons for Racan, Maynard, and a few other disciples.

At the turn of the century the emotional vehemence and the erudition of the Pléiade were already yielding ground to a kind of poetry which was more impersonal, more intellectual, and more careful in workmanship. Bertaut and Montchrétien showed this spirit as they corrected their works for new editions. Malherbe seized upon the trend, identified it with himself, forced it to greater extremes, and preached it arrogantly and dogmatically. He was part of the rationalistic current of *l'épuration de la langue* which is everywhere visible in the early seventeenth century—in the salons, in the Academy, in the work of critics and grammarians. Although he stands in the foreground, he fills only part of the picture, a fact which makes his importance very hard to assess. He undoubtedly contributed to the development of classical ideals in France, but, in some other form perhaps, they would have come into existence without him.

The problem of Malherbe's influence will not be solved in these few pages, but I hope to clarify its terms and point to future scholarship which can bring us closer to the truth. Even this modest goal would be very hard to attain were it not for the recent burgeoning of research on Malherbe, particularly on the occasion of the four hundredth anniversary of his birth in 1955.[1] The pioneer study of Malherbe's doctrine by Brunot[2] has at long last been followed by a revival of interest in the poetic reforms of the early seventeenth century—notably on the part of Professors Fromilhague and

[1] See the small but very valuable book by Mrs. Renée Winegarten, *French Poetry in the Age of Malherbe* (Manchester: Manchester University Press, 1954), and the two important theses by Professor René Fromilhague (Paris: Colin, 1954). One of these is biographical and does not concern us here. The other, *Malherbe: Technique et création poétique*, will be referred to repeatedly. See also the special issues of periodicals honoring Malherbe: *Annales de Normandie*, vol. VI (Jan., 1956); *XVIIe Siècle*, no. 31 (April, 1956); and *Publications des Annales de la Faculté de Lettres d'Aix-en-Provence*, n.s., no. 14 (1956).

[2] Ferdinand Brunot, *La Doctrine de Malherbe d'après son commentaire sur Desportes* (Paris: Masson, 1891). For a good, brief summary of Malherbe's rules, see Raymond Lebègue, "Malherbe Quintilius," *XVIIe Siècle*, no. 31, pp. 230–246.

Lebègue—so that there is good reason to hope for further progress. Two words of caution are perhaps in order. First, one must distinguish clearly between the early or provincial Malherbe and the later one who achieved a dominant position in the Parisian literary world. So much attention has recently been given to baroque literature that Malherbe the reformer is sometimes lost from sight. His most widely cited poem, nowadays, is "Les Larmes de Saint Pierre," a youthful work which he eventually regretted and disavowed. Secondly, many scholars have shown a tendency to confuse his theories as a critic with his practice as a poet, or his towering prestige with his impact on literature. It is these four matters—doctrine, technique, reputation, influence—which I propose to discuss.

DOCTRINE

It was soon after his arrival in Paris, in fact in the fall of 1605 or the first months of 1606, that Malherbe crossed out words or phrases and made marginal jottings in an edition of the poems by Desportes. It was an easy target, for Desportes was an aging man who belonged to an earlier school of poetry which was going out of style. Malherbe's sarcastic notes and slashes of the pen are nearly all expressions of disapproval or exasperation and do not constitute a system of ideas. However, by working backward from the negative to its opposite, Brunot succeeded in establishing what is known as *la doctrine de Malherbe*. The comments on Desportes deal partly with versification: caesura, hiatus, *enjambement,* and rhyme. They also make demands in the realms of vocabulary and grammar, such as proper spelling, *bienséance,* purity and clarity of expression, direct and forceful terminology, logic and restraint in the use of imagery. It has long been apparent that Malherbe conceived of poetry as an art of persuasion, as rhetoric with the added difficulties of rhyme and meter. Lebègue has verified this in his study of Malherbe as corrector of a lawyer's speech in prose: except for the requirements of versification there appears to be no difference whatever between his ideal for poetry and his ideal for oratory.[3]

We may be astonished today at such a definition of poetry, but it presumably filled a need, which Malherbe and some of his contemporaries felt, for a radical new emphasis on correctness of language and technique. Various reasons have been advanced to explain the nature of Malherbe's doctrine: not only the political and social aspirations of the age he lived in but also the spirit of the Renaissance, still very much alive, which he wanted to break and bring under control. Perhaps his own character counted for most, or at least gave him a position of leadership and originality: his deeply rooted Stoicism and acceptance of discipline, his rationalism and almost scientific search for perfect lucidity, his overbearing self-confidence and his contempt for the literature of the past, perhaps his very lack of poetic inspiration and ease of expression. As Fromilhague has put it, Malherbe was an extremely slow and unproductive writer; he could succeed as a poet only through vast personal effort, and he therefore made effort and difficulty the core of all his literary theories.[4]

As it has survived, his doctrine is striking above all as narrow and arbitrary. It applies to only one type of poetry, the serious, official, circumstantial poem—whether called *stances* or "ode" or even "sonnet"—and makes no room for other genres, although he himself sometimes wrote in a lighter vein. Implicitly it condemns inspiration, imagination, and ornamentation, but without saying why or setting precise limits. (At what point does the use of mythology become "excessive" or "too erudite"? How can one judge whether a metaphor is overlong, illogical, or inappropriate?) He has nothing to say about the function of poetry or the relationship between writer and reader. He insists on rightness and truth, but without any theory of imitation as their basis; if they are good in prose they are desirable in poetry too. Mal-

[3] Raymond Lebègue, *Malherbe et du Périer: Harangue pour le prince de Joinville* (Paris: Colin, 1956).
[4] René Fromilhague, (La Création poétique chez Malherbe," *XVIIe Siècle*, no. 31, pp. 247–268.

herbe commented repeatedly on what he considered bad rhymes and bad repetitions of sounds in Desportes, but his reasons are technical, even pedantic, and do not seem to spring from a deep concern for the musical qualities of verse —this in spite of the fact that some of his own poems were written to be sung or else recited to a musical accompaniment. His insistence on order and clarity is usually confined to individual lines, sentences, or stanzas; he does not explain his standards for the structure or organic unity of a poem as a whole.

These deficiencies—and the reader can doubtless think of others too—may point either to Malherbe's inadequacy as a literary theorist or else to an inadequacy of evidence with which to judge his thought. The commentary on Desportes is not a rewarding document, to be sure, but one may wonder whether it has been exploited to its utmost. Brunot and more recent scholars, too, have examined it mainly from a linguistic point of view—which is quite natural, since Malherbe was much interested in questions of syntax and vocabulary—but have they really probed it deeply in a search for artistic principles? If the same evidence were to be studied again, this time by a poet or a student of aesthetics, Malherbe's ideas on poetry would perhaps emerge in a fuller and truer light.

TECHNIQUE

Although incomplete, Malherbe's doctrine is probably better understood than is his art as a poet. Needless to say, his theory and practice were not identical, although they merged in many ways and contributed to one another. It is not uncommon to find him using rhymes or constructions or figures which he had condemned in Desportes. For example, he attacked repetitions of sounds and words, yet used this device himself with great effectiveness. He blamed Desportes for certain exaggerations which seemed extravagant, yet himself found in the hyperbole, the sweeping exaggeration, his favorite figure of speech. Despite his strictures on vocabulary he occasionally employed archaic words, or blunt words, which proved shocking and unpoetic to some of his readers.

All of us have certain impressions of Malherbe's poetic style. We are familiar with his organ tones, with his epic flow or rather epic waves; for he wrote not at length but always in a series of carefully measured stanzas, each one densely filled and progressing with a slow, steady beat. His main themes are political and not very numerous: praise for some royal personage, prayers or congratulations for some military campaign, wrath poured out on France's enemies. We have a feeling for the structure of his major poems, with their give and take between calamity and triumph, their fearful suppositions which are raised only to be rejected in favor of an opposite and fortunate vicissitude. We even have some access to his imagination by way of figures and images—such as the storm safely passed, one of his favorites—which are intellectual rather than visual, conveying little emotion but clearly suggesting an abstract idea of peace, or progress, or prosperity.

Such impressions are probably sound—at least they spring from careful reading and conscientious teaching—but few of them have been subjected to rigorous scrutiny or research. Only recently have scholars begun to analyze Malherbe's poetry with scientific objectivity. We are much indebted to the pioneer in this work, René Fromilhague. His thesis bears a broad and somewhat misleading title, *Malherbe: Technique et création poétique*. It is a very rich book, indeed, partly historical and partly analytical. The author succeeds admirably in situating Malherbe in the poetic and philosophical movements of the late sixteenth and early seventeenth centuries. But in dealing with the poet's technique he found himself obliged, in order to keep his study within reasonable bounds, to restrict himself to the exploration of stanza forms and rhymes. Consequently, one finds here almost no information on Malherbe's imagery, or themes, or trains of thought, or musical harmonies. Within his limits Fromilhague has provided an admirable quantitative investigation of the poet's various kinds of strophes and rhymes throughout the whole body of his works and also in comparison with certain other writers of the age. The method is illuminating. When Malherbe's performance is confronted with that of Desportes and Bertaut, his originality in versification becomes quite apparent. When it is confronted with that of Maynard and Racan, his immediate technical influence on his disciples (or sometimes lack of influence) comes clearly into focus. Fromilhague has rendered a particularly valuable service in showing Malherbe's metrical evolution, progressing to an ever stricter application of his rules to his own practice as a poet. His standards became increasingly difficult and tended to force him into silence. This explains the many fragments and preliminary drafts which never reached final form. It probably explains, also, why he came to abandon the ode written in lofty ten-line stanzas, the form to which he owed his greatest fame. He had set up so many rules and obstacles for the structure of this strophe that such odes became impossible to write, at least to his satisfaction.

Several other scholars have recently contributed, in smaller ways, to our understanding of Malherbe's poetry. In a perceptive article on aspects of the poet's vocabulary, Professor Wagner has pointed out the high proportion of abstract terms, the avoidance of descriptions of nature and of expressions which appeal to the senses, and the process of "sterilization"—or removal of the inherent images or associative power which many words possess.[5] From a different point of departure, the qualities of baroque poetry, two other critics, Jean Rousset and Marcel Raymond, have reached similar conclusions as to Malherbe's stark, unsensuous manner. They have suggested that, as his career progressed, he tended to use simpler, shorter metaphors; the building of a firm strophe was more important to him than the development and interplay of images.[6]

An article by Mia Gerhardt examines an ancient, hack-

[5] R.-L. Wagner, "Le Langage poétique (Réflexions sur le vocabulaire des poésies de Malherbe)," *XVIIe Siècle*, no. 31, pp. 269–295.

[6] Jean Rousset, "La Poésie baroque au temps de Malherbe: La métaphore," *XVIIe Siècle*, no. 31, pp. 353–370; and Marcel Raymond, "Esquisse d'un Malherbe," in *Baroque et Renaissance poétique* (Paris: Corti, 1955), pp. 153–167.

neyed theme—the invocation to the Muses—and finds Malherbe quite different from the poets who preceded him. He does not call on the Muses for inspiration and he never appeals to them in his love poetry. Rather he refers to them as the servants of his own powers of expression. When he mentions them it is in his odes in praise of famous people, people who will be immortalized because he has the Muses at his command.[7] Another kind of comparative study, by Renée Winegarten, deals with Malherbe and his Spanish contemporary, Góngora.[8] The two were vastly different, one belligerently modern, the other a lover of erudition and antiquity, one intent on austerity of style almost to the point of impoverishment, the other always searching for new and rich methods of ornamentation. Yet they had certain traits in common: their musicianship, their interest in metrical forms, and in their official poems a fondness for pomp and ceremony.

This is by no means an exhaustive survey of research on the works of Malherbe but it will serve to suggest that some very useful things have been done and that much remains to be undertaken. Few poets have suffered greater neglect. He deserves to have his writings scrutinized, analyzed, explicated. Lebègue has more than once mentioned the need for a complete and chronological repertory of Malherbean imagery as a tool for understanding his art and its presumable evolution toward classical sobriety. But not only imagery is important. His use of words, his sounds and rhythms, his ways of expressing ideas and emotions—all these and other aspects of his technique should be systematically investigated. How about his development of themes? Are his odes really well organized or was he embarrassed, as I think he must have been, by the multiplicity of topics and eulogies (the war, the peace, the king, the queen, the dauphin) which had to be included in these circumstantial poems? The relationship of Malherbe and his main disciples is fairly

[7] Mia I. Gerhardt, "Malherbe et les Muses," *Neophilologus*, XLI (1957), 8–15.

[8] Renée Winegarten, "Malherbe and Góngora," *Modern Language Review*, LIII (1958), 17–25.

well understood, but it would be desirable to have comparisons made between his verse and that of other poets of his era, such as Régnier and Théophile (adversaries who nevertheless have much in common with him), or Saint-Amant and Tristan L'Hermite (independent spirits but heirs to the Malherbean tradition). The reformer's poetry should be examined, also, in relationship with other serious literary genres of the period: not only the ode, but also tragedy and the epic. Fromilhague has pointed to some of the tasks remaining to be done and has invited the collaboration of *une équipe d'ouvriers*. Many hands will in fact be needed if we are to arrive at a clear comprehension of the stylistic qualities which made Malherbe's influence so important.

REPUTATION–THE MYTH OF MALHERBE

When dealing with a writer belonging to a distant age it is one thing, very good in itself, to study and appreciate his works as they exist for us today. It is far different and probably more difficult to reconstruct his image as it radiated among his own generation and those which followed. Careful statistical analysis, as carried out by Fromilhague, permits us to ascertain the nature and development of Malherbe's technique, but it cannot show how his influence operated. Poets of the seventeenth century did not count types of rhymes or stanza forms, yet they doubtless had a strong impression of what Malherbe stood for. Here is where the reformer's theory and practice and personality, or what was known about them, tend to merge into a blurred picture which can be called his reputation. In 1620 or 1630 a poet might have had firsthand information about Malherbe's literary principles and aspirations. A poet of 1660 or 1670 probably had a hazier idea, perhaps distorted or exaggerated, acquired partly through an accumulation of anecdotes and legends and in some cases through only a very limited contact with Malherbe's writings.

His success was swift. By 1610 he had his disciples grouped around him and he already held an awesome position in the world of letters. In 1620, with the publication of the *Second livre des Délices de la poésie française,* his triumph over the "irregular" poets was clearly consecrated. The *Recueil des plus beaux vers . . .* (1626 or 1627) was conceived of as an edition of his works—it contains over sixty of his poems—and of pieces by his avowed disciples. The posthumous edition of his works in 1630 carried with it Godeau's "Discours sur les oeuvres de Malherbe," full of expressions of boundless admiration. From this date onward there is less evidence to work with and various other types and schools of poetry make their presence felt. Renée Winegarten has noted that, from 1630 to 1660, only 14 poems by Malherbe were reprinted in anthologies. He fared better, with 31 poems, in the period 1660–1700. In the meantime Marot had been revived, Voiture was flourishing, and, although serious poetry did not disappear, it was crowded into the background by a torrent of verse that was gallant, precious, playful, or satirical. One senses that Malherbe's reputation suffered a serious eclipse for two or three decades, then returned to favor around 1660, although this would be hard to prove. Comments on him show that he never ceased to be held in high esteem, particularly as the unquestioned master of the official, high-sounding ode.

Among the many discussions of Malherbe, or tributes to him, there are several that stand out as particularly interesting. Some lines by Tristan L'Hermite are worth quoting because they are virtually unknown, not having appeared in print for over three hundred years, and also because Tristan, in certain elevated, meditative pieces, helped to perpetuate the Malherbean concept of poetic diction:

> Malherbe, qui fut sans pareil,
> A trouvé le dernier sommeil
> A la fin de ses doctes veilles,
> Lui dont les écrits, en nos jours,
> Sont des plus savantes oreilles
> Les délices et les amours.[9]

---

[9] From a series of stanzas where Tristan laments the passing of great men, in "Les Misères humaines," published in *La Lyre* (1641).

This is warm praise but rather vague: Malherbe is greatly
admired (sometime in the 1630's), at least by people of
culture and taste. Possibly the phrase "doctes veilles" shows
an appreciation for the hard labor which was the basis of
Malherbe's art. Around the same time, in 1640, Jean Chapelain—an incompetent poet but a gifted literary critic—expressed unusual reservations on Malherbe's contribution to
French verse. First, apparently speaking of his judgment or
tactics in combatting the poets of the Pléiade: "C'était un
borgne dans un royaume d'aveugles." Then, on Malherbe's
own abilities: "Ce qu'il a d'excellent et d'incomparable, c'est
l'élocution et le tour du vers et quelques élévations nettes
et pompeuses dans le détail qu'on pourra bien imiter, mais
jamais égaler." Chapelain adds that such verse can well be
called "de fort belle prose rimée."[10] This rather obscure text
seems to say that Malherbe is a matchless technician but a
limited poet; his craft lacks certain qualities (inspiration?
naturalness?) and comes close to the exaggerated eloquence
of oratorical prose.

This view is partially shared in some of La Fontaine's allusions to Malherbe—in "Clymène," in the "Épître à Huet."
Although he loved every kind of poetry he often expressed
particular admiration for the master of the ode, but with the
added commentary that this high art could not be successfully imitated and, to his regret, would no longer please the
reading public. Various critics of the classical period felt
called upon to discuss Malherbe's verse in some detail, a fact
which is no small tribute to its vitality. It could not be ig-
nored, and in fact was highly praised, by Chevreau in his
Remarques . . . (1660), by Ménage in his Observations . . .
(1666), but both these scholars found fault with various
details of versification and vocabulary. Similarly, in the
Recueil de poésies chrétiennes et diverses of 1670–1671,
some unidentified writer attempted to modernize Malherbe,
"correcting" some forty lines or stanzas so as to remove archaic expressions and, supposedly, bring new youth to a

---

[10] Written June 10, 1640, to Balzac; in Chapelain, Lettres, ed.
Tamizey de Larroque (Paris: Imprimerie Nationale, 1880–1883),
I, 637.

great but aging classic. Then, in 1674, Boileau, a second legislator on Parnassus, extolled his predecessor in a formula so striking and so positive that it became unforgettable. For the next two hundred years, whether rightly or wrongly, Malherbe's prestige was firmly established and his importance could not be denied. Only the irreverence of modern scholars has permitted a closer view of the facts behind the myth.

INFLUENCE

Here, without reaching any definitive conclusions, I should like to enumerate and discuss very briefly some of the complexities which make Malherbe's influence hard to measure. For one thing his tyrannical reign over French poetry did not go undisputed. There were members of the old guard, notably Hardy and Mlle de Gournay, who clung tenaciously to the language and style of the late sixteenth century. There were gifted artists, such as Régnier and Théophile de Viau, who respected Malherbe's abilities but who claimed the right to compose verse that was natural, freely expressed, and colorful in its use of descriptive details. Both these men lacked the professional prestige of Malherbe but probably enjoyed greater popularity, to judge from the fact that their works were reprinted more frequently than his. Corneille retained his independence and found himself blamed, in the *Cid* quarrel, for disregarding some of Malherbe's rules of prosody. (On the other hand, Corneille became increasingly concerned with purity of style; this can be seen in the general evolution of his technique and in the ways he eventually corrected passages in his early plays.) We have seen that many kinds of poetry continued to flourish: precious verse, witty verse, verse written by the amateur or *honnête homme*, verse in archaic forms such as the *rondeau* and the *ballade* or even in irregular meters. *Vers libres* were widely accepted by the time La Fontaine began using them in his tales and fables. By this time, also, aesthetic concepts had passed far beyond the teachings of Malherbe. Poets loved the literature of antiquity, which he did not, and they had arrived at a doctrine of imitation—or free inspiration based on well-known sources—which was quite alien to his thinking. Technical excellence, while still important, was subordinated to another classical ideal, *plaire et instruire*.

Despite all this, Malherbe exerted a powerful influence. His principles were somehow propagated without being published anywhere—of course they were partly exemplified in his own poetry—and they soon found acceptance among other critics and theorists. In 1610 Deimier's *Académie de l'art poétique*, although somewhat cautious and conciliatory, tended to favor Malherbe over his predecessors. Fromilhague has pointed out how Deimier minimizes the part played by inspiration in the composition of poetry; it is one of seven characteristics required of a good poem, the other six being matters of careful craftsmanship. The presence of Malherbe is also strongly felt in an anonymous *Introduction à la poésie* of 1620, which Renée Winegarten has studied. His ideas found their way into the salon of Mme de Rambouillet, where literary style was a frequent subject for discussion, and, after his death, into the new French Academy, which hoped, among its many projects, to draw up a poetics and a rhetoric for the legislation of literature. Some of his rules for versification (hiatus, *enjambement*) were widely adopted by the authors of epics and tragedies. His doctrine undoubtedly remained alive and helped to form the literary aspirations of the great classical writers. Their clarity, their dislike of facility, their care in questions of versification, their restraint in the use of imagery—all these ways of thought owe something to Malherbe's dogmatic insistence on labor and technique as the basis for poetry.

But what about the influence of his poems and their impact on later generations? Can this be separated from his theories or from the kind of mythical reputation he enjoyed? It is not hard to trace a certain current of overt, conscious imitation of Malherbe. The ten-line stanza which he made famous was, for a while, tried by many other poets. His particular kind of official, oratorical ode was accepted as a model and was frequently imitated. Even though this genre later declined in importance and departed from the strict metrical form which he had given it, his example lingered on whenever odes were written. La Fontaine's "Ode au Roi," of 1662 or 1663, is full of echoes of Malherbe, but it should be noted that the fabulist composed other odelike pieces in freer form and in a more playful manner. The odes of Boileau are also marked by reminiscences of Malherbe, although he intended one of them ("Sur la prise de Namur," 1693) to be an imitation of Pindar. I think it is safe to say (although the matter needs to be investigated) that a number of seventeenth-century poets show quite openly their indebtedness to themes and mannerisms found in Malherbe. Gomberville, Gombauld, Chapelain, Pellisson, Colletet, Boisrobert—some of whom had catholic tastes and admired Marot or Ronsard, too—seem well aware of the reformer's special gifts and willing on occasion to imitate them.

To these tangible influences must be added certain others, no less important, which can easily escape detection. Poets must have been impressed, perhaps unconsciously, by the musical qualities of Malherbe's lines and stanzas and by certain elusive characteristics of expression: eloquent sonorities, harmonious sequences of vowel and consonant sounds, firmness and density of diction, self-control in the expression of emotion, images with an abstract or intellectual coloring. Such qualities do not lend themselves easily to objective analysis. We know very little about the elements of style in Malherbe but, as I have tried to indicate, there is much that can be uncovered by the sensitive literary scholar. Unfortunately he will often have to express his results as probabilities rather than as established facts. It is to be hoped that students of versification and of phonetics will join in the search and perhaps develop methods for measuring the weight and resonance and particular tonalities which enter into the style of individual poets.

As one advances beyond the individual and into the channels and crosscurrents of literary history, the problem becomes infinitely complex. The imprint of Malherbe is not always distinguishable from that of other poets such as Corneille. And their successors were exposed to many other forces from all directions. Who can tell, with any precision, how memories of Malherbe may have prompted certain rhythms, certain restraints, certain attitudes, in La Fontaine or Racine? Again, to cite an extreme case, what did the tempestuous Baudelaire find to admire in the symmetrical measures of Malherbe, and was he in any way indebted to them?[11] Problems of literary influence may defy exact solutions but they are important and deserve to be explored, diligently, delicately, resourcefully. Scholars will need an adventurous spirit if they are to give full credit to Malherbe and to other great innovators who from time to time have launched French literature in new directions.

[11] "Les esprits simples s'ébahissent d'entendre Eugène Delacroix vanter sans cesse Racine, La Fontaine et Boileau. Je connais un poète, d'une nature toujours orageuse et vibrante, qu'un vers de Malherbe, symétrique et carré de mélodie, jette dans de longues extases" (Baudelaire, *Oeuvres complètes* [Paris: Bibliothèque de la Pléiade, 1954], p. 865).

SAINT-AMANT, *LE POETE SAUVE DES EAUX*

By Alain Seznec

Saint-Amant was born in Rouen, in 1594; not far from the *eaux précieuses* which

Abreuvent la contrée où proche de leur cour,
[Il] augmenta [sa] famille et [vit son] premier jour.

The ancestral home on the banks of the Seine will belong to him at his father's death; it will be the refuge where our seafaring Don Quixote will return after each of his peregrinations and where he will put on, poetically, Sancho Panza's robe and slippers. A sailor he will be, willy-nilly, a good part of his life; it is in his blood. His father had for more than twenty years commanded a naval squadron for Queen Elizabeth; his uncles, cousins, his two brothers even, all served at sea. The two brothers died in the course of duty, one *à l'embouchure de la mer Rouge*, the younger *dans le navire ennemi qu' il avait abordé*.

How could Saint-Amant resist such heredity? From the familiar Seine which will come "[pour] le voir à sa fenêtre" during the floods, to the exotic Vistula, from the Mediterranean and the Atlantic to the wild Baltic, our poet will cross the aquatic world on his precarious barque. In the "Avertissement au lecteur" of 1651 he recalls "les choses merveilleuses que j'ai vues dans mes voyages tant en l'Europe qu'en l'Afrique et en l'Amérique." It is for this continent that he set sail on his first trip after the completion of his studies in 1616. Alas, this precursor of Chateaubriand will bring back not a word from those mysterious shores. At most does he underline the perils of the voyage which, ironically, proved greater on the Seine than on the ocean. Thus he

> Qui sans crainte [a] bravé les dangers
> Et des bords naturels et des bords étrangers;
> Qui du large Océan [a] traversé le gouffre,

he who has witnessed "des sanglots de feu," has

> Sur la Seine . . . couru plus de fortune
> Que sur l'onde soumise au trident de Neptune.

On the first trip, he experienced the first encounter with death which lies in wait for every sailor.

At Belle-Isle-en-Mer, where he will sojourn a number of times (1617, 1622, 1626) as a *domestique* of the duc de Retz, he rediscovers the ocean, which he contemplates—with impunity now—from the height of a solitary rock. These periods of calm are soon to be disrupted. In 1626 he is afloat again, setting sail for Senegal as a member of an expedition organized by the Compagnies du Sénégal et du Cap Vert which will result, among other things, in the foundation of Saint-Louis-du-Sénégal. The first port of call is Lisbon, then the Canaries. Saint-Amant spent a number of months at sea giving vent to the *rêveries qui [entretenaient son] esprit dans l'oisiveté de la mer*. Quite naturally he evokes Arion, the poet victimized by the sea yet saved by a charitable dolphin. Like Arion, Saint-Amant came back from this trip safe and sound and ready for new adventures.

In 1628 we find him at the siege of La Rochelle and in Spain. In 1629 he accompanies Créqui on the Italian campaign. In the spring of 1631 he sails for the banks of the Thames as an officious ambassador to the court of England. Later, with Créqui, he boards, in Provence, galleys of the king bound for Ostia. The trip goes well, but upon his arrival Saint-Amant discovers a scrawny Tiber, an unworthy sight for the great traveler he has become. A short stay in Rome in 1633 is followed by a visit to Venice in January of 1634 before returning to Paris.

For a few months Saint-Amant stays put; but the urge is soon upon him: the comte d'Harcourt offers him participation in a great naval expedition. A considerable fleet has been gathered on Richelieu's orders at the Ile de Ré; its mission is to recapture the islands of Lérins from Spain. Passing by Gibraltar, Saint-Amant prepares for combat. Unfortunately the Spanish fortifications are stronger than imagined: the French fleet will have to hibernate in Sardinia. With spring comes a new attack—this one successful—and the islands of Lérins surrender in May of 1637. Saint-Amant comes back from this expedition with many bright memories, nor will this *Homère d'une nouvelle Odysée* forget that he is a sailor-poet.

From 1639 to 1642 he leaves the sea, but not adventure. We find him in the numerous campaigns led by D'Harcourt in Italy. It is also D'Harcourt (ambassador extraordinary to *l'orgueilleux Albion*) whom Saint-Amant accompanies in 1643 at the time of the English disorders. He spends a number of months on the foggy isle, leaving it with joy in the spring of 1644. In 1647 he is on the coast of the Mediterranean, at Collioure, in front of *la vaste mer*. The tumultuous waves serve as an inspiration, now tinged with disquiet.

In 1649 Saint-Amant embarks upon a final voyage fraught with endless mishaps. His purpose is to reach Warsaw and his principal patron, the queen of Poland. The first leg of the journey takes him to Flanders, where he is imprisoned, then released, by the Spaniards (according to him the *Moïse sauvé des eaux* almost became a *Moïse perdu*). He is off to Antwerp and Amsterdam. On the first of February he sets sail for Hamburg, Lübeck, Stettin, Danzig, and Warsaw, where he arrives after many vicissitudes in what is still the dead of winter. A few months later *l'éternel voyageur* has gone; Sweden is his new destination as the unofficial ambassador of the queen of Poland to Queen Christine. The Swedish winter is harsh and our poet dreams of more temperate climes; rather than return to Warsaw, as he had promised, he flees toward *les berges fleuries de la Seine*. He stops off at Amsterdam, then joins the Meuse and at last the Seine; "Ulysses" has come back.

These peregrinations have tired him considerably (he is fifty-seven years old). The time has come to settle down. His trips will now take him from Rouen to Paris, and his greatest excitement will be to see the Seine overrun the countryside. The adventure is over:

> Je n'oserai revoir le Tibre,
> L'ample Tamise encore moins
>   . . . . .
> Adieu Cybèle, adieu Neptune.

The last call is to the sea, companion and foe of a lifetime. Nine years later he was to die.

Homer of new odysseys, the reincarnation of Ulysses, Arion poet and sailor, Moses *sauvé des eaux*—such are some of Saint-Amant's guises. His road has led him over the Atlantic, the Channel, the Baltic, the Mediterranean; he has chanced many shipwrecks on the Seine, on the Thames, on the Meuse, on the Vistula. What remains of these experiences in his work?

His reminiscences are hardly tinged with local color. Despite a trip to Africa, Saint-Amant makes his Nile far from exotic—only one or two crocodiles prove that this is not the Vistula. He is not above error, for example, as he speaks of *la pourpre du Tage,* where the symbolic takes over from the concrete. On the whole he chooses to write about the ports of call rather than the sea or the rivers. On his trip to Senegal (a country which he never even mentions) he is inspired by the Canaries, not by the cruise. His attention is not focused on the seashore—we even forget that these are islands as he sings the praises of the vineyards. At Collioure, the same reaction: his eyes are drawn to the harbor and the mountains rather than to the sea. Local color appears only in land trips. In the *Polonaise,* for example, where *le gros Saint-Amanski* as he calls himself, discovers successive inns and brilliantly describes the food, the vestments, the furs, even the odors, of these wild lands.

His memory is also selective. Two trips to Amsterdam furnish two interesting poems, while Venice—the aquatic city—

will not appear, although Saint-Amant sojourned there. Yet
what a temptation for this poet of *villes bateaux* where stone
and sea fuse! Of the sea itself scattered precise memories remain: exotic animals, flying fish especially, which he mentions a number of times as in "L'Arion," where they listen to
the singing poet and *s'élancent haut en l'air d'allégresse in-
finie.* There are fishing scenes too, vividly described whether
in *Moïse* or in the "Epistre diversifiée" (sardine fishing).
Nautical terms finally, which Saint-Amant annotates, include,
in "Le Passage de Gibraltar": *faire pouge (aller vent-ar-
rière), faire orse (cingler près du vent), faire passe-vogue,
ramberge, rambade,* and many others. In his descriptions of
sailing maneuvers we feel the seaman's sharp glance; the
hoisting of the sails and the handling of the helm are all well
rendered.

There is, at times, the impression that classical reminiscences get in the way; they are literally laid over memories
drawn from real life. On one hand, there are mythological
references with their usual vocabulary and traditional gestures, e.g., the invocation to Phoebus so that he may scatter
la fureur des noires tempêtes; on the other, there is the vividness which comes from experience, as in "L'Arion":

> On lève aussitôt l'ancre, on laisse choir les voiles,
> Un vent frais et bruyant donne à plein dans les toiles;
> On invoque Thétis, Neptune et Polémon,
> Les nochers font jouer les ressorts du timon,
> La nef sillonne l'eau, qui, fuyant sa carrière,
> Court devant et tournoie à gros bouillon derrière.

The last lines briefly reveal two aspects of the suggestive
force drawn from poetic realism. The movement is expressed
by the accentuation: 1/5 division in the second hemistich
which accelerates *fuyant sa carrière* followed by the regular
3/3 *court devant et tournoie,* these two hemistichs elegantly
surrounded by two hemistichs which answer one another,
2/4 then 4/2. Hesitation, sliding, balancing, and disequilib-
rium are suggested. Alliterative sonorities echo each other
perfectly. These qualities appear in numerous passages—in-

cluding the following drawn from *Moïse*—in which the sense
of movement, the alternation of accentuated rhythms followed by regular meters expressing balance and pause,[1] in
which sonorities contrasting fricatives and liquids, the interior
rhymes echoing, all contribute to the total picture of a scene
taken from life:

> le double mouvement
> Que fait dessus le bord l'incertain élément
> Lorsque, tout blanc d'écume, il vient, onde après onde,
> Se rouler en bruyant sur l'arène inféconde,
> Et qu'avec le gravier, qui bouillonne et frémit,
> Il s'avalle soi-même et puis se revomit.

These qualities are present in the early poems, in "Solitude" for instance, where Saint-Amant had already acquired
great technical skill as evidenced in three lines balancing
sounds with an extraordinary intricacy:

> L'onde brouillant l'arène
> Murmure et frémit de courroux
> Se roulant dessus les cailloux.

In the descriptions of the sea just mentioned, it is the *contemplateur* who speaks rather than the *marin*. This is the
poet who has often sat facing the sea, letting his imagination
wander. It is in Saint-Amant's reactions to the sea and its
perils that one can find traces of the most haunting memories. His entire work is studded with descriptions of storms,
typhoons, shipwrecks, in which water appears as nature's
destructive element. Speaking to winter in "L'Hiver," he
pleads with it to protect the young queen of Poland about to
sail:

> Ne pense pas que l'on veuille commettre
> Ce beau trésor, . . .

---

[1] Specifically, after two lines somewhat unbalanced, 2/4, 3/3 and
2/4, 2/4, five consecutive regular hemistichs are suddenly broken
by the last in 2/4.

> A l'aventure, à la foi des dangers,
> Que sur les flots courent les pins légers.
> Ces grands périls de l'illustre ambassade,
> Sauvée à peine au doux sein d'une rade,
> Montrent assez que l'infidélité,
> Est de la mer la belle qualité.

The *pins légers* recall the fragile presence of man on the changeable deep. In the "Epistre diversifiée" he had spoken of ships as *des planches vagabondes* and had portrayed the dangers that awaited them on the sea. In an image still more compact and evocative, he remembers having imagined *le pin naval se changer en cyprès*. The ephemeral and death are very close here; they are transposed according to a scheme which is frequent in Saint-Amant.[2] In *Moïse* he will depict the cradle of reed floating on the Nile, not knowing if

> pour tromper le naufrage,
> il doit s'appeler un vaisseau
> Ou plutôt un cercueil, ou plutôt un berceau.

We are thus presented with a series of seafaring catastrophes taken from reality. Wasn't he almost swallowed by the Seine when, in his thirteenth year, the ice on which he was walking broke open? Had he not witnessed the near shipwreck of Henriette de France when she was returning in 1643 to fight the Roundheads:

> En quelle indicible peine
> Ces barbares ennemis
> Sur les eaux n'ont-ils point mis
> Une généreuse reine?
> Elle a couru des dangers
> Où tous ces démons légers
> Qu' Eole anime de glace

[2] Writing to the queen of Poland about his *Moïse*, Saint-Amant pleads with her to like his poem, or
> "Si pour ce héros le Nil fut sans écueil,
> L'onde du Borysthène en verra le naufrage
> Et son berceau flottant deviendra son cercueil."

> Auraient vu blêmir d'audace
> Des plus hardis passagers.

Had Saint-Amant, traveling to Poland, not changed routes
and elected to go by land—on a road not without risks—saying:

> La chance du cocher,
> Dans l'incertaine carrière,
> Vainquit celle du nocher.

True, on the expedition to the islands of Lérins we find him
jolly and quite martial (see "Le Passage de Gibraltar"), but
more often the view of large bodies of water depresses him.
Sometimes, in a melancholy mood, the landscape echoes his
own sadness:

> L'Elbe sut par mes regrets
> Mes ennuis les plus secrets:
> Ma douleur pesante et sombre
> Affligeait ses vastes bords.

Sometimes it provokes it, as in "Solitude," where he imagines
the sea *étalant sur ses bords . . . des gens noyés, des vaisseaux brisés du naufrage, des monstres morts.* At this point
the wandering poet is indeed Arion saved *in extremis* from
the waves. It is a precarious and endangered existence during
which the poet dreams that he will *serrer son luth d'ivoire en
son étui doré;* then, like Ulysses,[3] he will see

> ondoyer, par un décret fatal
> La fumée à flots noirs sur son vieux toit natal.

The image of water is prolonged as if the sea refused to

[3] Saint-Amant compares himself a number of times to Ulysses
either directly or, as below, when he speaks of the revisions of
Moise:
"Quand je suis venu à le regarder de pied ferme pour y mettre
la dernière main, et que j'en ai bien considéré toutes les parties,
j'ai fait comme celui qui, après de longs voyages tels qu'ont été
les miens, se retrouvant en sa propre maison champêtre et venant
à revoir son jardin, en change aussitôt toute la disposition."

release its prey, and even the familiar smoke recalls the storm reluctantly receding.

Past experiences can thus color the tone of certain poems, and parallels can be drawn between the work and the life of the poet; but it is not so much in the direct retelling of facts as in the incidental images that we find a revealing aspect of Saint-Amant: aquatic metaphors are characteristics of his style.

Rivers and seas are, at the simplest level, landmarks or rather geographic and naval boundaries. Thus the Ganges is the ultimate limit of the world, as is the Antarctic.[4] Water forms a vast network of transportation and communication which links the most distant points on the globe over and beyond national frontiers. Fountains, torrents, lakes, rivers, and seas flow into a single element. Describing the victories of the duc d'Enghien in 1644, Saint-Amant writes:

> Le Danube, à qui l'on conta
> Du Rhin soumis l'étrange histoire,
> Blêmit de crainte et se hâta
> De l'aller dire à la mer Noire.
> L'Océan l'apprit aussitôt
> Par la bouche du vaincu même,
> Et, dans l'abîme qui l'enclôt,
> Trembla pour son grand diadème.

Beyond mere personification of rivers appears the metaphor of fame—including the pun on *bouche*—which can be compared (as Durand Lapie suggests) to the much more *précieux* letter of Voiture, the so-called "Lettre de la commère la carpe [Voiture] à son compère le brochet [le duc d'Enghien]":

> Vous ne sauriez jusques où s'étend votre réputation, il n'y a point d'étangs, de fontaines, de ruisseaux, de

---

[4] In a poem reminiscent of the Hôtel de Rambouillet entitled "Le Tombeau de Marmousette" (a small dog which has just died), he exclaims:

> "Que de la Seine jusqu'au Gange
> L'on puisse envier son tombeau."

rivières, ni de mers, où vos victoires ne soient célébrées,
point d'eau dormante où l'on ne songe à vous, point
d'eau bruyante où il ne soit bruit de vous, votre nom
pénètre jusques au centre des mers, et vole sur la surface
des eaux, et l'océan qui borne le monde, ne borne pas
votre gloire.

At times, rivers serve as allegories of the countries they
water, but the literal meaning does not entirely disappear;
alluding to the war between Ladislas VII of Poland and the
Turks, Saint-Amant represents the soldiers of the king who
repoussent de l'Euxin le fier débordement.[5]

Finally the river can serve as a historical symbol as it so
often does in classical literature: the Thames symbol of England in "L'Ode à L.L.S.S. Majestés d'Angleterre," the Seine
in the "Pourvus bachiques" which during the war *dompte
en un an, le Rhin, le Neckar et la Lippe,* the Thames again
in "L'Albion" whose *vaste cours* and *onde libre et hautaine*
Saint-Amant cites. There is a nuance here: the river is not
only the sigil of the country, it reflects in its bearing the temperament of the nation. In the "Rome ridicule" where Saint-
Amant—like Du Bellay—looks in vain for Rome in Rome, we
find a pale and rickety Tiber, at the same time pretentious
and grotesque. On the contrary, opposing optimistically the
disorders of the Fronde to the situation in England, where
Cromwell has rebelled, Saint-Amant writes:

> Qu'on ne compare point les troubles de la Seine
> A ceux de la Tamise, où l'orgueil même agit;
> C'est un fleuve brutal qui sans cause mugit,
> Mais l'autre avec raison murmure en voix humaine.

Beyond symbolizing the nation, the poet fuses in a single

---

[5] Only allegory remains on the other hand in "Suspension
d'armes." Saint-Amant recalls the meeting between Mazarin and
Luis de Haro in 1659, which was to lead to the treaty of the Pyr-
enees:

> "Encore une fois et la Seine et le Tage,
> Au bien de l'univers, à l'honneur de cet âge,
> Veulent entrelacer les myrtes aux roseaux
> Qui leur parent le front sur leurs superbes eaux."

image a climatic observation with a psychological judgment. The Seine is above all human and reasonable. During its floods in 1658 Saint-Amant speaks to his companion in a friendly tone. He reproaches the Seine for its *désordres*, its *excès;* the civilized and rational Seine is in every sense of the word *hors d'elle même.* Visibly this is only a passing madness—despite the gravity of the situation there is not a word of terror in the whole poem—and the Seine, French par excellence, will remain a friend and refuge. It is more—the very frame of his poetic inspiration. In Stockholm, writing the preface to "La Vistulle sollicitée," he recalls that

> Les muses de la Seine étaient si délicates qu'elles ne m'avaient pu suivre dans une si pénible et si longue course; que la fatigue du chemin les avaient étonnées et qu'absolument il me fallait une retraite solitaire et naturelle où ces belles Vierges habitassent pour venir à bout de ce que j'avais projeté.

The Seine, haunted by the delicate muses has become the *France, mère des arts, des armes, et des loix,* inspiration and *nourrice* of Du Bellay.

All examples cited up to now are partial metaphors in which objective reality—here primarily geographic and historical—has not completely disappeared. There are many other pure metaphors, some borrowed from literary tradition, others curiously original.

The comparison may be solely visual as in the description (from "Joseph") in which Benjamin reentering the city finds himself, not without trepidation, surrounded by a *bruyante foule:*

> Comme un gros de poissons qui s'agite et se roule
> Tout autour d'un vaisseau, lorsque près d'un rocher,
> Il flotte sans timon, sans mats et sans nocher.[6]

Elsewhere it is essentially abstract, as in "La Vistulle sollicitée," where inspiration pushes his ship onward:

[6] Cf. in *Moïse* Laban's family seeing him angered and fleeing *de tous côtés* [*comme*] *les rapides poissons* [*devant*] *un monstre marin.*

> Peut-être que l'éclat de cette vive étoile
> Excitera ma nef à déployer sa voile.

It may become extremely complex and precious—metaphor within metaphor, puns, and the like—as in his description of a gift sent to him from afar under the guise of a *lettre de change* by his protector Marie Louise de Gonzague:

> Son beau Pactole, où se gagne la gloire,
> Changeant son onde en l'encre la plus noire,
> Et s'étant même à dessein travesti
> Pour éviter quelque mauvais parti,
> Loin du climat qui tremble près de l'ourse,
> A traversé cent terres en sa course,
> A vu la Seine, a réjoui ses flots,
> Encor qu'il fut dans un papier enclos,
> Puis tout à coup, sur la table où je mange,
> Quittant l'habit d'une lettre de change,
> M'a fait un compte, a repris sa couleur,
> Et de ma soif a noyé la douleur.[7]

Three subjects particularly tend to be illustrated by aquatic images, often traditional. First, of course, is love. The lover sits on the bank of a river which is both the confidante of his sorrows and the image of the ephemeral and the inconstant. It flees toward the sea *qui n'a rien de plus amer* than the despair of the poet, who will swell it with his tears. Water is also the element which can "put out" the "fire" burning in the lover. By contrast the lewd Tritons ogling their prey

> Au fond de leur poitrine attisent
> Un feu qui vit même dans l'eau.

And in a very sensuous poem Saint-Amant describes the body of his mistress, strangely metamorphosed into a seascape:

---

[7] Cf. what the poet writes to the duc d'Orléans about the latter's purse:

> "Tu fais couler ainsi que d'une source
> Un long ruisseau de qui les flots dorés
>   . . . charment la soif."

Quand je la vois, cette gorge ivoirine
Où l'oiseau-dieu souvent va se nicher
Comme un goéland qui sur quelque rocher,
Fait ses petits au bord de la marine.[8]

The beauty of this woman literally melts the lover and *plonge [ses] sens dans un doux fleuve d'aise*. Water is again associated with sexuality in a passage in which Saint-Amant evokes an aviary. The birds flitting with more and more excitement finally *plongent*

Dans l'onde, où brille leur image,
Meurent d'aise, et pensent
Sein contre sein baiser d'autres oiseaux.

The contact with the water, the *plongeon*, suggests sexual penetration rendered more ambiguous here by the latent narcissism.

In a completely different domain, politics and government, aquatic images are frequent. War is most often a storm at sea pushing hither and yon the fragile barks before it. Radizievsky, the traitor rebelling against the Polish sovereigns

a suscité l'Occident et le Nord,
Il a couru de port en port
Pour nous livrer à la tempête;
Il presse le naufrage, et veut que notre tête
En sente le dernier effort.

Writing to the Princesse Palatine, Saint-Amant reminds her of the *écueils* which await any government ("ship of state"), the *tempêtes de la politique*, and so forth. On the contrary, the same ship sails on calm waters in times of peace. The return to Paris of young Louis XIV from his exile in Rueil is thus announced:

Paris aime le Roi, Paris aime la Reine,
Son auguste sénat pour leur bien le régit
Et mon oeil est trompé si sa nef ne surgit
Dans le port où sa gloire est promise à la peine.

[8] This recalls "La Géante" of Baudelaire.

In "L'Albion," Saint-Amant recalls the end of the Hundred
Years' War and forecasts the unification of France under a
firm monarchy:

> On vit voguer notre nef
> Sous des auspices illustres:
> L'air désarmé de courroux,
> L'onde calme, les vents doux,
> Favorisèrent nos voiles,
> Et le bonheur des étoiles
> N'éclata plus que pour nous.

Fate will now favor the French ship and abandon the English one. The life of a nation is represented as a long and
perilous journey on a hostile and unpredictable sea. The ship-
nation whose helm is held by the government at times sails
against the storm searching for a haven; at times rests on ap-
peased waves. Images of stability—the stars, the lighthouses,
the lanterns—guide the ship. In the same way Richelieu

> Est à la France dans l'orage
> Ce qu'au navire est le f[a]nal.[9]

Transposing these images to the philosophical and religious domains, Saint-Amant applies them to the destiny of the
individual. He too looks for the harbor, guided by divine
lights, avoiding the reefs and storms of existence. Despite turmoils and partial defeats, man can reach his roal if *au milieu
des hasards* he replaces the flags flying on his masts by the
cross:

[9] Tempest, harbor, lighthouse, also appear in purely social con-
texts. In "L'Epître héroï-comique," Saint-Amant warns the duc
d'Orléans of the speeches which will be made in his honor when
he returns from war:
> "L'un te plaira, l'autre te fera rire;
> L'autre, égaré sur la mer du bien dire,
> Et ne sachant en quel havre surgir
> Te feras même et suer et rougir."

See also the very precious description of the princesse de Conti:
> "Dont la sagesse est un célèbre phare
> Qui sert de guide au sexe qu'on adore
> Pour en former d'autres phares encore,
> Le retirant des flots des passions."

La seule lumière celeste
Encore qu'invisible, éclairant à ses pas,
   Lui fera du second trépas
Eviter le chemin spacieux et funeste;
Il la suivra partout, et, cinglant vers ce nord,
En conduira sa barque au véritable port.

   Que l'orage emporte ses voiles,
Que ses mats soient rompus, son gouvernail détruit,
   Que l'horreur d'une épaisse nuit

A ses yeux pour un temps dérobe les étoiles,
Ses yeux verront ce phare, adorable aux nochers,
Et son faible vaisseau domptera les rochers.

We think of René feverishly pacing the shore beneath the convent of Amélie:

La tempête sur les flots, le calme dans la retraite; des hommes brisés sur des écueils, au pied de l'asile que rien ne peut troubler; l'infini de l'autre côté du mur d'une cellule; les fanaux agités des vaisseaux, le phare immobile du couvent; l'incertitude des destinées du navigateur, . . . un naufrage plus affreux que celui du marinier . . .

In "Le Contemplateur," Saint-Amant, by the sea, lets his mind *changeant de projet* dream in front of the ever fluctuating spectacle. Soon he is *obsédé* by the movement of the sea, *le flux et le reflux* in which he loses himself. The sea—deep and unfathomable—recalls the mysteries of existence, but especially the uncertainty. The poet imagines *les nefs sillonnant la plaine liquide au gré du vent*. There too, in the middle of the changing elements, is an image of salvation, the *miraculeux* compass. He contrasts its *pierre dure*—but constant—to the heart of man restlessly turning away from his rightful road.

Supreme image of human destiny, the spectacle of an uncertain sea recalls the flood: Noah *choisi des cieux*, the only survivor of divine wrath, on *le premier logis flottant [dans lequel] le genre humain eut son refuge*. The image has

reached the level of religious symbolism. The sea becomes
the instrument of celestial vengeance and the ship the last
refuge of innocence. Moses, too, is *l'élu des cieux;* a defenseless child thrown on hostile waters (all the more hostile because the Nile is also the symbol of Egypt), he will triumph
over the elements. Aaron prophesies that his tribulations will
be *passagers,* that the *tempêtes* will not prevail; Moses will
fulfill his destiny. Thus, *sauvé des eaux* takes on a mystical
meaning. Moses, like Noah, will be saved by his innocence.
Water is the image of the destruction of humanity, the physical and spiritual death, the *gouffre* in which man, at any moment, can be swallowed up.[10]

In *Moïse,* too, among the great plagues which are about to
fall on Egypt, Saint-Amant speaks in detail about only one:
the Nile *mue en bouillons de sang ses bouillons de cristal.* It
is a vision of terror in which the aquatic element divides itself,
the sea struggling against the river. An awesome sight, the
world is turned upside down; the fish abandon the water.
One fish tries

> D'éviter le trépas en sautant sur le bord
> Mais la peur de mourir lui fait trouver la mort.

The other—the reversal is even more striking—*se noye.*

In the episode of the crossing of the Red Sea, Saint-Amant
depicts the sea, unleashed, about to punish forever *le tyran
impie,* the pharaoh. Adversary of divine will, he will be *reclu
en un tombeau flottant.* The sea at the height of its anger recalls the fury of the Flood. The other elements seem to flee in
terror, and Pharaoh, last survivor, is going to die, after a desperate struggle against *un monstrueux poisson.* The sea, once
again, will have taken its revenge on the earth and on men.[11]

The ultimate destruction of the world appears in "Le Con-

---

[10] The persecution of the Jews by the Egyptians is also described
as *un si sanglant déluge.*

[11] Often there are monsters who appear out of river or sea:
l'amphibie énorme which Elisaph must affront in *Moïse,* in "L'Andromède" the combat between Perseus and the marine monster.
The scene cited above recalls the "Récit de Théramène" in *Phèdre*
both on the elemental plane and on the plane of religious symbolism.

templateur." The Apocalypse is represented as a storm at sea. The elements are again opposed to one another and fire invades water and air: "la mer brûle comme eau de vie."[12] The mineral reign is metamorphosed:

> Les métaux, ensemble fondus,
> Font des rivières précieuses;
> Leurs flots bouillants sont épandus
> Par les campagnes spacieuses.
> Dans ce feu, le dernier des maux,
> Tous les terrestres animaux
> Se consolent en quelque sorte,
> Du déluge à demi vengés,
> En voyant ceux que l'onde porte
> Aussi bien comme eux affligés.

These curious lines seem to make of the fish the last representative of life. Is it a recall of early Christian symbolism or more simply the natural bent of Saint-Amant's poetic vision? The element of life and destruction, water, ceaselessly menacing our precarious existences—barks and sailors—makes of the fish a privileged being. He travels without danger, letting himself be carried by the tide or fighting with impunity against it. At the moment of the final catastrophe he too is destroyed. The metamorphosis of the elements—such as the reversal of nature [drowning fish]—is a sign of his end and, thereby, of the end of the world.

Sensuality, changeableness, terror, are associated with marine landscapes. From memories to visions of Apocalypse, common characteristics unite Saint-Amant's universe. To these must be added the general ambiguity of seascapes and their subjacent violence.

The ambiguity results from the uncertain limits which separate or unite the elements. The sea invades space: rising toward the sky it fuses with it as it does with the earth when it covers its shores. The impression of a constant struggle is reflected either by warlike images or by a mimesis which is con-

[12] Is *eau de vie* only literal?

scious on the part of the sea. In "Le Passage de Gibraltar,"
for example:

> Pour faire au ciel la guerre,
> Les Tritons, fâchés du tonnerre,
> Entassant monts sur monts flottants,
> Veullent qu'aussi bien que la terre
> La mer fasse voir des Titans.

In "La Vistulle sollicitée," *l'ambre doré* of the sea suggests
l'or de Cérès en paille

> Et semble dire à l'oeil que la mer et la terre
> De leur muette haine et de leur vieille guerre
> Voudraient bien étouffer la dure opinion,
> En des baisers d'amour, de paix et d'union.

More than once there is an exchange of descriptive terminology—often according to classical tradition—whereby the sea
becomes a field and the earth (the harvest in particular)
evokes the liquid element.

Water can also become the mirror in which earth and sky
are reflected. It thus seems to have captured the ambient elements and presents us with an upside-down world in which
the normal boundaries have ceased to exist.

In Collioure, Saint-Amant looks at the reflection of the Pyr-
enees in the sea. The earth dominates here, and the *pieds* of
the mountains *triomphent des ondes*. In "La Généreuse" we
find a symptomatic landscape: the poet is dreaming of the
fate of Marie Louise de Gonzague, queen of Poland, and he
looks at trees rising on the banks of a river. They represent in
his mind the strength and constancy of the queen. Yet the
river, like a magician's mirror, gives a clue to the future:

> Ces frênes hauts et droits qui bordent ces ruisseaux,
> Aussi bien que les arbrisseaux,
> Me semblent renversés dans l'onde,
>
> . . . . .
>
> Mais comme en la seule apparence
> Leur sommet est précipité,
> L'erreur même et la vérité

M'instruisent de leur différence.
Ils sont toujours debout, ils souffrent cent débats,
Ils s'obstinent dans les combats
Des plus effroyables tempêtes;
Ils portent jusqu'au ciel les honneurs de leurs faites,
Et rien ne les peut mettre à bas.

The double vision allows the poet to predict optimistically
the stubborn resistance of the trees—those on the bank (the
"real" ones)—which will hold despite the storm, yet fore-
shadow the uncertainty of the future through the reflection of
the trees, infinitely more fragile and dependent upon forces
it cannot control. Suddenly the spell is broken, the mirror becomes blurred:

Mais quoi, cette glace liquide
Où je les voyais jusqu'au fond,
Toutes leurs images confond,
Se change, se trouble et se ride.
Ce n'est plus qu'un torrent qui dédaigne ses bords,
Un fier torrent dont les efforts,
Sous ces bois tristes et sombres,
Semblent en leur murmure, ayant détruit les ombres,
Parler de détruire les corps.

Here then is a double destruction. The image of the trees is
distorted in the inconstant mirror, and the real trees are menaced by a real flood which may carry them away. Water, by
reflecting the world which is outside of it, captures it, then
symbolically disfigures it—the first indication of its power.

Thus water becomes the lying element which provokes hal-
lucinations by upturning the world. Saint-Amant describes a
river

Où j'ai vu, en la trompeuse glace,
Des poissons et des oiseaux.[13]

The sun itself is caught in the trap and the sea, *miroir flottant,*

[13] This so called "baroque process" by which the poet deliberately confuses two elements is carried to its extreme limits by young
Racine in "De l'étang."

> représente à l'instant
> Encore d'autres cieux sous l'onde.
> Le soleil s'y fait si bien voir,
> Y contemplant son beau visage,
> Qu'on est quelque temps à savoir
> Si c'est lui-même, ou son image,
> Et d'abord il semble à nos yeux
> Qu'il s'est laissé tomber des cieux.

It is, literally, in the sea that the sun retires at night:

> Phébus quitte les cieux
> Pour se cacher sous l'onde.

At times, even, the sea—the fatal snare—can become a tomb. Speaking of the sun, it is with great relief that Saint-Amant sees it rise again in "Le Contemplateur":

> Je l'observe au sortir des flots,
> Sous qui la nuit, étant enclos,
> Il semblait être en sépulture;
> Et, voyant son premier rayon,
> Bénis l'auteur de la nature.

The sun emerging from the sea recalls Christ's rising up from the dead.

In two lovely poems on Amsterdam another sort of ambiguity is underlined. The limits of stone and water are not clearly marked, and the city arises from the struggle in which

> Cybèle et Thétis s'entrusurpent leurs bords;
> Où leur sceptre est douteux, et de qui les discords
> Exigent des humains les veilles assidues.

This *petit univers* is neither completely the earth nor the sea. Beside the *arbres morts*, which can be seen underneath the surface of the sea, and the *arbres verts*, which line the banks, one can see *les arbres secs qui fleurissent sur l'onde*. The city itself is a ship ready to brave the perils of the deep:

> J'admire . . . ces plaines confondues,
> Ces lieux où les maisons sont presqu'autant de ports,

Ces havres dont les nefs sont les mobiles forts
Qui bravent l'Océan à voiles étendues.

All waterscapes suggest possible change and movement—instability. The islands are banks ready to set forth whether *l'île Tibérine* in Rome, *que l'on prendrait pour un bateau,* or the islands, *cousines de la Seine,* which during floods may be *déracinées* and become *des îles errantes.* Even motionless and calm, a marine landscape hides a possible metamorphosis which gives it dramatic tension. In "L'Andromède," the sea monster vanquished by Perseus feels himself turning to ice, his body little by little hardens, and at last he ceases to move; his great tail, barely apparent over the waves, has been transformed into rocks. Rocks are no longer passive minerals then, but marine monsters which have been petrified and may come back to life; the menace remains.

Violence is present in seascapes even when it is not directly associated with the sea, for example, the hunt, which Saint-Amant describes in "Le Contemplateur." Above all a surprise—underlined in the poem below by the place of *tombent*—death, as on the sea, is brutal and sudden:

> je tire aux cormorans,
> Qui bas dans les flots murmurant
> Tombent percés du plomb qui tue;
> Ils se débattent sur ce bord,
> Et leur vie en vain s'évertue
> D'échapper des mains de la Mort.

The fish too is drawn by the mirage of the lure. It will be a fatal illusion, and the dorado pursuing the hook will find out, but too late, that

> La chose même qu'il chasse
> Enfin l'attrappe en le fuyant.[14]

In the "Epistre diversifiée," Saint-Amant describes a fishing expedition, and the dramatic intensity, the ironic intent, go far beyond the picturesque. The fishing takes place at night

[14] Compare also with the breathtaking fishing scene in *Moïse.*

with lanterns, and it accentuates the cruelty of an illusory world and the suddenness of death:

> Je vois des feux se promener sur l'eau,
> Des feux rusés, qui de mainte chaloupe
> Font en des fers luire dehors la poupe
> Pour attirer les poissons au trépas,
> Les aveuglant d'un lumineux appas.
> A ce beau piège, à l'embûche brillante,
> Des innocents la presse fourmillante
> Donne soudain dans le filet tendu,
> Et leur plaisir leur est bien cher vendu.

This scene is followed by the arrival of a galley whose sight haunts Saint-Amant. For more than a hundred lines he depicts *les forçats qui suent*, the hardships of their existence (they, too, have been caught in the trap), the brutality of the guards, and so on. The sea is once again associated with the cruelty of fate and the bitterness of life.

By comparison, in "Solitude," the aquatic landscape is all the more peaceful because no menace weighs upon it:

> Là cent mille oiseaux aquatiques
> Vivent, sans craindre, en leur repos.

There too:

> Jamais chevreuil désespéré
> N'y finit sa vie à la chasse
> Et jamais le traitre hameçon
> N'en fit sortir aucun poisson.

A few lines earlier in the same poem Saint-Amant had shown us this *marais paisible* as

> tout bordé d'aliziers,
> D'aulnes, de saules et d'osiers

and this brings us to a final consideration, the manner in which Saint-Amant opposes calm and peaceful landscapes to a world of violence. In the lines first quoted, we can vaguely perceive the image of a barrier: the trees *bordent le marais* and in that sense contain it. When Joseph in his dream sees the fatted calves, it is in a prosperous and happy countryside watered by

> Un fleuve inconnu, mais clair et spacieux
> Et planté des deux bords d'arbres délicieux.

One could multiply the examples in which trees and flowers, the earth even, serve as reassuring limits of the aquatic domain.[15] A bank hedged by regularly spaced trees—incidentally the most notable characteristic of the French countryside—becomes a guarantee of stability and rationality.

The river just cited was also *claire*, and the luminosity of the water is another indication of beauty and calm. It is in the domain of metals and minerals that Saint-Amant usually finds his descriptive terms when he evokes the beauty of a seascape,[16] *argent liquide, crystal*. These are conventional terms, but Saint-Amant goes further. Imagining what the Tiber may look like, he lends great beauty to it. Each element of the landscape is transformed into a glittering mineral, the *cailloux* are *diamants*, the *fange* becomes *du pur gravier d'or*, even the flora and fauna suggest the mineral:

> Le sucre emplissait vos roseaux
> Le saumon brillait dans vos eaux
> Avec des écailles de nacre.

After his trip to Rome he opposes the brilliance of his dream to what he has seen: the Tiber is lusterless and *visqueux*. The gleam has disappeared leaving behind it gray reality. Metal and mineral evoke not only clarity, limpidity, but by their hardness oppose themselves to the changing element. They suggest stability in front of fluidity. A river which has metallic gleams is no longer fully water.

A last image of water—a water which has lost its inherent qualities and thus is no longer dangerous—can be found in "La Seine extravagante." Saint-Amant seeing the floods of

[15] Among others, the shore at Belle-Ile-en-Mer. Saint-Amant writes that *la mer endure les bornes de la terre;* it has been *mise en prison.*

[16] See also "La Mer" of Tristan.

the Seine remembers with nostalgia the winters in which it froze:

> Ha! que mes yeux seraient ravis
> De revoir l'onde sèche et dure
> Comme naguères je la vis
> Sous les rigueurs de la froidure.

Here is the ultimate limit, water is at last *sèche* and *dure*. Man is totally safe; he can, looking at the water, *rire de son audace*. Water has for once been subdued. Playing on the word *fers*, Saint-Amant shows us the Seine *soumise aux fers des patins*.

We have examined the personal memories, the real-life experiences, such as they appear in Saint-Amant's poetry and have tried to regroup the principal comparisons and metaphors, inspired in part by these experiences, in order to suggest some constants which unite these images. As a conclusion let us examine three suggestive passages in which these characteristics reveal an aspect of Saint-Amant's poetic vision.

In a passage of *Moïse* in which the Flood appears, Jocabel with her *aiguille savante* is depicting in tapestry work the moment *où l'horrible déluge engloutit l'univers*. We are suddenly thrust in the very midst of the tapestry which comes alive in front of our eyes:

> Là, de pieds et de mains, les hommes noirs de crimes
> Des arbres les plus hauts gagnaient les vertes cimes;
> L'effroi désespéré redoublait leurs efforts,
> Et l'on voyait pâlir leurs membres et leurs corps.
> Ici, l'un au milieu de sa vaine entreprise,
> Pour son peu de vigueur contraint à lâcher prise,
> Blême, regarde en bas, hurle,
>   . . . . . .
> Là, l'autre, plus robuste, empoignant une branche
> Fait que la branche feinte et s'éclate et gémit,
> Et trébuche avec eux dans l'onde qui frémit.

The *bêtes éperdues* are not spared either, and their rending outcry is joined to the *cris et aux sanglots des nageurs vains*

et nus qu'on voyait sur les flots. Despite the violence, the irresistible movement is in fact *endigué.* Surrounding the unleashed ocean one can see:

> le beau rempart d'une riche bordure
> De fruits, de papillons, de fleurs et de verdure
> Qui semblait s'opposer au déluge dépeint.

Rempart, bordure, are significant. There is a curious contrast
here between a factitious nature (which is defined by the ex-
igencies of tapestry styling and not by the dictates of nature)
and the dramatic and fully realistic violence of the center of
the canvas. Saint-Amant deliberately plays on the notions of
reality and artifice. Showing the deluge in the middle of the
picture, he speaks of it as of a real landscape. Then, at the
highest point of his description, when the deluge seems about
to invade the whole world, he suddenly reminds us that it is
only a canvas:

> Les plus proches objets, selon la perspective,
> Etaient d'une manière et plus forte et plus vive;
> Mais de loin en plus loin la forme s'effaçait,
> Et dans le bleu perdu tout s'évanouissait.

Thus, abruptly the force of the floods is controlled by the artist who was only playing with a nightmare and can dispel it
at will. To put a delirious sea on a canvas, to surround it by
une bordure de fruits, de fleurs, de papillons, is in fact no
more than to reduce it, to frame it.

Toward the end of *Moïse* we find another series of landscapes no less revealing. After the turmoils of the first nine
books, which are filled with shipwrecks, storms, drownings,
aquatic monsters, we discover the gentle joys of existence.
First comes the description of an idyllic haven not far from
Memphis. In opposition to the *ravages* of the river, we find
le repos et les plaisirs innocents in the favorite retreat of
Pharaoh's daughter. The garden especially—which recalls the
French and Italian gardens of Saint-Amant's age—is notable
for its luminosity, its quasi-geometric order, and specifically
for the impression it gives of a nature which has been tamed.
Everything is channeled, *divisé par le plomb,* mineralized.

Even animal life has been supremely domesticated: the *poissons rares*—rare as artifices—and swans, conscious, no doubt, of their roles as moving statues:

> Tantôt, dans un jardin enrichi de statues,
> De grottes, de canaux et de masses pointues,
> Où l'on voyait l'orgueil d'un porphire éclatant,
>
> • • • • •
>
> Tantôt, sous des lauriers repliés en arcades,
> Elle prenait plaisir à voir mille cascades,
> Que, par art et de front, les claires eaux faisaient
> Vis-à-vis de la place où ses beaux yeux luisaient.
> Ces charmes, composés d'une onde vive et pure,
> Semblaient en descendant avec un doux murmure,
> Offrir à sa grandeur des degrés de cristal
> Pour l'induire à monter sur leur tertre natal;
> Tandis que d'autres eaux, par le plomb divisées,
> Sortaient de cent bassins en forme de fusées,
> Et que d'autres encore allaient en cent façons
> Grossir un bel étang plein de rares poissons,
> Un étang précieux dont seulement les cygnes
> Entre tous les oiseaux s'osaient réputer dignes.

So many details remind us of Baudelaire's "Rêve parisien," a dream of stone and canals, of *métal* and *marbre* and *eau;* a dream of a natural world subjected to the domination of man who can make

> Sous un tunnel de pierreries
> Passer un océan dompté.

It is of Baudelaire also—a Baudelaire who said, "L'eau en liberté m'est insupportable; je la veux prisonnière, au carcan, dans les murs géométriques d'un quai"—that we think when, a few pages later, Saint-Amant evokes the daughter of Pharaoh bathing in the waters of the Nile. It is precisely in *une branche du Nil avec art ménagé* which

> Isole une prairie où les plus rares fleurs
> Faisant briller l'émail des plus vives couleurs

Présentent aux regards . . .
Tout ce qu'ont nos jardins d'exquis et de superbe.

Here the Nile is vanquished, *nature* is beautiful because it is
exquise like a civilized garden. It is not really in the Nile that
the princess bathes but in a swimming pool made up of *un
long et droit canal que ce beau pré renferme* and which

S'ornait de deux beaux ponts qui de la terre ferme
Aboutissaient à l'île, et l'art y faisait voir
Des plus rares ouvriers l'industrieux savoir.

It is ornamented by sculptured figures, marble arches, pro-
tecting ramparts, and

Deux longs rangs de barreaux, faits du premier métal,
Sur des murs de porphyre en gardaient le cristal;
Entre ces barreaux d'or cent piliers magnifiques,
Sous des vases de jaspe ornés d'hyéroglifiques,
De distance en distance arrêtaient les regards
Et d'un albâtre pur luisaient de toutes parts.

Man's triumph is complete. The Nile, only a moment ago so
powerful and ill-intentioned, seems here literally buried in a
funeral monument of stone. The *fleuve* has become *un canal,*
cased in metal, compartmented, set in precious stones,

l'onde fortunée
. . . pour être plus libre était emprisonnée.

The whole scene hardens into an engraved miniature. *Le noble ruisseau d'or sur le fluide d'argent* receives the nude body
of the princess which is metamorphosed into *ivoire souple*
and *marbre flottant.* Nature's violence has been exorcized,
artifice triumphs.

A last passage taken from the fifth book of *Moïse* concerns
the crossing of the Red Sea by the nations of Israel:

L'abime, au coup donné, s'ouvre jusqu'aux entrailles;
De liquides rubis il se fait deux murailles
Dont l'espace nouveau se remplit à l'instant
Par le peuple qui suit le pilier éclatant.

D'un et d'autre côté ravi d'aise il se mire;
De ce fond découvert le sentier il admire,
Sentier que la nature a d'un soin libéral
Paré de sablon d'or, et d'arbres de corail,
Qui, plantés tout de rang, forment comme une allée
Etendue au travers d'une riche vallée,
Et d'où l'ambre découle ainsi qu'on vit le miel
Distiler des sapins sous l'heur du jeune ciel.

What strikes here is not simply the transformation of a seascape into a landscape, but rather the characteristics of this
terre. In a way "realism" is preserved: the sand and the coral
recall the bottom of the sea. But the impression of a *jardin à
la française* is clearly superimposed. The *sentier* is *une allée;*
the coral resembles *des arbres plantés en rang;* the golden
sablon itself is waiting for the rake. The verbs *parer* and
planter also remind us of artifice. This is further a *riche vallée*
in which *le miel distillé* suggests the promised land, the fertile
earth which will replace the sterile sea. Saint-Amant shows us
sheep and oxen passing *où naguères flottaient les dauphins et
le thon.*[17] Man's creatures, domesticated animals, have re-
placed *les monstres marins.* Man repossesses the earth. We
have come back to the origins of time, soon after the Flood,
when the sea, having receded, also left *des fertiles vallées,*
signs of the covenant between man and his creator. Even
more, we are back to the creation of the earth itself—this
earth which grew out of the seas, as day came from darkness
—this earth which has never since relinquished its struggle
against the sea, instrument of divine wrath.[18] Man and the
sea are *des frères ennemis*, Noah, Moses, Arion, Andromeda,

[17] Saint-Amant underlines the fact that this narrow corridor, this
earth canal as it were, is held up by the will of God. Water is here
again mastered—see above *murailles*—fixed by *des remparts que
l'oeil peut transpercer, [à travers lesquels] les poissons ébahis re-
gardent passer.* These lines, so harshly condemned by Boileau as
absurd, are therefore less naïve than they seemed. They are the
logical consequence of Saint-Amant's poetic vision.
[18] It is significant that in descriptions of the Flood, Saint-Amant
never mentions the great rains pouring down from the sky, but only
the sea rising out of itself to cover the earth. The sea is the only
enemy.

Ulysses, are all images of humanity. Faced by the instability, the hostility, of the watery elements, man holds on precariously to his fragile craft; but he dreams of the earth, of palaces of stone, of gardens in which his art triumphs, of canals, of fountains—symbols of his mastery—and he, perchance, recalls the words of Genesis:

La terre était informe et tout nue, les ténèbres couvraient la face de l'abime; et l'esprit de Dieu était porté sur les eaux. Dieu dit: que les eaux qui sont sous le ciel se rassemblent en un seul lieu et que l'élément aride paraisse. Dieu donna à l'élément aride le nom de terre et il appela Mers toutes ces eaux rassemblées. Et il vit que cela était bon. Dieu dit encore: que la terre produise de l'herbe verte qui porte la graine, et des arbres fruitiers qui portent des fruits chacun selon son espèce, et qui renferment leur semence en eux-mêmes pour se produire sur la terre. Et cela se fit ainsi . . . et Dieu vit que cela était bon.[19]

[19] *La Sainte Bible*, traduite en français sur la Vulgate, par Monsieur de Sacy.

CORNEILLE'S *HORACE*:
A STUDY IN TRAGIC AND
ARTISTIC AMBIVALENCE

By Lawrence E. Harvey

In his study of *Horace*, Louis Herland writes of the *dissonance fondamentale* on which the play is constructed.[1] Such a phrase might be used equally well to describe the nature of much recent criticism of *Horace*. The problem is posed most clearly no doubt by the hero's murder of his sister: does this act damn Horace and everything he represents or can it be explained in some way so that his glory remains untarnished? Guy Michaud works toward the latter solution by making Horace a tool of destiny: "La volonté du jeune Horace n'est réelle et efficace que dans la mesure où elle est au service de la volonté divine."[2] This places him above ordinary law and morality and absolves him of crime. Herland himself moves in the same direction through a psychological analysis of the characters that attempts to lessen our sympathy for Camille and Curiace and to establish the innocence of Horace. The criticism of Octave Nadal also tends, though in a different way, to justify Horace. In his view the central subject of the play has to do with the destruction of the individual by the state. Horace, in this perspective, becomes a victim along with Camille, Sabine, and Curiace.[3] Although disagreeing radically with the two preceding critics about the "future" of Horace, Georges May stresses, as they do, the positive qualities of the

1 *Horace ou naissance de l'homme* (Paris: Ed. de Minuit, 1952), pp. 14–15.
2 *L'Oeuvre et ses techniques* (Paris: Nizet, 1957), p. 225.
3 *Le Sentiment de l'amour dans l'oeuvre de Pierre Corneille* (Paris: Gallimard, 1948), pp. 194–196.

hero and minimizes the negative. In this view, apparently, nothing really irreparable has occurred, at least from the point of view of the protagonist:

> On sent fort bien que, n'eût été une guerre et le choix malencontreux de Rome, Horace aurait vécu heureux entre sa soeur Camille et sa femme Sabine, entre ses deux frères et ses trois beaux-frères. . . . En fait, on sent bien que, lorsque la tragédie est terminée, Horace et Sabine vivront heureux. . . . Leurs malheurs furent accidentels, anormaux; une fois passés, ils seront oubliés.[4]

A number of other recent studies, explicitly or by implication, hold Horace to be an out-and-out villain. Perhaps the most extreme statement of the case has been made by Peter Newmark, who views him as a representative of amoral (if not immoral) statism.[5] In this interpretation the play becomes an ironic attack by Corneille on something very similar to what the twentieth century calls totalitarianism:

> The constant recital and repetition of the Roman abstractions, the pompous tone, the refusal to mention Camille, leave no doubt of the indirect criticism intended by Corneille. "Gloire" and "honneur" are mere counters of State phraseology. . . . The long humourless tirades [teach] the lesson that the essence of states which are based on violence internally and externally does not change, and big words still hide mean deeds.[6]

Other critics, such as W. H. Barber and W. A. Nitze, while less extreme in this direction, tend to slight the glory of Horace and emphasize his ambition, pride, or arrogance.

The persistence of such diametrically opposed views is very instructive, both of the nature of the play and of the critical stances that have been adopted in dealing with it. In consid-

[4] *Tragédie cornélienne, tragédie racinienne* (*Illinois Studies in Language and Literature*, XXXII, no. 4; Urbana: University of Illinois Press, 1948).

[5] "A New View of *Horace*," *French Studies*, X (Jan., 1956), 1–10.

[6] *Ibid.*, pp. 9–10.

ering first of all the latter, I should like to make it clear that I am aware that every critical position, including the ontological approach, which I shall utilize in this study, has its advantages as well as its limitations. My purpose in pointing to limitations is not to disparage the valuable work done by the critics mentioned but rather to justify the need for further discussion of an already-much-discussed drama.

A first group of critics is concerned with the entire theatrical production of Corneille and, of course, with generalizing about it. Nothing could be more legitimate. The danger, often recognized by these same critics, lies in failing to realize that no generalization applying to the whole of Corneille can hope to account adequately for all that is particular to a given play. A conviction that the theatre of Corneille constitutes a school for greatness no doubt lies behind the unwillingness of some critics to admit any guilt on the part of Horace. A great deal had been said about the devotion to duty of the Cornelian hero before Brunetière pointed out that some of these heroes were not exactly models of virtuous conduct and substituted the idea of will for that of duty. Similarly, we have been made aware of the inadequacy of the Lansonian generalization by the studies of subsequent critics following the lead of Péguy.

If these critics, in focusing on Cornelian drama as a whole, run the risk of distorting the individual work, a second group compounds the danger by dividing its attention between the drama and something other than the drama.[7] As a number of writers have pointed out, *Horace* is often produced in France in times of national crisis. Obviously such a patriotic slant will hardly stress the guilt of the protagonist. On the other hand, the modern revulsion to war, already alluded to, has given rise to interpretations that scarcely do justice to the greatness

---

[7] Paul Bénichou states the problem very well in the introduction to his excellent study, *Morales du grand siècle* (Paris: Gallimard, 1948): "Le danger, pour qui veut définir ces rapports complexes de la vie sociale et de la pensée, est d'attenter à l'individualité des grands écrivains en prétendant les intégrer dans un ensemble impersonnel qui les dépasse. On risque ainsi, en poursuivant une systématisation hasardeuse, de défigurer ces réalités particulières, mais privilégiées du point de vue du patrimoine humain, que sont les grands hommes et les grandes oeuvres."

of Horace. A modern bias may, however, be only relatively less damaging than a historical one which, viewing literature as no more than a reflection of patterns found in seventeenth-century moral, social, or political life, forces the work to make it fit the pattern. Paul Bénichou writes:

> Quant au problème moral que l'ensemble de l'oeuvre invite à poser, c'est celui de la concordance possible ou non entre l'exaltation du moi et la vertu. Le mouvement essentiel du sublime cornélien consiste à donner à cette question une réponse favorable, naturellement formulée en termes de philosophie idéaliste: le moi s'affirme, et s'épure en même temps, dans le sens du bien.

While this problem, which is that of the feudal aristocracy in France under Louis XIII, no doubt finds such a solution in many of Corneille's plays, this formulation, by suggesting the innocence of Horace, fails to do full justice to the play.[8] Another divided focus that may have similar consequences appears in comparative studies, often contrasting Corneille and Racine, or the greatness of man and his corruption.[9] Finally, phenomenological and psychological criticism, unless practiced with considerable discretion, may deform the play by attempting to make it conform to extrinsic patterns. The confusion between a dramatic character and a living human being, no doubt a vestige of nineteenth-century historical realism, may lead the phenomenological critic to expand imprudently upon the data of the play. Thus Herland's vindication of Horace depends to a large degree on his interpretation of the silences in the play, of what Horace thinks and feels but never says:

> Il avait dit, il est vrai—ou plutôt il n'avait pas dit, il avait pensé du moins, nous l'avons vu, les mêmes choses en

---

[8] *Ibid.*, p. 51. In all fairness it must be pointed out that Bénichou does not attempt to deal with the particular problem of *Horace* and that he does point out (p. 45) that Camille is a notable exception to the general absence of rebellion against familial authority in Corneille and in the serious literature of the time.

[9] The books of Paul Bénichou and Georges May are among the most recent and certainly the best of such studies.

présence de Camille. Mais enfin il ne les avait pas dites, il n'avait pas réussi à les dire, à trouver les paroles amies qui désarment.[10]

Il a bien dit *rougir;* il n'a pas dit *souffrir:* mais c'est *souffrir* qu'il faut comprendre.[11]

Il l'analyse, il la définit, il ne la *sent* pas: il se grise de mots justement pour ne pas la sentir.[12]

Still more perilous is the negative evaluation of Paul Goodman, who condemns Horace, and the play, for failing to reflect perfectly a pattern taken from Gestalt psychology.

A final group of critics in centering their attention on something less than the whole play—a character, an idea, a technique—may jeopardize their results by neglecting the context within which, and only within which, the isolated part assumes its full meaning. The approach adopted by the historian of ideas leads Nadal in his study of love in Corneille to concentrate on the role of Camille. His sympathy for her as victim suggests antagonism for the *toute-puissance de l'Etat.* From this point to considering all the characters, including Horace, as innocent victims is a short step, one which he does not hesitate to take. Carlo François, concerned with the idea of the conscientious objector, focuses his attention on Curiace, to the detriment of Horace, while, for Newmark, Sabine is the only tragic character in the play. In his study of Corneille and Racine, May operates a fairly radical separation of form and content, which leads to a curious depreciation of this *forme mélodramatique . . . une enveloppe extérieure destinée à séduire, mais dont l'apparence ne permet en aucune manière de préjuger du contenu.*[13] In this view, suffering, dangers, obstacles become mere technical devices meaningless in themselves and destined only to enhance the greatness of the hero. (The terms *arbitraire . . . fortuit . . . adven-*

---

[10] Herland, *op. cit.,* pp. 175–176.
[11] *Ibid.,* p. 163.
[12] *Ibid.,* p. 105.
[13] May, *op. cit.,* p. 231.

tice[14] are revealing.) It is easy to understand, then, how the death of Camille and the resultant guilt of the hero fade into insignificance and Horace and Sabine can live happily ever after.

In attempting to assess some of the reasons why critics have favored one of two polar interpretations of *Horace*, one senses beneath individual variations a general view that identifies literature and moral message. The play tends to become either a satire or a eulogy of personal and military idealism: "Comme tout artiste, [Corneille] avait dû écrire son message sur du papier doré sur tranche. Mais c'est bel et bien le message, la substance intime même, qui est passé à la postérité; la dorure est oubliée, ternie. . . ."[15] Here, I should like to support a different view of literature, one that argues the interpenetration of form and content and, without denying literary meaning, stresses its indirect and often problematical nature. The need for such a view in the interpretation of *Horace* arises from the play itself but is underlined by the critical controversy in which each of the opposed readings is not so much wrong as incomplete. Only with a more comprehensive approach does it seem possible to achieve a synthesis that can do greater justice to the complexity of Corneille's masterpiece.

Several critics who tend to view the play as monocentric mention, nonetheless, one or more aspects in which it is ambivalent,[16] but no one, to my knowledge, has seen ambivalence as essential to the very meaning and structure of this tragedy or explored its artistic implications. Perhaps this can be explained in part by the attitude of Corneille himself, who, although quite aware of the double plot of *Horace*, con-

[14] *Ibid.*, p. 234.

[15] *Ibid.*, p. 232.

[16] W. A. Nitze, for example, notes with approval the remark of Martin Turnell that "it is one of the signs of Corneille's maturity that these standards are never accepted passively; his attitude towards them is always critical" (Turnell, *The Classical Moment* [London: Hamilton, 1947], p. 30). And Octave Nadal writes: "Telle est la rançon de la gloire, qu'elle impose au plus vivant d'entre les vivants des actes qui l'amènent à haïr la vie. Corneille ne pouvait pas ne pas s'étonner de ces contradictions douloureuses et inéluctables" (*op. cit.*, p. 196).

demned it as a violation of the rule of the unity of action.[17]
It is worthwhile insisting on the fact that there are two centers in the plot, two principal episodes in tension—the victory
over the Curiaces and the murder of Camille, the gain and
the loss of Horace—and that the unity of the play cannot be
achieved by dismissing either. The salient characteristic of
the play, the primary shock that disturbs and puzzles everyone on initial contact with the play, is precisely this paradoxical coexistence of contraries. Our task is not to obfuscate this
fact but rather to search out its significance and comprehend
it.

As we read the play again and examine it more closely, we
begin to understand that the double plot is not an accidental
structure—a lapse on the part of the poet or a slavish imitation of the historical account in Livy and Dionysius. The internal economy of the play makes it clear that the tension
within the plot is reflected in all the other aspects of the
tragedy—characters, style, structure, themes, images, and
emotions.

THE TRIPLE COMBAT: FLIGHT AND CONQUEST

Flight and conquest in this most unusual and improbable
combat are the two moments, causally bound together, that
distinguish it and, more than its doubly triple nature, set it
apart from more realistic duels.[18] One senses, in fact, that in

[17] "Le second défaut est que cette mort fait une action double,
par le second péril où tombe Horace après être sorti du premier"
(*Oeuvres de P. Corneille*, ed. C. Marty-Laveaux [Paris: Hachette,
1862], III, 275). It is quite possible to argue that Corneille was
more interested in dramatic polemics than in an objective evaluation of his play at this point or, as Herland does, that he is a better
playwright than critic: "Le poète de théâtre procède par intuitions,
et trop d'esprit d'analyse le desservirait plutôt. Ce don au reste man-
quait singulièrement à Corneille; on le voit par ses Examens, où il
se révèle si maladroit à expliquer ses personnages" (*op. cit.*, p.
183). At any rate, while Corneille's negative evaluation is unac-
ceptable, the fact of the double plot is indisputable.

[18] Jacques Scherer in *La Dramaturgie classique en France*
(Paris: Nizet, n.d.) writes: "L'invraisemblance politique passe par-

the play this triple aspect functions primarily as a device to make possible the surprising flight-conquest pattern. Corneille highlights the latter by the interrupted account of the battle. Julie's premature departure permits the dramatic buildup that sets the stage for Valère's climactic recital of the true outcome. Flight and conquest are linked elsewhere in the play. Toward the end of the second act, after the very moving attack and plea of Sabine, the elder Horace warns his son and Curiace that flight is the only way to strength and victory:

> Qu'est-ceci, mes enfants? écoutez-vous vos flammes,
> Et perdez-vous encor le temps avec des femmes?
> Prêts à verser du sang, regardez-vous des pleurs?
> *Fuyez*, et laissez-les déplorer leurs malheurs.
> Leurs plaintes ont pour vous trop d'art et de tendresse.
> Elles vous feroient part enfin de leur foiblesse,
> *Et ce n'est qu'en fuyant qu'on pare de tels coups.*[19]
>
> [679–685]

This passage clearly forecasts the coming combat. The use of military terminology (*pare de tels coups*) links the passage to this critical episode, and the psychological content of the speech establishes the connection between that episode and the more generally human theme of the nature of the idealistic mentality, which lies at the very heart of the play. Flight is one way of narrowing the focus of one's attention and eliminating all but the essential. Such a concentration is at the source of the energy and strength of idealism. And it constitutes, at the same time, its greatest danger.[20] The theme of

---

fois aussi inaperçue du public classique que l'invraisemblance psychologique. Il faudra attendre Schlegel pour qu'on remarque combien le choix des champions d'Albe et de Rome, qui fait le fondement d'*Horace* de Corneille, est peu croyable" (p. 374). Such an episode as the combat, then, evidently invites and demands something more than a literal interpretation.

[19] All quotations are taken from the Marty-Laveaux edition (see footnote 17) and are followed immediately by the line reference. Italics are mine.

[20] It is perhaps not inappropriate to suggest here a relationship between this idealistic concentration that Corneille understood so

flight as a way to victory occurs again at the end of Act IV
after the death of Camille and after Sabine entreats Horace
to kill her as well:

> Quelle injustice aux Dieux d'abandonner aux femmes
> Un empire si grand sur les plus belles âmes,
> Et de se plaire à voir de si foibles vainqueurs
> Régner si puissamment sur les plus nobles coeurs!
> A quel point ma vertu devient-elle réduite!
> *Rien ne la sauroit plus garantir que la fuite.*
>
> [1391–1396]

Flight, which serves Horace so well before, during, and after
the battle, was the obvious course of action before the im-
precations of Camille. The elder Horace clearly implies that
this was the way of avoiding the dishonor and shame of his
act when he agrees that Camille was guilty and should have
been punished—but not by Horace:

> Son crime, quoique énorme et digne du trépas,
> Etoit mieux impuni que puni par ton bras.
>
> [1417–1418]

THE IDEALISTIC DISCIPLINE: GAIN
AND LOSS

Flight is only one of a number of manifestations of the
narrowing of focus in *Horace*. The image of blindness is another. The protagonist rejects the idea of the backward glance
to happier days (488) and accepts *aveuglément* (492) what

---

well and the nature of his art. Much has been made in recent years
of the baroque side of Corneille's theatre on the one hand and its
realistic aspect on the other. Everything is relative, but Corneille's
theatre is certainly not so close to that of Shakespeare (or the
nineteenth-century naturalists!) as to that of Racine. The relative
economy of means, the tight interrelation of parts that leads to an
aesthetic of analogies and symbols, that eliminates extraneous materials and scarcely ever indulges in realism for its own sake—this
idealistic (or classical) art, which follows from the idealistic mentality, is Corneille's as well as Racine's. (For an admirable discussion of this art in Racine, see J. D. Hubert, *Essai d'exégèse racinienne: Les secrets témoins* [Paris: Nizet, 1956].)

the present has to offer. "Je n'examine rien" (498), he says, and later Julie reports:

> Et ce désir d'honneur qui leur ferme les yeux
> Tout aveugle qu'il est, respecte encor les Dieux.
>
> [821–822]

The idea behind limiting the field of vision, putting on intellectual blinders, recurs in the image of smothering or stifling. Horace calls on Curiace to *étouffer . . . tous autres sentiments* (494) except that of joyously accepted duty. Later he urges this same "direction of attention" on Camille:

> Tes flammes désormais doivent être étouffées;
> Bannis-les de ton âme, et songe à mes trophées.
>
> [1275–1276]

The repeated image of the altar and immolation functions in a similar way to express this sacrifice of one side of the self in order to heighten another. Horace speaks of the courage required in order to *vouloir au public immoler ce qu'on aime* (443), and during the battle he cries:

> Rome aura le dernier de mes trois adversaires,
> C'est à ses intérêts que je vais l'immoler.
>
> [1132–1133]

As Valère describes it, this third Curiace

> comme une victime aux marches de l'autel,
> . . . sembloit présenter sa gorge au coup mortel.
>
> [1137–1138]

It is impossible not to associate this theme with the sacrifice of Camille by Horace. She too is a victim offered to Rome, and, since the gods have decreed the destiny of Rome, it is fitting that the play end on this essential theme of sacrifice to them and that this sacrifice should be linked ironically to the death of Camille. One more reflection of the idea of limitation or restriction occurs when Horace asks his father to keep Sabine and Camille in their quarters during the combat:

> Mon père, retenez des femmes qui s'emportent,
> Et de grâce empêchez surtout qu'elles ne sortent.
> [695–696]

Their physical absence corresponds to their absence in the mind of Horace, the difficult and painful achievement of the idealistic discipline.

The psychological mechanism represented by these images is described, and advocated or condemned, by all the major characters in the play. Sabine understands very well that it offers a way to victory, a means of internal control over external contingencies and hence a liberation from indecision and suffering, a way out of her dilemma. She also understands that such a victory has its price. If love expands being to include others, the idealistic discipline contracts and diminishes by eliminating all external dangers to internal mastery. This two-edged sword of idealism calls forth such opposed parallels as the following in which Sabine weighs in the balance gain and loss, glory and tribulation:

> Songeons pour quelle cause,
>   et non par quelles mains;
> Revoyons les vainqueurs,
>   sans penser qu'à la gloire
> Que toute leur maison
>   reçoit de leur victoire;
> Et sans considérer
>   aux dépens de quel sang
> Leur vertu les élève
>   en cet illustre rang,
> Faisons nos intérêts
>   de ceux de leur famille:
> En l'une je suis femme,
>   en l'autre je suis fille,
> Et tiens à toutes deux
>   par de si forts liens,
> Qu'on ne peut triompher
>   que par les bras des miens.
> Fortune, quelques maux
>   que ta rigueur m'envoie,

> Quand je songe à leur mort,
>   quoi que je me propose,
> Je songe par quels bras,
>   et non pour quelle cause,
> Et ne vois les vainqueurs
>   en leur illustre rang
> Que pour considérer
>   aux dépens de quel sang.
> La maison des vaincus
>   touche seule mon âme:
> En l'une je suis fille,
>   en l'autre je suis femme,
> Et tiens à toutes deux
>   par de si forts liens,
> Qu'on ne peut triompher
>   que par la mort des miens.
> C'est là donc cette paix
>   que j'ai tant souhaitée!
> Trop favorables Dieux,
>   vous m'avez écoutée!

J'ai trouvé les moyens   Quels foudres lancez-vous
   d'en tirer de la joie   quand vous vous irritez,
Et puis voir aujourd'hui   Si même vos faveurs
   le combat sans terreur   ont tant de cruautés?
         [726-737]   [751-762]

Returning now to the triple combat, we can understand
how it figures not only the glory of Horace but also his loss.
While the narrowed focus made possible by flight saves
Horace and enables him to win glory, it also results in the
death of his long-time friend, his friend's brothers, and ultimately his sister.[21] Now, although this is so, it must be admitted that the emphasis in the combat itself falls on the side
of *la gloire*. Loss occurs, but its full magnitude and implications remain to be developed, both dramatically and psychologically. And herein lies the necessity and justification
of the other major episode of the play, the murder of Camille.

THE DEATH OF CAMILLE: *LE REVERS DE LA MEDAILLE*

The two most striking examples in the play of the narrowing mechanism are, significantly enough, its two most famous
passages, often cited as examples of the sublime in Corneille.
The first, the *Qu'il mourût* (1021) of the elder Horace, takes
for granted an idealistic discipline that scorns self-preserva-
tion (and it provides a living example of an idealist who
radically subordinates his paternal love to the ideal). The
second sums up symbolically the central meaning of the
play:

HORACE: . . . Albe vous a nommé, je ne vous connois plus.
CURIACE: Je vous connois encore, et c'est ce qui me tue.
                           [502-503]

Once again, Corneille exteriorizes the psychological in dramatic action. The words of Horace eliminate Curiace as
friend from his consciousness, and this initial death is sub-

[21] One is reminded of the phrase of Curiace that includes *longue
amitié, amour,* and *alliance* (463).

sequently represented by the physical death of Curiace during the triple combat.[22] Similarly, the words of Curiace must be taken literally as well as figuratively. His refusal to accept the intellectual discipline urged on him by Horace weakens him and, on the symbolic level, accounts for his defeat in battle. His words here are clearly a forecast of his coming death. The inability or unwillingness to kill the Horace in his heart is a prelude to the inevitable result—the inability to kill him on the battlefield. This symbolism is not symbolism for its own sake, of course, nor is its significance confined to the military sphere, which in the play is itself symbolic of a more universal experience of life. It corresponds, rather, to the profound intuition of the relationship between thought and action, of the value and danger of idealism.[23]

In a sense Camille is a second Curiace—not only because she is betrothed to him and one with him in love but also because they both represent a side of Horace that his mind and will have eliminated. Horace and Rome have become identified. Therefore Camille's magnificent rhetorical attack on Rome—no less an attack than the military assault of Curiace—is at the same time the most telling of her thrusts against Horace:

> Rome, l'unique objet de mon ressentiment!
> Rome, à qui vient ton bras d'immoler mon amant!
> Rome qui t'a vu naître, et que ton coeur adore!
> Rome enfin que je hais parce qu'elle t'honore! [etc.]
> [1301–1304]

The fundamental identity between the psychological weap-

---

[22] It is no doubt significant, incidentally, that Curiace the friend is the hardest of the three brothers to vanquish, for such a friendship is more difficult to extirpate from the heart than the interfamilial ties represented in potential by the other two Curiaces. Livy does not tell us which Curiace is which, while Corneille makes a point of it (1115). It is also, of course, dramatically fitting and necessary that the major character have the major part in the action.

[23] In our time the film version of The Bridge on the River Kwai is an impressive treatment of the same theme—and, like Horace, profoundly ambiguous.

ons of Sabine and Camille and the military weapons of the men is clearly established both explicitly and by the imagery that associates tears and arms:

> Julie, on nous renferme, on a peur de nos larmes;
> Sans cela nous serions au milieu de leurs armes.
>
> [775–776]

If Camille and Curiace become identified as "the enemy," it is as the internal as well as the external enemy. Thus, on the extraliteral level, Camille-Curiace represents an aspect of the self of Horace, one which must be exorcized. Horace states this in so many words when he speaks of his fight against Curiace as a *combat contre un autre soi-même* (444) and explains the elimination of Camille in terms that apply more to psychological struggle than to physical conflict:

> Et ce souhait impie, encore qu'impuissant,
> Est un monstre qu'il faut étouffer en naissant.
>
> [1333–1334][24]

They both represent, to different degrees, the temptation to personal rather than political idealism, that part of him that must be destroyed. Thus glory is balanced by dishonor, joy by sorrow, gain by loss, and the episode of the triple combat by the episode of Camille's murder.

THE CHARACTERS AS FIGURES OF THE DIVIDED SELF

The double plot, while it is a central manifestation of the basically ambiguous nature of the human experience ex-

---

[24] It is, of course, legitimate to view the play through the eyes of Camille, although aesthetically such a point of view must be subordinated to one in which Horace, the protagonist for whom the play is named, assumes his central place. Even in the former perspective, however, Camille is another Horace, as radically idealistic as he, who has simply chosen the ideal that Horace has rejected and rejected the one he has chosen.

> "Oui, je lui ferai voir, par d'infaillibles marques,
> Qu'un véritable amour brave la main des Parques"
>
> [1195–1196]

is as true to Horace as it is to Camille, who says it.

pressed by the play, is by no means the only such manifestation. The theme of division, in fact, occurs in a number of different forms throughout the tragedy. In the first line of Act II, Curiace notes that Rome *n'a point séparé son estime* (347) in choosing all three champions from the same family, and we are reminded of the divisive tactics of Horace in combat, when he does separate the three Curiaces. Their physical separation, of course, mirrors the internal division of Curiace, which he expresses when he first comes on stage:

> Tant qu'a duré la guerre, on m'a vu constamment
> Aussi bon citoyen que véritable amant.
> D'Albe avec mon amour j'accordais la querelle:
> Je soupirais pour vous en combattant pour elle;
> Et s'il fallait encor que l'on en vînt aux coups,
> Je combattrais pour elle en soupirant pour vous.
>
> [265–270]

The repetition in lines 268 and 270 stresses his ambivalent feelings, and the inversion is a very expressive stylistic device that reinforces our sense of the balanced nature of the tension. If Camille is mentioned in the first hemistich of line 268, it is not that the scales are tipped in her favor, for Albe in turn receives first mention in line 270. Needless to say, such divided loyalties do not make for military effectiveness.

The recurrent phrases *rompre les noeuds* and *rompre les liens* (447 and 497, for example) carry out this theme of disunity. With Horace, however, breaking ties is equivalent to throwing off bonds, to rejecting one-half of the self in order to reestablish a new unity that is both less and more than the previous one. He seeks to resolve the tension that Curiace and Sabine choose to maintain. Her resolve is evident in the first scene of the play, when she asserts that even after the final decision there will be no true resolution for her:

> Et je garde, au milieu de tant d'âpres rigueurs,
> Mes larmes aux vaincus, et ma haine aux vainqueurs.
>
> [93–94]

This is, in effect, a means of prolonging the tension or righting the balance. The decision that goes one way in physical combat will go another in the affective struggle waged by Sabine. As we have seen before, both men and women join battle, each with his own weapons.

It is Camille, however, who carries out the threat of Sabine and, by her death, ruins the great attempt of Horace to abolish the duality that, we must finally admit, is inherent in the human condition. While Curiace and Sabine harbor opposites within themselves, Horace and Camille, in eliminating respectively the private and the public ideal, merely balance each other and together constitute a restatement of the same opposition.[25] Every extreme engenders its opposite, and escape from the human dilemma is shown to be impossible.[26] Thus at the end of the play Camille has sealed forever the ineluctable law of destiny and left Sabine with no alternative but to express again the insoluble predicament.[27] Critics have explained the "death wish" of Sabine and of Horace in a psychological perspective, but there is also the very good aesthetic reason that their parts are complete. They have said and done what they had to, and the final act is not really their act.

THE STRUCTURE OF THE PLAY

Corneille, and most critics after him, criticize this last act as being *tout en plaidoyers*, whereas the fifth act *doit plus*

[25] Earlier in the play Camille too had expressed this opposition as an inner tension:

"Nos sentiments entre eux demeurent suspendus,
Nostre choix impossible, et nos voeux confondus."
[889-890]

[26] Pascal wrote, "L'homme n'est ni ange ni bête, et le malheur veut que qui veut faire l'ange fait la bête." Corneille, in *Horace*, seems to say that man *can* be great, but only at great cost. Neither the admiration for the attempt nor the pity at the cost are so apparent in the Pascalian statement.

[27] The denouement of the play in the original edition consisted of a restatement of the veiled prophecy of the oracle that foretold the death of Camille. Whatever disadvantages such an ending entailed, it did serve admirably to point up the relationship between the death of Camille and the edicts of the higher powers that determine the nature of the human condition.

agir que discourir.[28] If we think in terms of the linear development of a dramatic story, this is no doubt a valid judgment. Such a perspective, however, seems especially inappropriate in a play like *Horace*, which can hardly be said to have any such linear structure. The play is built, rather, around a central pair of events linked closely together in the fourth act. The alternating hopeful and fearful reactions of the different characters toward the uncertain future fill out the first three acts, and each reaction may be referred to this center. It is more fitting, therefore, to speak of a circular structure than of a linear plot development.[29] From this point of view the importance of the last act becomes clear, for it functions, as do all other parts of the play, as a mirror that reflects the central ambiguity from a new angle, deepening our understanding of its implications and significance. The sureness of Corneille's poetic (as opposed to his critical) instinct is evident here, for what better correlative of the ambivalent center could there be than the trial with its prosecution set against its defense? And what trial could serve better than this one in which the judgment handed down, while sparing Horace for the ends of the state, justifies both the prosecution and the defense and maintains the paradoxical, and very human, union of contraries in the guilt and the glory of Horace?

[28] *Oeuvres*, ed. Marty-Laveaux, III, 279.

[29] Georges Poulet writes: "Dans l'ordre de la vie volontaire il n'y a point de causalité temporelle" (*Etudes sur le temps humain* [Paris: Plon, 1950], p. 101). What is psychologically true of the Cornelian hero is aesthetically true of the author's dramatic structure. Poulet points this out when he says of the *durée objective* of the plot: "Ce qui lui enlève presque toute signification, c'est qu'elle n'est jamais qu'une durée antécédente. Elle prépare le présent, mais elle ne l'amène point, ne le fait point" (p. 100). It is not within the scope of his study to explore types of structure other than the causal and temporal, and we can only be grateful for the insight that established the link between the free will of the protagonist and the noncausal nature of the plot. However, from the aesthetic point of view the events of the play can hardly be said to lack *presque toute signification*. They function as analogies and symbols of a central human experience within a "circular" structure that, far better than would a causal chain of happenings, reflects the theology of freedom within the framework of which Corneille's theatre was written.

If we can speak of a linear development at all, it is probably in the tension that mounts through the oscillations of the first three acts and culminates in the explosive actions of the fourth act. This tension must abate finally. The meaning of particular words and events must be universalized in a poetic catharsis or calming that makes possible our acceptance of the human destiny revealed in the play. The pace must slow and contemplative distance succeed empathetic engagement. Once again, the trial scenes, analogous in part to the chorus scenes in Greek tragedy, are admirably suited to these ends.

Although the oscillations between hope and fear, illusion and reality, serve, as May has pointed out in his discussion of the *fausse piste*,[30] to maintain suspense and engender surprise in the audience, they also have a substantive purpose. The illusions of the characters, as long as they last, have a certain reality that enriches the rather meager material of the play. They provide hypothetical alternative situations each of which must be tested on the yardstick of personal and public idealism. Thus the elder Horace, under the illusion that his son has fled the field of battle, shows the full measure of his *vertu*. Camille, thinking Curiace has deserted his country for love of her, reveals her lack of adhesion to the ideal of her brother. Such an aesthetic makes for classical economy in the plot and at the same time favors emotional vicissitude and intellectual complexity.

Structure is not simply technique, however. In a literary masterpiece it should be expressive of meaning as well, and this is perhaps its most important function in *Horace*. That Corneille was fully conscious of the significance of structure is hard to doubt in light of the following speech of Camille, which is in part a commentary by the artist on his art:

> En vit-on jamais un [sort] dont les rudes traverses
> Prissent en moins de rien tant de faces diverses,
> Qui fût doux tant de fois, et tant de fois cruel,
> Et portât tant de coups avant le coup mortel?

[30] *Op. cit.*, p. 104.

Vit-on jamais une âme en un jour plus atteinte
De joie et de douleur, d'espérance et de crainte,
Asservie en esclave à plus d'événements,
Et le piteux jouet de plus de changements?

[1203–1210]

In the next twenty-four lines she becomes quite specific in
what amounts to a veritable summary of the entire play. This
lengthy monologue which immediately precedes her final
meeting with her brother and her death is extremely important because it establishes quite clearly the link between
structure and meaning in the play. In it we have a picture of
man caught up in flux and subject to all the vicissitudes of
fortune, the slave and plaything of destiny. Such a picture
of fickle change is associated elsewhere in the play with *le
peuple stupide*:

Sa voix tumultueuse assez souvent fait bruit;
Mais un moment l'élève, un moment le détruit;
Et ce qu'il contribue à notre renommée
Toujours en moins de rien se dissipe en fumée.

[1713–1716]

Against this "superficial" view of life (*Le peuple, qui voit
tout seulement par l'écorce* . . . 1559) is pitted an inner
idealism that frees man from the control of external vicissitudes. Now it is Sabine and Camille who, by making happiness their goal and by making this happiness depend on
other human beings, destroy their own freedom. Such an attitude is closely akin to the "pastoral" mentality which, although it rebels idealistically against the passage of time, still
puts its faith in an exterior world whose joys are emotional
and sensuous and most subject to flux. The profound distrust
of *les sens* that is evident in Corneille's first play, *Mélite*, is
an index of the gulf that separates the idealistic orientation
of this play (which has, on occasion, been termed a *pas-
torale*) from the pastoral vision of life.[31] In *Horace* the plot

---

[31] For a fuller discussion of this problem, see L. E. Harvey, "The
Intellectual Art of the Early Corneille" (Harvard dissertation,
1955), chap. iv.

structure serves to express a similar vision, the hallmarks of which are *bonheur, passion* (in its etymological meaning), *change, illusion, les sens,* and, in general, dependence on what is external to the self. In tension with it, heroic idealism can be recognized in such recurrent expressions as *vertu, immuable, loi, devoir,* and *constance,* and its contrasting characteristics are inwardness and immutability:

> Je sais trop comme agit la vertu véritable:
> C'est sans en triompher que le nombre l'accable;
> Et sa mâle vigueur, toujours en même point,
> Succombe sous la force, et ne lui cède point.
>
> [1067–1070]

THE HISTORICAL SETTING

Very little has been written of the historical setting of *Horace* and its relation to the meaning of the play. In the background is the *ordre éternel* (980) of destiny that guarantees the glorious future of Rome: "Les Dieux à notre Enée ont promis cette gloire" (991). It is this higher immutability that corresponds to and authorizes the constancy of the human ideal. The opposition between Albe and Rome expands the meaning of the battle between the Curiaces and the Horaces, and here it is important to note, first of all, that Albe is the mother-city of Rome:

> Mais respecte une ville à qui tu dois Romule.
> Ingrate, souviens-toi que du sang de ses rois
> Tu tiens ton nom, tes murs, et tes premières lois.
> Albe est ton origine: arrête, et considère
> Que tu portes le fer dans le sein de ta mère.
> Tourne ailleurs les efforts de tes bras triomphants;
> Sa joie éclatera dans l'heur de ses enfants;
> Et se laissant ravir à l'amour maternelle,
> Ses voeux seront pour toi, si tu n'es plus contre elle.
>
> [52–60]

The image of close familial ties is one more instance of Corneille's insistence on this theme. As he invented Sabine and thereby drew the two cities more closely together, so here he stresses the fact that the people of Rome are descendants of Albans and relatives of Albans. The two cities are two parts of a single people, as the forces they represent are two aspects of the protagonist and of every man. The war is a civil war, one people torn internally:

Nous ne sommes qu'un sang et qu'un peuple en deux villes:
Pourquoi nous déchirer par des guerres civiles?

[291–292]

This theme of internal *divorces* (299) is reinforced by the recurrent parricide motif. In the passage above Rome is a child that will kill its mother. Later Curiace recalls the motif in describing the reaction of the warriors to the speech of the Alban leader:

Il semble qu'à ces mots notre discorde expire:
Chacun, jetant les yeux dans un rang ennemi,
Reconnoît un beau-frère, un cousin, un ami;
Ils s'étonnent comment leurs mains, de sang avides,
Voloient, sans y penser, à tant de parricides.

[316–320]

Camille asks Curiace not to *aspirer au nom de fratricide* (600), and Valère at the end of the play echoes the civil war theme (1492–1498) and refers twice to the *main parricide* of Horace (1522; 1532). All this is, of course, borne out, for Rome does kill Albe, and Horace his sister. Tulle does well to remind us at the end of the play that Rome is under the sign of Romulus, who killed his twin (his other self), Remus (1755–1758). Horace is, in effect, the second founder of Rome, and the price he has to pay is the same. The greatness of Corneille lies in transferring this story of the cost of greatness from the plane of external events (which become analogies and symbols) to the plane of the mind, in showing us two Horaces (called Horace and Camille-Curiace), one of whom must be sacrificed to the other. The relationship between the idealistic discipline that accomplishes this and the symbolic murder that figures it is beautifully expressed by Camille when she refuses to banish

the memory of Curiace from her mind: "Tigre altéré de sang
. . . qui veut que . . . moi-même je le tue une seconde fois!"
(1287–1290). The vision of Rome's suicide that she con-
jures up is a logical extension of this pattern of imagery:

> Qu'elle-même sur soi renverse ses murailles,
> Et de ses propres mains déchire ses entrailles!
>
> [1311–1312]

It is curious that in L. M. Riddle's study of the sources of
Horace there is no attempt to explain Corneille's choice of
the names Sabine and Camille.[32] Models for Sabine in Lope
de Vega, La Calprenède, Mairet, and Dionysius of Hali-
carnassus are discussed, yet if one is aware of the significance
of the civil war theme in the play, it becomes obvious that
the source is elsewhere. Since, as stated explicitly in the text,
the tragedy is part of the legendary story of Aeneas and the
founding of Rome, it would seem logical, in any case, to look
first into the account of this founding in Livy (cited by
Corneille as his source) and Dionysius. In doing this, one is
struck immediately by the tale of the battle between the
followers of Romulus and the Sabines following the rape of
the Sabine women two generations before the battle between
Rome and Albe under Tulle, who, it is worth noting, is linked
by Livy to this earlier war, since he is said to be the grand-
son of a warrior who fought against the Sabines. We are
struck more particularly by the following passage:

Then the Sabine women, whose wrong had given rise
to the war, with loosened hair and torn garments, their
woman's timidity lost in a sense of their misfortune,
dared to go amongst the flying missiles, and rushing in
from the side, to part the hostile forces and disarm them
of their anger, beseeching their fathers on this side, on
that their husbands, that fathers-in-law and sons-in-law
should not stain themselves with impious bloodshed,

---

[32] *The Genesis and Sources of Pierre Corneille's Tragedies from*
Médée *to* Pertharite (Johns Hopkins Studies in Romance Litera-
tures and Languages, vol. III; Baltimore, 1926), chap. iii.

nor pollute with parricide the suppliants' children, grand-
sons to one party and sons to the other.[33]

The analogous civil war situation, the parricide theme, the
intercession by the Sabine women, which Corneille's Sabine
echoes when she says:

> J'aurai trop de moyens pour y forcer vos mains.
> Vous ne les aurez point au combat occupées,
> Que ce corps au milieu n'arrête vos épées;
>
> [658–660]

the anxiety of Horace lest she and Camille appear on the
battlefield to interfere with the fight by their cries and tears,
and, in general, the mediating role of Sabine provide overwhelming evidence that we need search no further for Corneille's source. The invention of Sabine is first and foremost
a way of reflecting, reinforcing, and expanding the significance of the human dilemma that lies at the heart of the
tragedy.[34]

[33] Livy, *Histories* (2), I, ed. B. O. Foster (London, New York,
1919), 47–48.

[34] In a very sensible article, "L'Invention chez Corneille" in *Yale
Romanic Studies*, vol. XXII (New Haven: Yale University Press,
1943), Jean Boorsch points out a general tendency in the creative
imagination of Corneille to invent characters not found in his
sources, usually in order to introduce amorous rivalries. I am in
agreement with Boorsch on his important conclusion that this leads
to artistic complexity, but would go further in attempting to show
that this complexity is part and parcel of an aesthetic of analogies
and symbols. (For further evidence favoring this view, see the recent article, "Intellectualism in Corneille: The Symbolism of Proper
Names in *La Suivante*" in the Fall, 1959, issue of *Symposium*).
Boorsch writes: "Cette tendance était déjà marquée nettement
dans *Horace* avec l'invention de Sabine. . . . Le public a bien pu
couvrir Sabine de son approbation; de quelque côté qu'on regarde
ce personnage, il est indéniable qu'il viole l'unité d'action, et il
nous paraît utile de noter le besoin que dès ce moment Corneille
éprouvait, de faire cette double alliance, mais sans avoir pu, selon
son expression 'incorporer' Sabine dans la pièce, autrement que par
l'artifice des liaisons de scènes" (pp. 124–125). It would appear, on
the contrary, that Sabine is admirably incorporated into the play, if
our definition of dramatic unity is taken from Corneille's practice
rather than from seventeenth-century dramatic theory. A negative

The problem of the name of Camille is somewhat different. The name does not appear in Dionysius nor in Livy, where she is called *Horatia*, but the person does. It is, then, the source of the name and not the character that is in question. Obviously, Corneille could scarcely use *Horatia*, which, along with *Horatius*, would produce Horace, making five of them and creating a feminine designation unlikely to be accepted seriously by a French audience. Since, once again, the play is under the sign of the promise made to Aeneas, the Camilla of Virgil's *Aeneid* seems a likely possibility. She is a warrior maiden, which supports the Cornelian imagery that unites physical combat and psychological warfare. She leads the Volsci against the men of Aeneas, the Volsci who in the time of Tulle remain a danger to Rome, waiting on the periphery to attack the weakened victors in the fight between Albe and Rome, as Corneille's Camille attacks the victorious Horace and, in him, Rome, the offspring through Albe of the Lavinium of Aeneas. If this enemy of Rome is within the walls of the city and a Roman in *Horace*, this is in keeping with the general interiorization of the play. She becomes the enemy within Rome and, as we have seen, within Horace himself, who in one sense personifies Rome. Beyond this, there is a note of tragic irony in the fact that Virgil's Camilla has been consecrated by her father to the service of Diana. Like Camille, she is destined for eternal virginity. The violence of her nature and the pity that her death inspires are no doubt further reasons for Corneille's choice. Finally, it is well to note that Camille's vision of the future destruction of Rome, which counters the vision of Aeneas, begins with the attack of the Latin peoples:

> Puissent tous ses voisins ensemble conjurés
> Saper ses fondements encor mal assurés!
>
> [1305–1306]

judgment of this kind is one more illustration of the danger of measuring a work against some extrinsic standard instead of seeking to comprehend it on its own terms.

TIME AND THE TWO CITIES: SABINE *vs.* CAMILLE

If the parent is conservative and the child idealistic, if the former looks to a utopian past and the latter to a glorious future, if parents are divided between their own interests and those of their children, while the children are more selfishly single-minded, if youth, in a profound sense, must always replace age, yet suffer loss as well as gain in doing so, then the image that compares Albe and Rome to mother and son is an appropriate and richly suggestive one. Something of the human attitude represented by the older city can be seen in Sabine's brief but lyric vision of the golden age of childhood:

> Albe, où j'ai commencé de respirer le jour,
> Albe, mon cher pays, et mon premier amour;
> [29–30]

and in her refusal to accept the dictum that *pour suivre un mari l'on quitte ses parents* (886). Indeed, for Curiace as well as Sabine, since they are both Albans, the personal and the public each has its rights, with Sabine inclined to the personal and Curiace to the public, as their sexes dictate. The youthful extremism of Rome makes Camille, the feminine extension of Sabine, more exclusively on the side of the personal and Horace, the masculine extension of Curiace, more absolute in his adherence to the public ideal. It is in this architecture, involving two cities, two sexes, and four characters, that we find the justification for the fourth scene of the third act, which brings Sabine into opposition with Camille. One critic, who feels that these two feminine characters are mouthpieces for Corneille's attack on amoral statism, is at a loss to explain this scene except as a failure on the part of Corneille or a concession to political expediency:

Both these characters indulge in tiresome and pointless mutual recrimination in Act III, scene 4, an interlude which betrays all Corneille's deficiencies, his hairsplitting, his weakness for sterile antithesis and futile *raison-nement*, but which may have been deliberately "placed" in order to weaken the appeal of such subversive characters.[35]

The scene is, one may argue, no more tiresome, pointless, sterile, nor futile than most of the other scenes in the play. It has dramatic power as well as a kind of emotional appeal lacking up to this point in the tragedy. And it has a structural *raison d'être* in the ambiguous situation of Camille, at once a Roman and an enemy of Rome. Until this scene the differences between the woman and the girl have seemed less important than their common cause and suffering. Each has expressed an aspect of what we have called the "pastoral" attitude.[36] But Camille is also a Roman with the youthful idealism and violence of Rome and its orientation toward the future rather than the past. While she does not yet completely reject the mature Alban vision that admits reasons on both sides, her impatience with such divided loyalties and the absolute nature of her love are apparent in her depreciation of early familial ties:

> L'hymen qui nous attache en une autre famille
> Nous détache de celle où l'on a vécu fille,
>
> [883–884]

and in her apology of love that begins with the famous and cruel lines:

> Je le vois bien, ma soeur, vous n'aimâtes jamais;
> Vous ne connoissez point ni l'amour ni ses traits.
>
> [917–918]

Both these statements serve at once to mark her as a Roman and to prepare the audience for her ultimate rejection of Rome and her Roman family in a final and tragic homage to love.

[35] Newmark, *op. cit.*, p. 8.
[36] Another interesting analogy exists between the pastoral rejection of the city in favor of personal happiness in the country and the tension in *Horace* between public and private goods.

OTHER MANIFESTATIONS OF DUALITY

The central meaning of the play grows also from other elements of its form, such as critical vocabulary. The key words in the play cluster around two central word pairs: *faible-généreux*, which mirrors the basic tension between the private and the public from the point of view of Horace and Rome, and, balancing it, *humain-barbare*, which reflects the same conflict seen through Alban eyes.[37] The use of oxymoron is another device that serves the same purpose: *funeste honneur* (533), *cruels généreux* (798), *brutale vertu* (1237), and on the other side *noble criminel* (1602). Rhymes like *vanité-immortalité* (457–458), *fumée-renommée* (459–460), and *Romain-humain* (481–482) function in the same way. Even a play on words is not scorned by Corneille when he has Camille say:

> Dégénérons, mon coeur, d'un si vertueux père;
> Soyons indigne soeur d'un si généreux frère.
>   [1239–1240]

Such irony is only one example of many similar instances in the play, for irony, in its apparent agreement and real opposition, is one more means of accentuating the central tension of the play.[38]

The Alexandrine line is so widely used in classical literature that we rarely stop to ponder its aesthetic function in a particular work of literature. If Corneille delights in playing

[37] For a basic statistical study of the vocabulary of *Horace*, see Pierre Guiraud, *Index du vocabulaire du théâtre classique: Corneille III* (Paris: Klincksieck, 1956). Needless to say, such information, though very useful, does not lead automatically to valid interpretation. Frequency, even in the rhyming position, does not always correlate with importance. Once again, isolation from the total context can be a dangerous procedure.

[38] For Newmark "the pompous tone" of the speeches of Horace and his father is a sign of Corneille's ironic attack on Roman idealism. This is undoubtedly a projection of a twentieth-century anti-rhetorical bias on a rhetorical age. The occasional irony of Camille, Curiace, and especially Sabine in Act II, scene 6, on the other hand, is undeniable.

one hemistich against another in ringing antitheses in all his plays, their poetic expressiveness is nonetheless admirable in *Horace*, where they contribute not a little to the architecture of ambivalence that gives the play its form and meaning:

CURIACE: J'aime ce qu'il me donne, et je plains ce qu'il m'ôte;
[479]
SABINE: Je ne suis point pour Albe, et ne suis plus pour Rome;
[88]
Je prendrai part aux maux sans en prendre à la gloire;
[92]
LE VIEIL HORACE: Nos plaisirs les plus doux ne vont point sans tristesse;
Il mêle à nos vertus des marques de faiblesse.
[1407-1408]

The antitheses come often one to a line but occur also one to a hemistich ("De joie et de douleur, d'espérance et de crainte . . ." [1208]), one to two lines (1213-1214). They are frequently arranged in impressive series:

Ce jour nous fut propice et funeste à la fois:
Unissant nos maisons, il désunit nos rois;
Un même instant conclut notre hymen et la guerre,
Fit naître notre espoir et le jeta par terre,
Nous ôta tout, sitôt qu'il nous eut tout promis,
Et nous faisant amants, il nous fit ennemis.
[173-178]

Sometimes we have antitheses within antitheses:

Quelle horreur d'embrasser un homme dont l'épée
De toute ma famille a la trame coupée!
Et quelle impiété de haïr un époux
Pour avoir bien servi les siens, l'Etat et vous!
[1615-1618]

Such conflicts also take place in larger units of structure, the monologue of interior division, the dialogue and the stich-omythic dialogue (IV, 2). No reader of *Horace* can fail to be struck by the density of the various manifestations of tension. The style and structure, at all levels and all times, express by their very nature the tragic human dilemma that is the core of the play.

CONCLUSION: CORNELIAN ART AND THE NATURE OF TRAGEDY

In his early comedies Corneille often uses his characters to represent alternative attitudes toward a central problem. The obstacles raised by such attitudes create dramatic tensions, which he resolves finally into a hierarchy of values. The dilemmas are only apparent, and we learn through the actions of the ideal couple the way to a happiness that is heightened by the difficulties overcome in its pursuit. The dramatic art is the same in *Horace* but the dilemma is no longer illusory. It has become a fissure in human nature itself.

In *Oedipus Rex* pity and fear are met by an emotion, less often recognized, that is more positive. In his inherent nobility and his transcendent acceptance of his fate Oedipus inspires something closely akin to admiration. And such a response is clearly authorized by *Oedipus at Colonus*. Similar emotions are in balance in *Horace*. Within the play there is an audience, which no doubt corresponds to the theatre audience and functions as a model, responding as Corneille would have the real audience respond. It is composed of the two armies which are spectators of the triple combat, and Julie reports its reactions:

> L'un s'émeut de pitié, l'autre est saisi d'horreur,
> L'autre d'un si grand zèle admire la fureur.
>
> [785-786]

The same combination occurs in the phrase *ce triste et fier honneur* (478), which reflects the dual emotions elicited by the two actions of Horace, the admiration his heroism arouses and the fear and pity evoked by his shameful murder: "je te plains . . . d'avoir par sa mort déshonoré ta main" (1412-1414).

These ambivalent emotions come into play, of course, before the spectacle of man's greatness and his weakness. Since most of the human race can probably be divided into two groups, those who stress man's greatness or goodness and those who emphasize his weakness or depravity, it is not surprising that critics of *Horace* have often seen him as either hero or villain, idealist or fanatic. All the evidence in the play, nevertheless, forbids us to make such a choice. Tulle sums it up when he says to the elder Horace:

> Beaucoup par un long âge ont appris comme vous
> Que le malheur succède au bonheur le plus doux,
>
> [1461–1462]

and the elder Horace had said it to his son:

> Quand la gloire nous enfle, il [le jugement céleste] sait
>   bien comme il faut
> Confondre notre orgueil qui s'élève trop haut.
> Nos plaisirs les plus doux ne vont point sans tristesse;
> Il mêle à nos vertus des marques de faiblesse,
> Et rarement accorde à notre ambition
> L'entier et pur honneur d'une bonne action.
>
> [1405–1410]

Although Horace does not refer to the death of his sister, he too recognizes this general law of the human condition that makes the fall inevitable:

> L'honneur des premiers faits se perd par les seconds;
> Et quand la renommée a passé l'ordinaire,
> Si l'on n'en veut déchoir, il faut ne plus rien faire.
>
> [1570–1572]

Man cannot, with impunity, assault heaven nor regain his lost paradise (although he cannot cease trying either).[39]

[39] Dionysius writes: "But it was ordained after all that even he, as he was but a mortal, should not be fortunate in everything, but should feel some stroke of the envious god who, having from an insignificant man made him great in a brief moment of time and raised him to wonderful and unexpected distinction, plunged him the same day into the unhappy state of being his sister's murderer" (*The Roman Antiquities* [London: Heinemann, 1939], II, 79).

In the play this prohibition is expressed in the idea of the separation of heaven and earth,

> Le ciel agit sans nous en ces événements,
> Et ne les règle point dessus nos sentiments
> [861–862]

which the enigmatic oracle fails to bridge. Although the six combatants will the combat and refuse to relinquish their positions as champions of their countries, the gods, as Camille suggests, inspire the choice of the champions and it is they who confirm their choice and the triple combat. Sabine emphasizes the role of fate in all that has happened: "Et je m'en prends au sort plutôt qu'à ton devoir" (1366). It is destiny, in fact, that guarantees the future glory of Rome and will permit, as Camille's vision suggests, its subsequent destruction; and the future fate of Rome is foretold in the present fate of Horace. The king, in sealing both his greatness and his fall, acts in the name of this higher power (840–846; 1469–1470; 1476–1478) and, aesthetically, symbolizes it. To stress the role of destiny is by no means to absolve Horace, of course, for in the play destiny itself is merely a name that designates man's dilemma and suggests its inevitability.

If it is easy to find arguments in favor of Horace, it is just as easy to find arguments against him, and the same is true of the other characters in the play. But the greatness of the tragedy lies precisely in the fact that it is neither a facile humanistic hymn to man's glory nor an equally facile condemnation of his corruption. It is, rather, an artistically impressive re-creation of his essentially tragic predicament. Only when this has been firmly established, is it legitimate to admit that the balance may incline to the side of man's greatness and say with King Tulle

> Vis donc, Horace, vis guerrier trop magnanime:
> Ta vertu met ta gloire au-dessus de ton crime;
> Sa chaleur généreuse a produit ton forfait;
> D'une cause si belle il faut souffrir l'effet.
> [1759–1762]

And even then, when we note that *généreuse* was changed to *dangereuse* in the edition of 1656, we realize anew how essential it is to avoid resolving in one direction or the other a tension that Corneille was careful to maintain unresolved.

Every artist negates something in order to affirm something else. The great artist, however, is loath to reject what he negates and reluctant to accept unreservedly what he affirms. Such ambivalence is built into the very fiber of *Horace*, where each human position is tested in the fire of an opposition and the inadequacy of each is measured against its excellence. This is an art and a subject that have much to offer in a time like ours that understands so well, though in other terms, the joy and anguish of man's eternal pursuit of an eternally elusive ideal.

ATTILA REDIVIVUS

By Georges May

Après l'Agésilas,
Hélas!
Mais après l'Attila,
Holà!

It has become an unwritten, but almost unbroken rule never
to discuss Corneille's *Attila* without first quoting Boileau's
epigram. The totally unrewarding aspect of this practice is
made obvious by the healthy lack of agreement existing
among scholars as to the meaning of the two lines concerning *Attila*.[1] Whether Boileau meant to express his admira-

---

[1] The first systematic attempt to elicit from Boileau's lines a favorable judgment on *Attila* is to be found in René Talamon, "Deux
épigrammes de Boileau," *MLN*, XLVIII (1933), 283–291. But the
idea was not new: half a century earlier the belief that Boileau
meant to express his admiration for *Attila* was voiced by Henri de
Bornier, "Attila: à propos d'une tragédie nouvelle," *Le Correspon-
dant*, Feb. 10, 1880, pp. 493–494. Ten years before Talamon's
methodical weighing of evidence, further doubts had been raised
by Henry Lyonnet: ". . . à moins que le 'Holà' ne soit pris ici
comme un cri d'admiration?" (*Les Premières de P. Corneille*
[Paris: Delagrave, 1923], p. 212). More recently Daniel Mornet,
despite his own lack of enthusiasm for *Attila*, considered *tout à fait
probable* that Boileau's lines were meant to express admiration
(*"Andromaque" de Jean Racine* [Paris: Mellottée, 1947], p. 91). A
recent survey of this little problem can be found in Georges Couton,
La Vieillesse de Corneille (1658–1684) (Paris: Deshayes, 1949),
pp. 138–144. This article was already set up in print before the
author could get hold of a study by Professor Arnaldo Pizzorusso
of the University of Pisa: "Sull' *Attila* di Corneille," in *Studi in
onore di V. Lugli e D. Valeri*, II (Venice, 1961).

tion or his indignation, whether he did not simply succumb to the irresistible attraction of clever rhymes, rather than heed the appeal of reason and respect the rule of clarity, is far from sure. All that can be said is that, if Boileau's reputation for unfailing critical judgment is to be vindicated in this instance, his *Holà* had better mean: "Stop quibbling about *Attila* which, unlike *Agésilas*, is a true masterpiece," for *Attila*, as the ensuing pages will attempt to show, is among Corneille's most original, representative, and effective plays.

In point of fact, it no longer is eccentric or paradoxical nowadays to admire a play so long despised and unjustly smeared by lazy or blind critics. Admirers of *Attila* can be found without inordinate effort.

Most of the very few meaningful contemporary accounts of the play were, indeed, favorable. Saint-Evremond, who read rather than saw *Attila*, went as far as to imply, in a well-known essay, that he placed it above *Andromaque*, performed eight months later,[2] but failed to spell out his reasons. Another stanch Corneille supporter, Edme Boursault wrote a brief piece on *Attila*, which is beyond doubt the most substantial of the contemporary reviews. This piece, cast in the form of a familiar letter to his girl friend Babet, concludes emphatically: "Enfin, Babet, c'est un ouvrage à voir, et si tu veux que je te retienne une loge pour vendredi, j'y retournerai encore."[3]

Admittedly, it is more difficult to find admiring readers of *Attila* in the eighteenth century. Judging from Voltaire's own disparaging comments, which unfortunately set the keynote of Corneille criticism for many years, one may even wonder whether *Attila* was ever read during this period. For Voltaire, of course, did not take the trouble to scan beyond the first act when he wrote his often inept *Commentaires*.[4]

---

[2] Letter to Count de Lionne, in his *Oeuvres* (Londres: J. Tonson, 1711), II, 260–261; quoted by Pierre Mélèse, *Le Théâtre et le public à Paris sous Louis XIV* (*1659–1715*) (Paris: Droz, 1934), pp. 330–331.

[3] Edme Boursault, *Lettres nouvelles* (Paris: F. Le Breton, 1709), III, 201. Substantial parts of the text are quoted by Mélèse, *op. cit.*, p. 260, n. 1.

[4] For once in his long fight against Voltaire, Emile Faguet was

Then came Stendhal, who must be considered one of Corneille's most enlightened and original critics, and who is said to have seen *Attila* performed no fewer than fourteen times.[5] It is abundantly clear from his various references to *Attila* that it was among Stendhal's favorite Corneille plays.[6]

Of all the scholarly critics of our century who examined *Attila* without undue bias, Emile Faguet was perhaps the first to "rediscover" the play. In 1913 he called it a *tragédie fort estimable*[7] and discussed it with sympathy and understanding. Gustave Lanson was soon to follow suit in 1916–1917, thus correcting his own earlier prejudices and misconceptions.[8] Finally, in the last quarter-century *Attila* has elicited some measure of approval from almost all critics and historians of literature who have taken the trouble to read it.

The two best-known commentators of Corneille in the 1930's, Jean Schlumberger and Robert Brasillach, both still remained somewhat cool toward *Attila*, to which they tended

entirely right when he wrote in the *Journal des débats* (July 22, 1907): "Vers la fin de son travail sur Corneille, Voltaire en avait assez de son entreprise et il n'a pas lu *Tite et Bérénice*, non plus qu'il n'a pas lu *Agésilas*, ni *Attila*, ni *Pulchérie*, ni *Suréna*. Vous pouvez m'en croire absolument" (reprinted in *Propos de théâtre* [5th ser.; Paris: Société Française d'Imprimerie et de Librairie, 1910], p. 120). Cf. also Emile Faguet, *En lisant Corneille* (Paris: Hachette, 1913), p. 214.

[5] "Stendhal . . . avait quatorze fois vu représenter *Attila*" (Pierre Lièvre, *Corneille et son oeuvre* [Paris: Divan, 1937], p. 60). One may wonder where these performances took place, since *Attila* was not staged even once at the Comédie Française during Stendhal's lifetime.

[6] E.g., *Pensées* (Paris: Divan, 1927), I, 298–299. A quick survey of Stendhal's reactions as a reader of Corneille is available in Victor del Litto, *La Vie intellectuelle de Stendhal; Genèse et évolution de ses idées* (1802–1821) (Paris: P.U.F., 1959), *passim* and pp. 62–67 and 230–232. Cf. also Lièvre, *op. cit., passim*.

[7] *En lisant Corneille*, p. 214.

[8] In his *Esquisse d'une histoire de la tragédie française* (New York: Columbia University Press, 1920, pp. 98–99; and Paris: Champion, 1927, pp. 120–122), based on his lectures given at Columbia University in 1916–1917, Lanson acknowledged the value of *Attila*, which he had misrepresented and underestimated, both in his *Boileau* (Paris: Hachette, 1892, p. 76), and in his *Corneille* (Paris: Hachette, 1898, p. 84).

to prefer *Othon, Sophonisbe,* perhaps even *Agésilas.*[9] But about the same time H. C. Lancaster expressed his admiration especially for the play's structure,[10] an opinion voiced even more strongly by Léon Lemonnier in 1945: "une des mieux composées parmi les tragédies de Corneille."[11] In his monumental study of Corneille's last period, Georges Couton stood fast on a position of strict historical impartiality and remained rather noncommittal.[12] Finally, Bernard Dort, in one of the most recent and original monographs on Corneille, concluded his enthusiastic, brilliant, and profound—if not always crystal-clear—essay on *Attila* by the unexpected assertion that this play is Corneille's one and only tragedy, at least according to the concept of tragedy evolved by Lukàcs and elaborated by Lucien Goldmann.[13]

Thus the way seems clear now to a better understanding of *Attila roi des Huns,* Corneille's twenty-ninth play and one of the three or four of his total production of thirty-two which he placed, at one time or another, above all others.[14] Yet even in the case of a play as relatively unknown as *Attila,* our knowledge of Corneille and of his works is still so cluttered with unverified legends, half-truths, and gross prejudices that a bit of housecleaning is first necessary.

Let us recall that, in spite of what the majority of commentators who have allegedly *read* the play keep repeating, the protagonist of Corneille's *Attila* does not die of a nosebleed. Even as careful a scholar as Lanson initially dismissed the play with this unfortunate statement: "Il ne reste rien de

[9] Jean Schlumberger, *Plaisir à Corneille* (Paris: Gallimard, 1936), pp. 224–233; Robert Brasillach, *Corneille* (Paris: Fayard, 1938), pp. 410–413.

[10] Henry Carrington Lancaster, *A History of French Dramatic Literature in the Seventeenth Century* (Baltimore: Johns Hopkins Press), III (1936), 593.

[11] Léon Lemonnier, *Corneille* (Paris: Tallandier, 1945), p. 245.

[12] Couton, *op. cit.,* pp. 128–136.

[13] Bernard Dort, *Pierre Corneille dramaturge* (Paris: Arche, 1957), pp. 100–108.

[14] "Corneille a dit souvent qu'*Attila* était sa meilleure pièce" (Abbé Dubos, *Réflexions critiques sur la poésie et la peinture* [Paris: J. Mariette, 1719], pt. 2, chap. xii).

réel dans *Attila* que le saignement de nez."[15] And the same careless error has since been made over and over again, and most probably will still be made many times in the future.[16] Of course it is quite true that historians traditionally ascribe Attila's death to unchecked epistaxis, but Corneille took care to tamper with historical data and to adjust them to his purposes: although he has his protagonist bleed to death at the end of the play, he is careful not to mention his nose anywhere. Attila is not Cyrano.

Stendhal demonstrates the care with which he examined *Attila* by his statement that the hero *périt d'une espèce d'apoplexie*.[17] And Lemonnier was entirely right to castigate hasty readers attempting to ridicule Corneille for having done what he studiously avoided doing: "On ne doit pas, pour un dénouement mal lu, tourner en ridicule cette pièce."[18] For not only is the particular way Corneille has Attila die at the end of his play highly relevant to an assessment of its meaning, but the repeated error of so many commentators helps demonstrate the negligence with which they read the play and invites us to dismiss their perfunctory remarks. This applies not only to Voltaire, but to many of his lesser-known followers.

Another pitfall we must avoid is the temptation which led several critics to recognize in Corneille's Attila the prototype of various more recent despots and conquerors whom it was their intention to reprove. Hence Henri de Bornier's attempt to compare Attila's career to that of Napoleon;[19] or Auguste

---

[15] *Corneille*, pp. 80 and 84.

[16] A few years after taking Voltaire to task for not having read *Attila*, Faguet (*op. cit.*, p. 216) demonstrated his own insufficient or forgotten reading by an unfortunate reference to Attila's fatal nosebleed. Of the same play Brasillach (*op. cit.*, p. 410) wrote: "Il est dommage qu'elle se termine par un saignement de nez." Likewise, authors of a recent French textbook still state that the play's hero "meurt d'un saignement de nez" (Pierre-Georges Castex and Paul Surer, *Manuel des études littéraires françaises: XVIIe siècle* [Paris: Hachette, 1947], p. 52).

[17] Stendhal, *Pensées*, ed. Divan, I, 299.

[18] Lemonnier, *op. cit.*, p. 250.

[19] Bornier, *loc. cit.*, pp. 487–488.

Dorchain's nationalistic outburst in which he sees Wilhelm II
as a new avatar of the infamous Hunnish king and the battle
of the Catalaunian plain as an early rehearsal—on the same
stage!—of the first battle of the Marne![20] Even though Dorchain was writing during World War I, which may be an
excuse for such delusions, vagaries of this kind must be absolutely condemned, for they hamper an appreciation of an
essential aspect of Corneille's play: the moral ambiguity of
his portrayal of Attila.

Whether or not *Attila* was successful when first performed
in 1667 by Molière's company on the stage of the Palais-
Royal theatre is another moot point among historians of the
drama, even though the precise number of performances and
the box-office receipts are accurately known to us, thanks to
La Grange's *Registre*. Antoine Adam talks in terms of a genuine flop:

> Sur *Attila* . . . nous sommes exactement renseignés, et
> le chiffre des recettes ne permet aucune illusion. Seule la
> première représentation atteignit les mille livres. Dès la
> seconde, la chute fut certaine. . . . L'*Alexandre* de Ra-
> cine, qui fut un des grands succès du Palais-Royal, fit
> 5.502 livres dans les six premières représentations. *Tite
> et Bérénice* fit 7.468 livres pour le même nombre de
> chambrées. Les six premières d'*Attila* n'avaient donné
> que 3.781 livres.[21]

Couton concurs that twenty performances in a row, followed
by three more before the end of the year, was but a mediocre
success.[22] Yet Marty-Laveaux considered these very same
figures to add up to *un véritable succès;*[23] and Lancaster
remarked about *Attila* that Molière "produced it more often
than any other of its author's plays except *Sertorius* and

---

[20] Auguste Dorchain, *Corneille* (Paris: Garnier, 1918), pp. 406–
407.
[21] Antoine Adam, *Histoire de la littérature française au XVII*ᵉ
siècle (Paris: Domat), IV (1954), 221–222 and 223, n. 9.
[22] Couton, *op. cit.*, p. 138.
[23] *Oeuvres de P. Corneille*, ed. C. Marty-Laveaux (Paris: Hachette, 1862), VII, 101.

Rodogune."[24] Moreover, Pierre Mélèse, who may be considered the most expert authority on these matters, recalling that long runs were exceptional in the seventeenth century, noted: "On cite comme des succès remarquables les 44 représentations consécutives des *Précieuses* en 1659, les 27 de *Sganarelle* en 1660, les 23 d'*Attila* en 1667, les 30 d'*Amphitryon* en 1668 ou les 40 d'*Iphigénie* en 1675."[25] The same scholar argued further that the amount of time which lapsed between the first performance of *Attila* on March 4, 1667, and its publication on November 20 is much greater than average and may be viewed as a good yardstick with which to measure the play's success.[26] Finally, if we observe that the last performance of *Attila* on the Palais-Royal stage coincided with Marquise Duparc's severance from Molière's company to join that of the Hôtel de Bourgogne on March 29, we may conjecture that, had it not been for this serious blow, *Attila* might have had an even longer run. For it is probable that la Duparc played one of the leading parts in *Attila*,[27] and it seems clear that Molière had given *Attila* a most careful production designed to outdo the Hôtel de Bourgogne.[28] In other words, available evidence may be construed to mean that the play failed only in the eyes of those modern critics who consider that it did not deserve a better fate. The more objective historians can only conclude that *Attila* met with

---

[24] Lancaster, *op. cit.*, III, 590.

[25] Mélèse, *op. cit.*, p. 282, n. 1.

[26] *Ibid.*, p. 297, n. 2.

[27] Armand Le Corbeiller (*Pierre Corneille intime* [Paris: SFELT, 1936], pp. 234–235), following in the footsteps of Brasillach (*op. cit.*, p. 410), stated unequivocally that Marquise Duparc played the part of the Frankish princess Ildione but failed to document his assertion; H. C. Lancaster was more circumspect: "As it [*Attila*] has two important rôles for women, neither of which was taken by Molière's wife, it is highly probable that la Du Parc played one of them" ("La Du Parc," in his *Adventures of a Literary Historian* [Baltimore: Johns Hopkins Press, 1942], p. 90). As a matter of fact, the only actors who can be identified with certainty are La Thorillière, who played Attila, and Armande Molière, who performed the minor role of Flavie.

[28] Cf. Subligny's verse letter of March 19, 1667, as quoted by Mélèse, *op. cit.*, p. 190.

what René Bray termed a *demi-succès*,[29] Louis Herland a
succès honorable,[30] and René Jasinski *mieux qu'un succès
d'estime*.[31]

A final bone of contention among *Attila* scholars has to do
with Corneille's historical sources. In his own preface ("Au
lecteur"), Corneille acknowledged only the sixteenth-century
historian Count Marcellinus. Marty-Laveaux, however, believed that he had also used the *De Getarum rebus gestis* by
the sixth-century Bishop Jordanes. Lancaster reasoned that

> all the material with which Jordanes and Marcellinus
> might have supplied Corneille passed into Mézeray
> (*Histoire de France*, ed. of 1685, I, 211–218), and, as
> the French historian mentioned his indebtedness to Mar-
> cellinus, Corneille could have indicated the latter as his
> source without having read his text.[32]

Finally, Couton vindicated Corneille of this suspicion of "Je-
suitic" prevarication and added to the names of these three
historians, who, he believed, were consulted by Corneille,
that of Père Caussin, whose then widely read and profusely
reprinted *La Cour sainte* (1643) appears indeed as a very
likely additional source.[33]

This debate, of interest only to those concerned with Corneille's scholarship and documentation, is quite irrelevant to
an appreciation of his play; as indeed is the case of most of
the problems which have just been reviewed. These problems, however, have stimulated much scholarly activity, too
often, unfortunately, at the expense of an empirical examination of the play. What is of genuine literary interest in the
problem of the historical sources of *Attila* is not to identify
them, but to study Corneille's particular selection from among

[29] René Bray, *Molière homme de théâtre* (Paris: Mercure de
France, 1954), pp. 124–125.

[30] Louis Herland, *Corneille par lui-même* (Paris, Editions du
Seuil, 1954), p. 36.

[31] René Jasinski, *Vers le vrai Racine* (Paris: A. Colin, 1958),
I, 224.

[32] Lancaster, *History*, III, 590.

[33] Couton, *op. cit.*, pp. 128–29 and 334, nn. 36–37.

the confused maze of legends then constituting Hunnish history and to analyze the twists which he gave them in order to fulfill his purpose. It is remarkable in this respect that Corneille's own frank testimony in his preface is more helpful than all that scholars have added to it since. The changes he confesses are accurate, truthful, and, if not exhaustive,[34] sufficient and meaningful: he suppressed Attila's polygamy; he imagined that Ildione, Attila's last wife whose origins are unknown, was the sister of the Frankish king Mérovée; he refrained from having Ildione kill Attila, as in a widely accepted version of his death, but made her simply toy with the idea of this murder; finally, instead of having Attila die of indigestion, as in another version of his death, he had him die in a fit of rage. As we proceed, these four avowed alterations will be shown all to be highly significant and to yield important clues to an understanding of Corneille's purpose when he wrote *Attila*.

Attila roi des Huns being surely one of Corneille's lesser-known works, a brief plot summary is probably necessary at this point.

The action takes place in Attila's Illyrian camp, shortly after his defeat in the Catalaunian plain (451) at the hand of a coalition led by the Roman general Aetius and including among others the Franks of Mérovée. Seeking revenge, Attila plans to resort to matrimonial diplomacy rather than military force. Two royal fiancées are present in his camp: Honorie, sister of the Roman emperor Valentinian III, and Ildione, sister of *Mérovée, roi de France*. Attila aims at controlling both Valentinian and Mérovée by marrying one of the girls and holding the other as hostage.

Whether his bride will be Ildione, whom he secretly loves and in whose hands he is, therefore, afraid of surrendering his freedom, or Honorie, who leaves him suitably indifferent, Attila cannot decide. He consults on this point his two royal

[34] Lancaster (*History*, III, 590) listed the following alterations which Corneille failed to mention in his preface: "the presence of Honoria in Attila's camp, the love of these princesses [Ildione and Honorie] for the Gothic kings, the Hun's desire of being rid of his two allies, his dying before he marries Ildico and after Aetius."

allies and satellites, Ardaric and Valamir, Gothic kings practically held prisoners in the Hun's camp. They give him contradictory advices, which he shrewdly and correctly interprets as reflecting the fact that they each love one of the two princesses.

Honorie, who returns Valamir's love, is too proud to marry either a puppet king (Valamir) or a true sovereign (Attila) once Ildione has rejected him. Conversely Ildione, who returns Ardaric's love, is prepared to accept Attila's choice, toying with the idea of killing him if he chooses her.

Still undecided, Attila offers each of the two kings the girl he loves, provided he kills the other king, thus freeing one of the two princesses to marry him. This fiendish scheme is worthy of the Scourge of God, who, as is recalled more than once in the play, did not hesitate to murder his own brother and six kings and who never ceases demonstrating a robust sense of *humour noir*. Ardaric and Valamir, who always display much less energy than their princesses, confer together and agree that Attila's proposal creates an impasse.

Faced with the irresoluteness of the other four characters, Ildione breaks the deadlock unilaterally and boldly offers herself to Attila. Although he fully realizes that she is deceiving him and that he would be politically wiser to acquire as a brother-in-law the Roman emperor than the Frankish king, Attila accepts. But, enraged by his own weakness and thirsty for revenge against Honorie, who has haughtily vituperated him, he falls victim to his own anger: as he leads Ildione off to marry her, Attila dies of excessive loss of blood, a mysterious disease from which he has been suffering in moments of intense emotions ever since he committed his first heinous crimes. The two kings share his spoils and prepare to marry their princesses.

The plot of *Attila* is a relatively simple one, free of the mysteries, unexpected events, and complications of which Corneille of late had grown increasingly fond. There is only one minor subplot, consisting of a romance between Honorie's lady-in-waiting, Flavie, and Attila's aide-de-camp, Octar, who attempts to betray his master. This in no way detracts from the more central topics of interest, thus illustrating Corneille's increasing mastery of the construction of tightly knit dramas not requiring the conventional type of confidants. In his *Pulchérie* (1672), Corneille will finally manage to do away with these entirely. In this respect, *Attila*, with its two minor characters, is distinctly more advanced than Racine's *Andromaque*, in which each of the four main characters is usually escorted by a confidant.

In spite of the simplicity of the plot, the action of *Attila* is constantly kept interesting by a clever handling of suspense. Aware of the fact that something is bound to happen, the public is curious to watch how the various characters are trying to control their future. Not only is Attila opposed to the other principal characters and, therefore, secretive and devious in his encounters with them, but the two princesses, unlike the two flaccid kings, have the energy of being healthily jealous of each other and not unwilling to resort to treachery. This game of compounded deception adds to the power of the play to stimulate and retain interest, while spreading it out over more than one character. Even though Attila is clearly the protagonist, he appears in fewer scenes than Ardaric, Valamir, or Honorie and is entirely absent in Act II, as are Honorie and Ildione in Act I, and Ardaric and Valamir in Act III. In this respect *Attila* is representative of its era, for, according to Jacques Scherer, the number of plays in which the parts of the main characters are evenly distributed tended to increase as the century progressed. This, in his opinion, testifies to the increasing distinction of acting companies no longer limited to a single star; but it also is a sign of growing mastery on the part of increasingly sophisticated dramatists.[35] When it comes to the author of *Attila*, other evidence of his growing technical skill can be seen in such accomplishments as the clear simplicity and naturalness of the introductory scenes and the scarcity of monologues (only one, of 16 lines) or of narrative speeches (again only one, of 41 lines, describing the hero's death).[36]

[35] Jacques Scherer, *La Dramaturgie classique en France* (Paris: Nizet, 1950), pp. 27–28.

[36] Other similar remarks applicable to Corneille's last plays are to be found in Couton, *op. cit.*, pp. 239–242.

As for the composition of *Attila*, Boursault demonstrated his insight as a critic when he immediately expressed his admiration for this particular aspect of the play. In spite of his partiality for the third act—a preference shared by several leading modern critics, such as Octave Nadal or Bernard Dort —and of his feeling that the second act was not quite as full as the other four, Boursault asserted quite pointedly: "Quiconque voudrait s'appliquer à faire l'anatomie de sa pièce, trouverait à la dissection des scènes, qu'il n'y en a guère d'inutiles."[37] In fact, the structure of the play is effectively contrived to afford the public successive and alternate views of all the facets of a single but powerfully conceived dramatic problem. It is as remarkable for its simplicity as it is for its variety and balance.

Act I presents Attila and the two kings in a smooth-flowing sequence of three scenes: (1) Attila and his aide-de-camp —a traditional play opening;[38] (2) Attila and the two kings; (3) the two kings alone.

Act II, the only one in which Attila does not appear, manages to present all the other elements defining the initial dramatic situation, especially where the ladies are concerned. This is done through a clever succession of three duets: two scenes between lovers separated by one between the two kings. Each time a character comes on stage, one has to walk off. Honorie is talking with her lady-in-waiting when her suitor Valamir enters. After a brief conversation, Honorie leaves the stage as Ardaric enters. After an even briefer conversation between the two kings, it is Valamir's turn to exit, leaving Ardaric with Attila's aide-de-camp, who has just entered and who, in turn, abandons the stage to Ildione, who concludes the act by a long scene with her suitor. Nowhere in his career has Corneille more skillfully managed to have so many characters enter and exit with precision and naturalness.

Act III, symmetrical with Act I, shows Attila confronting the two princesses as he had confronted the two kings, both

---

[37] Boursault, *op. cit.*, p. 200; quoted in Mélèse, *op. cit.*, p. 260, n. 1.

[38] Cf. Scherer, *op. cit.*, p. 60.

separately and together. In his scene with Ildione, Attila shrewdly learns of her love for Ardaric, just as, in the final scene with Honorie, he learns of her love for Valamir. In the middle of the act, in a scene where he faces both princesses, Attila manages to have them reveal their reciprocal jealousy. In full possession of all the elements of information, he can now act swiftly.

Act IV, accordingly, sees the plot reach its climax with Attila's barbarous bargain with the two kings. The first three scenes revolve around Honorie, who betrays Ildione's love to Attila, suggesting that he punish her by having her marry a commoner. Attila counters by suggesting sarcastically that Honorie herself may be made to marry his aide-de-camp Octar. Honorie walks out as Ardaric enters. In the fourth and central scene of the act, Attila, showing his awareness of all the lovers' secrets, demands that Ardaric kill Valamir. The last three scenes revolve around Ildione, who has entered at the end of the fourth scene. Attila urges her to talk Ardaric into fulfilling the condition necessary to his marriage with her. Ildione then recommends to Ardaric that he consult Valamir on some common action, and, as though she realized his passiveness, she concludes the act by a soliloquy in which she envisages killing Attila herself.

Act V witnesses a noticeable quickening of the tempo as the denouement draws nearer. After an initial conference of the two Gothic kings agreeing on their mutual inability to solve the problem, each ensuing scene starts with the entrance of one more character until scene 5, in which, for the first and last time, all five protagonists are on stage to hear Attila accept Ildione's unexpected offer to marry him. The very short final scenes (92 lines for all three) allow for Attila's death offstage, for a realistic report of his death by Valamir, and for a quick sketch of future developments.

The feeling of acceleration generated by the play as it progresses toward its ending is largely due to its structure, and especially to the greater number of scenes during the last two acts, in which the plot reaches its climax and denouement. This in itself is one of the important structural features of French classical dramaturgy as analyzed by Jacques

Scherer: there should be in the fifth act at least as many scenes as in the fourth, and more in the fourth than in any of the first three.[39] As the following table will show, not only is this the case in *Attila*, but the quickening of the dramatic tempo is made even more perceptible by the following two devices: the final act is noticeably shorter than any of the previous ones, and the number of characters on the stage is conversely much higher. In order to make this latter point apparent, the figures in the last column on the right represent the totals of the number of characters appearing in the total of the scenes of a given act.

	Number of lines	Number of scenes	Number of characters
Act I	360	3	8
Act II	352	6	13
Act III	372	4	12
Act IV	368	7	16
Act V	336	7	26
	1,788		

Beyond these computable features which can be analyzed in a table, another more subtle but parallel development takes place as the play progresses: the emotional tension increases. This point has been carefully established by Jean Boorsch in his rich study of Corneille's dramatic technique. Boorsch shows how the first act apparently leads the public to believe that the central dramatic problem will be to know which princess Attila will choose, whereas the second does nothing to answer this question and misleads the public into thinking that Ildione may murder Attila. The third act brings forth a number of conflicting threats on the part of Attila and the princesses. The fourth act, containing the revelation of Attila's fiendish plan, *va nous fournir des sentiments encore plus tendus et plus extrêmes;*[40] and finally, in the last act, *la situation a dès lors été utilisée dans toutes ses possi-*

---

[39] *Ibid.*, p. 199.
[40] Jean Boorsch, "Remarques sur la technique dramatique de Corneille," *Yale Romanic Studies*, XVIII (1941), 158.

*bilités. C'est désormais une impasse, dont on ne peut s'échap-
per que par un coup de théâtre.*[41]

Attila's sudden death may well be a *coup de théâtre*, but,
as will be seen later, by no means a gratuitous one; carefully
prepared by several allusions spread throughout the play,
the particular and not historical way in which Attila meets
his death is highly significant. The same remark, however,
does not apply to the force which triggers the dramatic action in the first act. Why Attila must choose his bride at this
particular moment is not explained by any compelling reason.
Attila merely tells the two kings:

> Le choix m'en embarrasse, il est temps de le faire;
> Depuis leur arrivée en vain je le diffère:
> Il faut enfin résoudre.
>
> [I, ii, 85–87]

In the meaningless and arbitrary *il est temps* and *il faut*
may well be detected the single technical flaw of the play.
Racine will display more skill in his *Andromaque* by compelling Pyrrhus to make a similar choice—likewise long post-
poned—by having the Greek ambassador, Oreste, force the
issue.

Analyses such as Boorsch's quite rightly assume that the
emotions of the characters are exploited by Corneille, not so
much because of their intrinsic interest, as because they are
powerful forces which, by their shifting combinations, gener-
ate dramatic action and thereby play on the public's own
emotions. This is not meant to belittle the psychological or
moral nature of these emotional forces. Far from it: the originality and supremacy of Corneille's dramatic genius stem
from his choice and treatment of these forces as much as it
does from his technical virtuosity.[42]

This particular choice in *Attila* leads to what might be
called an ideological formula of great originality and effec-

---

[41] *Ibid.*, p. 159.
[42] Reacting against studies limited to dramatic technique, Adam
(*op. cit.*, IV, 250) badly overstated the point by asserting: "L'in-
térêt d'une oeuvre authentique ne peut jamais être dans sa technique."

tiveness. As he was probably already working on this play, Corneille wrote in a letter thanking Saint-Evremond for his kind words in his published essay on Racine's *Alexandre*:

> J'ai cru jusques ici que l'amour était une passion trop chargée de faiblesse pour être la dominante dans une pièce héroïque; j'aime qu'elle y serve d'ornement, et non pas de corps, et que les grandes âmes ne la laissent agir qu'autant qu'elle est compatible avec de plus nobles impressions.[43]

These lines are often quoted in an attempt to contrast Racine and Corneille. Concerning Racine's position on the place of love in tragedy, his own son Louis wrote that *il jugea au contraire qu'il fallait, ou ne lui en donner aucune, ou lui donner la première.*[44] As early as 1685 Pierre Bayle had already developed this much oversimplified judgment:

> [Racine] étudiait avec soin et avec grand succès le goût que l'on avait alors pour la tendresse, au lieu que Mr. Corneille dédaignait d'avoir cette condescendance pour le public, et ne voulait point sortir de sa noblesse ordinaire, ni de la grandeur romaine. Ainsi *Attila, Bérénice, Pulchérie, Suréna*, quoique pleines de choses inimitables n'eurent pas l'éclat du *Cid* ou d'*Horace*.[45]

Fontenelle eventually contributed to the spreading of this inaccurate legend as he expatiated in his *Vie de Corneille* on Corneille's assumed reaction against Racinian love tragedy and the *doucereux* and *enjoué*.

The ineptitude of this conception of Corneille's treatment of love has, of course, been expertly demonstrated by Nadal.[46] Yet, the very fact that Bayle mentioned *Suréna*—where, in the eyes of any unprejudiced reader, the role of love is just as essential as in any of Racine's tragedies—would

---

[43] Ed. Marty-Laveaux, X, 498.

[44] Louis Racine, *Remarques sur les tragédies de Jean Racine*, in his *Oeuvres* (Paris: Le Normant, 1808), V, 346.

[45] *Nouvelles de la république des lettres*, Jan., 1685; quoted by Mélèse, *op. cit.*, p. 123.

[46] *Le Sentiment de l'amour dans l'oeuvre de Pierre Corneille* (Paris: Gallimard, 1948).

be enough to discard such a sweeping judgment. As for Corneille's own statement in his letter of 1666 to Saint-Evremond, scholars have often been too prone to neglect the fact that he qualified it with a *jusques ici* which leaves the yet-unwritten, or at best unfinished, *Attila* out of this retrospective definition.

As a matter of fact, in his preface to the 1668 edition of *Attila*, Corneille went as far as to admit that love usually is at the core of modern drama. And his admirer Boursault systematically emphasized the love scenes of *Attila* in his letter to Babet, especially the last scene of the second act, in which Ildione warns Ardaric that, notwithstanding her love for him, she would marry Attila if he chose her:

> Une princesse que l'on donne à ce qu'elle n'aime pas, et qui aime ce qu'elle ne peut avoir; qui est obligée de donner à sa naissance, ce qu'elle n'oserait accorder à son amour; et qui a autant de peine à prononcer *J'aime*, que j'ai de plaisir à te le dire, est quelque chose de si touchant et de si délicat à traiter, qu'il fallait la plume de Corneille pour en venir glorieusement à bout.[47]

The love theme is therefore an essential one in *Attila*, as though the current new fashion exemplified in Racine's *Alexandre* (1665) could justify Corneille's reverting to the love drama which he had had to tone down since the censure of *le Cid*. But, showing at the same time the humiliation brought on by love to Attila and Honorie, Corneille perhaps meant also to imply a subtle but effective criticism of the very dramatic trend of which he was taking advantage to indulge his own taste. Such a practice of having his cake and eating it would by no means be unusual for Corneille. As he puts it in his preface, "L'amour dans le malheur n'excite que la pitié, et est plus capable de purger en nous cette passion que de nous en faire envie."

Of course it is true that Attila tries to dominate his own passion for Ildione and that, like Alidor in *La Place Royale* (1634)—the analogy has been noted by Nadal—he is afraid of loving because he shuns subjection:

[47] Boursault, *op. cit.*, pp. 200–201.

L'amour chez Attila n'est pas un bon suffrage;
Ce qu'on m'en donnerait me tiendrait lieu d'outrage,
Et tout exprès ailleurs je porterais ma foi,
De peur qu'on n'eût par là trop de pouvoir sur moi.

[I, ii, 117–120]

Yet in spite of his tentative decision to marry Honorie, he immediately accepts Ildione's offer, thus sacrificing everything to his passion. For the originality of *Attila* lies precisely in the balance of forces between love and the conventional political and *glorieux* interests. As Nadal puts it: "Tous les actes d'Attila sont marqués d'une double inquiétude: conserver la puissance en même temps que l'amour."[48] Likewise, the particular charm of the character of Attila stems from the unexpected grafting of Louis XIV *tendresse* on the traditional barbaric components of his personality—a device based on anachronism and exploited since, especially by Giraudoux.[49] It is this rather original blend of love, as it appears as early as the first act of *Attila*, which disconcerted many a critic and led as intelligent and sympathetic a reader as Faguet to write that Attila *n'aime pas les femmes, et il le dit nettement*,[50] an obviously ludicrous judgment.

This highly successful mixture of *galanterie* and ruthlessness, whose appeal was obscured by a long tradition of critical bias and an almost complete lack of fresh unprejudiced reading, did not escape at least one member of the contemporary audience, the young Jean Racine, then working on his first masterpiece, *Andromaque*. Much of Racine's masterful portrayal of Pyrrhus betrays his careful study of Attila: the counterpoint of *tendresse* and violence, the opposition between the barbarian and the smug Greeks, the recollection of his early bloody deeds, and so forth. Pyrrhus' conversations with Phoenix, who attempts to have his master concentrate on his political rather than romantic interests, clearly recall

[48] Nadal, *op. cit.*, p. 248.

[49] Discussing other aspects of the play, Brasillach, an outspoken admirer of Giraudoux, could write: "Le dix-septième siècle pouvait regarder *Attila* dans l'esprit où nous applaudissons une pièce de Jean Giraudoux" (*op. cit.*, p. 412).

[50] *En lisant Corneille*, p. 214.

Attila's similar conversation with his aide-de-camp Octar which ends as Ildione walks in:

> Octar, je l'aperçois. Quel nouveau coup de foudre!
> O raison confondue, orgueil presque étouffé,
> Avant ce coup fatal que n'as-tu triomphé!
>
> [III, i, 794–796]

If not the tone, at least the vocabulary is already that of Racine. Likewise, the following scene between Attila and Ildione had not been forgotten by Racine when he wrote the great scene between Pyrrhus and his captive Andromaque in the first act of his play. The parallel can even be carried further by recalling that Ildione's part may have been written for the same Marquise Duparc, who is suspected of having then just borne a daughter to Racine[51] and who was to perform a few months later the tailor-made part of Andromaque. So that Pyrrhus' love speeches to Andromaque, which must reflect Racine's passion for Marquise Duparc,[52] are in more ways than one the echoes of Attila's magnificent ode to Ildione:

> Ah! Vous me charmez trop, moi de qui l'âme altière
> Cherche à voir sous mes pas trembler la terre entière:
> Moi qui veux pouvoir tout, sitôt que je vous voi,
> Malgré tout cet orgueil, je ne puis rien sur moi.
> Je veux, je tâche en vain d'éviter par la fuite
> Ce charme dominant qui marche à votre suite:
> Mes plus heureux succès ne font qu'enfoncer mieux
> L'inévitable trait dont me percent vos yeux.
> Un regard imprévu leur fait une victoire;
> Leur moindre souvenir l'emportent sur ma gloire:

51 Cf. Jasinski, *op. cit.*, I, 146.
52 Cf. *ibid.*, pp. 183 ff. It must be pointed out, however, that the truth about Corneille's relationship with la Duparc is not known, and the story of the poet's infatuation for the actress is based on conjecture and the rather tenuous evidence of the few love poems collected by Sercy. Moreover, as has been pointed out above (cf. footnote 27), it has not been positively established that Marquise Duparc played the part of Ildione.

Il s'empare et du coeur et des soins les plus doux;
Et j'oublie Attila, dès que je pense à vous.

[III, ii, 817–828]

Thus Corneille's notion of love in *Attila* is already that of an irresistible force, akin to destiny, a notion which will reach full development in his last masterpiece, *Suréna*, but is already recognized as such by the Hunnish king:

O beauté, qui te fais adorer en tous lieux,
Cruel poison de l'âme, et doux charme des yeux,
Que devient, quand tu veux, l'autorité suprême,
Si tu prends malgré moi l'empire de moi-même,
Et si cette fierté qui fait partout la loi
Ne peut me garantir de la prendre de toi?

[III, i, 763–768]

This truly tragic conception of love, against which reason is powerless despite the lover's sober lucidity, is traditionally associated with the works of Racine, but was of course already present in some of Molière's comedies, as can be seen in such characters as Alceste and even Arnolphe.[53] It is, therefore, worth emphasizing here how it binds together three of the greatest plays of the age, first performed within a year and a half of each other: *Le Misanthrope*, June 4, 1666; *Attila*, March 4, 1667; and *Andromaque*, November 17, 1667.

Ah! traîtresse, mon faible est étrange pour vous!
Vous me trompez sans doute avec des mots si doux;
Mais il n'importe, il faut suivre ma destinée;
A votre foi mon âme est toute abandonnée.

[Alceste to Célimène, *Le Misanthrope*, IV, v, 1415–1418.]

Vous me trompez, Madame;
Mais l'amour par vos yeux me sait si bien dompter,
Que je ferme les miens pour n'y plus résister.
N'abusez pas pourtant d'un si puissant empire.

[Attila to Ildione, *Attila*, V, iv, 1654–1657.]

[53] Cf. Judd D. Hubert, "*L'Ecole des femmes*, tragédie burlesque?" *Revue des sciences humaines*, Jan.–March, 1960, pp. 41–52.

Mais cet amour l'emporte; et, par un coup funeste,
Andromaque m'arrache un coeur qu'elle déteste:
L'un par l'autre entraînés, nous courons à l'autel
Nous jurer malgré nous un amour immortel.

[Pyrrhus to Hermione, *Andromaque*, IV, v, 1297–1300.][54]

It is, therefore, quite impossible to agree with Mornet, who
concluded his analysis of *Attila* by saying: "Un pareil com-
promis de tragédie grande et de tragédie galante n'a exercé
aucune influence sur *Andromaque*."[55] Quite the opposite:
the time seems ripe now to reexamine, in the light of much
recent Corneille criticism, the whole problem of Corneille's
influence on Racine. This study is likely to be particularly
rewarding where Corneille's later plays are concerned, for
these were probably seen by Racine on the stage and may
have exercised a more durable effect: it seems quite obvious,
for instance, that the impact of *Attila* was still felt on Racine
when he wrote *Mithridate* (1672–1673).[56]

Moreover this little Racinian detour also shows that, even
when dealing with a play as expertly constructed as *Attila*,
the study of characterization is in every way as valid and as
rewarding as in the so-called "great" Corneille plays. This

[54] Discussing the scene in *Andromaque* (II, v) in which Pyrrhus
expresses to Phoenix his desire to see Andromaque again in order to
"la braver à sa vue," Louis Racine (*op. cit.*, V, 391) also quoted
Le Misanthrope: "Le Misanthrope de Molière vient, une lettre à
la main, pour confondre Célimène; il donne une libre étendue à
sa colère en lui disant:
     Que le sort, les démons et le ciel en courroux
     N'ont jamais rien produit de si méchant que vous.
Et après tant d'injures, et malgré la preuve qu'il a de son infidélité,
c'est lui qui demande pardon." The same Louis Racine, in his
Mémoires sur la vie de Jean Racine (*ibid.*, p. 35), mentioning
again *Le Misanthrope*, recalled his father's admiration for Molière
and quotes him as saying: "Il est impossible que Molière ait fait
une mauvaise pièce."

[55] Mornet, *op. cit.*, p. 102.

[56] Some further indications concerning *Attila*'s possible influence
on Racine are to be found in Talamon, *loc. cit.*, p. 289; and Lancaster, *History*, III, 594, n. 9. Signs of Corneille's influence on *La
Thébaïde* and on *Alexandre* are presented by Couton, *op. cit.*, pp.
109–110 and 332–333, n. 22.

does not mean that Boorsch was necessarily wrong when he wrote: "Il nous paraît qu'appliquer l'analyse 'psychologique' à une pièce comme *Attila*, amène à des vues fort contestables, à propos desquelles on peut disputer à perte de vue sans beaucoup de profit."[57] What he had in mind, as his own discussion makes clear, is the type of study which strives toward definitions, rather than analyses or explanations. For it seems clear that the outstanding structural excellence of *Attila* would come to nought—as was the case of *Théodore*, a well-constructed but ludicrous play—if it were not also for the quality of its substance.

Let us, therefore, revert to Corneille's characterization of Attila, surely one of his most remarkable achievements. This portrayal goes very far indeed beyond the views upheld by traditional Corneille scholars, and first expounded with calculated malice by Racine in his first preface to *Britannicus* (1670): "Héros ivre, qui se voudrait faire haïr de sa maîtresse de gaieté de coeur." Even when Attila's paradoxical attitude toward love has been extolled, even when Nadal's admiration has been shared, other remarkable aspects of this character remain to be appreciated.

A consideration of the way in which Corneille tampered with historical data will serve as an effective clue, just as his suppression of *la pluralité des femmes* of the historical Attila had a more constructive dramatic result than a mere concern for *bienséances*. Take, for instance, Corneille's concept of power politics as he ascribes it to his hero. In his preface he states that Attila *était plus homme de tête que de main, tâchait à diviser ses ennemis, ravageait les peuples indéfendus, pour donner de la terreur aux autres, et tirer tribut de leur épouvante*. It is quite obvious that, whether the play is considered as a dramatic work or as a historical piece, this notion of Attila is immensely more satisfactory than the presentation of a blood-thirsty brute, fed on raw meat and drinking his enemies' blood from their own skulls. Bornier, who had then just written his own *Noces d'Attila*, was prompt to single out this aspect of his predecessor's play. Corneille,

---

[57] Boorsch, *loc. cit.*, p. 159.

wrote Bornier, *s'est proposé de peindre l'Attila diplomate et non l'Attila conquérant.*[58] Still smarting from his military defeat on the Catalaunian plain, Corneille's hero realizes that his only chance of revenge is to maneuver shrewdly by suitable propaganda. As he tells his aide-de-camp:

> La noble ardeur d'envahir tant d'Etats
> Doit combattre de tête encor plus que de bras,
> Entre ses ennemis rompre l'intelligence,
> Y jeter du désordre et de la défiance,
> Et ne rien hasarder qu'on n'ait de toutes parts,
> Autant qu'il est possible, enchaîné les hasards.
>
> [I, i, 39–44]

This basic rule of power diplomacy succeeds rather well: Ildione and Honorie are gratifyingly jealous of each other, and Ardaric and Valamir are only too weak and cowardly to emulate their ladies. But Attila's master stroke of secret diplomacy is to have the Roman emperor send to his death Aetius, his own general and Attila's successful opponent on the Catalaunian plain:

> ATTILA: Apprends d'autres nouvelles.
> Ce grand chef des Romains, l'illustre Aétius,
> Le seul que je craignais, Octar, il ne vit plus.
> OCTAR: Qui vous en a défait?
> ATTILA: Valentinian même.
> Craignant qu'il n'usurpât jusqu'à son diadème,
> *Et pressé des soupçons où j'ai su l'engager,*
> Lui-même, àses yeux même, il l'a fait égorger.
>
> [III, i, 739–744]

The line italicized above, which contains one of Corneille's additions to historical accuracy, is highly symptomatic of the poet's conception of Attila's cunning intelligence.

Likewise Attila is shown in the play to be especially eager to earn a terrifying reputation, because terrorized enemies are likely to capitulate without fighting. This amazingly modern theory of psychological warfare, which Adam terms a *vue*

[58] Bornier, *loc. cit.*, p. 495.

géniale,[59] is unveiled to Honorie by Octar, once he has betrayed Attila:

> Il aime à conquérir, mais il hait les batailles:
> Il veut que son nom seul renverse les murailles;
> Et plus grand politique encor que grand guerrier,
> Il tient que les combats sentent l'aventurier.
> Il veut que de ses gens le déluge effroyable
> Atterre impunément les peuples qu'il accable;
> Et prodigue de sang, il épargne celui
> Que tant de combattants exposeraient pour lui.
>
> [IV, ii, 1109–1116]

This explains why, far from resenting his reputation as the
Scourge of God, Corneille's hero is careful to cultivate it:

> On me craint, on me hait; on me nomme en tout lieu
> La terreur des mortels et le fléau de Dieu.
>
> [III, ii, 883–884]

This also accounts for much of the ironical aspect of Corneille's Attila, and especially for his predominantly sarcastic
tone:

HONORIE: Tu pourrais être lâche et cruel jusque là?
ATTILA: Encor plus s'il le faut, mais toujours Attila,
           Toujours l'heureux objet de la haine publique,
           Fidèle au grand dépôt du pouvoir tyrannique,
           Toujours . . .
HONORIE: Achève, et dis que tu veux en tout lieu
           Etre l'effroi du monde, et le fléau de Dieu.
           Etale, insolemment l'épouvantable image
           De ces fleuves de sang où se baignait ta rage.
           Fais voir . . .
ATTILA: Que vous perdez de mots injurieux
           A me faire un reproche et doux et glorieux.
>
> [V, iii, 1563–1572]

This leads us in turn to a final series of remarks centered
around the basic critical error which is still too often made in

[59] Adam, *op. cit.*, IV, 235.

the interpretation of Corneille's plays, and especially of his last ones: this error consists in assuming that all of the poet's works may or indeed must be judged on the basis of criteria derived from a perfunctory study of his traditionally acknowledged masterpieces. In spite of convincing studies demonstrating the fallacy of this assumption, much remains to be done, even after Brasillach, Nadal, Herland, or Dort, to offset more than two centuries of blindness and laziness.

Many of the good points of *Attila* will remain unfelt unless an effort is made to realize that Corneille is among the most versatile and unpredictable French poets. The very dramatic formula of the play, that careful balance of political and love motivations, cannot be noticed or understood by a reader satisfied with the simple view that politics are Corneille's field and love, Racine's. Mornet's reaction is a rather typical one in this respect: "Attila est tout autant Céladon que fléau de Dieu; . . . son tonnerre devient constamment chanson de rossignol et murmures de brise langoureuse."[60]

Likewise, much of the plot development will appear either obscure, illogical, or inconsistent to a reader assuming that Corneille is always an exponent of rationalistic drama. For his characters are simply not pure rational beings. Attila's superstition, mentioned in the preface, is emphasized throughout the play. Both he and the Gothic kings lend their credulous ears to the predictions of seers and soothsayers. Moreover, as still remains to be examined, Attila himself is motivated by various forces, some of which are far from being clear and rational. Even Faguet had to confess, in his sympathetic analysis of the play: "A partir de l'acte IV, la pièce devient étrange et un peu ridicule parce que Attila devient un monstre incohérent."[61] Whether a monster remains monstrous when becoming coherent is a question Faguet did not consider. Another favorable reader, Bornier, experienced similar difficulties: "J'accorde que l'action en est d'abord confuse et qu'il faut beaucoup d'attention pour bien saisir le jeu de tous les ressorts imaginés par le poète."[62]

60 Mornet, *op. cit.*, p. 100.
61 Faguet, *op. cit.*, p. 215.
62 Bornier, *loc. cit.*, pp. 495–496.

It may be also that Corneille's too exclusive reputation as
the singer of Roman heroes and heroines did not facilitate
the appreciation of a play in which the only character true
to the tradition of *la fierté romaine* (II, iii, 502), Honorie,
ranks but third, after the Hunnish king and the Frankish
princess, among heroes whom Corneille intends for us to
"admire." This explains up to a certain point Bayle's judgment quoted above. It also obscures the interesting fact that
Corneille may be considered among the fathers of French
tragédie nationale, an honor often undeservedly bestowed
on Voltaire. For Corneille's intentions in this respect are
made quite clear in his preface: "Il [Attila] épousa Ildione,
dont tous les historiens marquent la beauté, sans parler de la
naissance. C'est ce qui m'a enhardi à la faire soeur d'un de
nos premiers rois, afin d'opposer la France naissante au dé-
clin de l'Empire"; a statement immortalized by the impressive
couplet uttered by Valamir:

> Un grand destin commence, un grand destin s'achève:
> L'empire est prêt à choir, et la France s'élève.
>
> [I, ii, 141–142]

The obvious and numerous allusions to Louis XIV, the
young Dauphin, French military and diplomatic ventures,
and the like need hardly be recalled at great length:

> Derrière Mérovée, fondateur de la dynastie régnante,
> Louis XIV reste bien visible. On reconnaît les prin-
> cipaux actes du jeune roi: la querelle des préséances
> avec l'Espagne, la tension avec le Saint-Siège, les grandes
> revues qui annoncent un tournant politique. Pour la
> quatrième fois, le roi est félicité de ne laisser prendre
> aux ministres que l'importance qu'il veut bien leur ac-
> corder. Le portrait sent son poète pensionné.[63]

> Je l'ai vu dans la paix, je l'ai vu dans la guerre,
> Porter partout un front de maître de la terre.

[63] Georges Couton, *Corneille, l'homme et l'oeuvre* (Paris: Hatier,
1958), p. 167. Cf. also the same author's *La Vieillesse de Corneille*,
pp. 134–135.

J'ai vu plus d'une fois de fières nations
Désarmer son courroux par leurs soumissions.
J'ai vu tous les plaisirs de son âme héroïque
N'avoir rien que d'auguste et que de magnifique;
Et ses illustres soins ouvrir à ses sujets
L'école de la guerre au milieu de la paix.

. . . . . .

Je l'ai vu, tout couvert de poudre et de fumée,
Donner le grand exemple à toute son armée,
Semer par ses périls l'effroi de toutes parts,
Bouleverser les murs d'un seul de ses regards,
Et sur l'orgueil brisé des plus superbes têtes
De sa course rapide entasser les conquêtes.

[II, v, 557–564 and 569–574]

It is true that it may be judged clumsy of Corneille to oppose a play entitled *Attila* to Racine's *Alexandre,* an openly
avowed portrayal of the young king. But credit must be
given to the superior originality he displayed in seeking a
historical figure capable of embodying Louis XIV's virtues
among his own predecessors on the Frankish throne, rather
than among the traditional heroes of classical antiquity. In
so doing, Corneille dared introduce on the serious stage a
device successfully used by some contemporary novelists,
notably in La Calprenède's *Faramond* (1661). In fact,
Corneille's innovation was too bold to be fully appreciated
by the contemporary public. As Fontenelle noted in his *Vie
de Corneille:* "Il ne pouvait mieux braver son siècle, qu'en
lui donnant *Attila,* digne roi des Huns";[64] which faithfully
echoes Saint-Evremond's second letter on the subject to
Count de Lionne: "Le vérité est que la pièce est moins propre au goût de votre cour, qu'à celui de l'antiquité."[65]

The same holds true of Corneille's obvious relish at insert-
ing into his well-controlled alexandrines the unwonted and
barbaric sounding names of so many of Attila's contemporaries. Blind to the fact that Corneille did not stumble
clumsily and unconsciously into these barbarians, too many

[64] Fontenelle, *Oeuvres* (Paris: Salmon, 1825), IV, 223.
[65] Quoted by Mélèse, *op. cit.,* p. 331.

readers, sorry to see him abandon the familiar Roman names, failed to appreciate some surprisingly successful and romantic-like effects achieved in *Attila*:

> Faut-il vous immoler l'orgueil de Torrismond?
> Faut-il teindre l'Arar du sang de Sigismond?
> [IV, v, 1311–1312]

If, on the other hand, Corneille felt the need to modify the historical name of Ildione, it was not because it sounded harsh and ridiculous, as Voltaire pretends: "Elle s'appelait Ildecone à la première représentation: on changea ensuite ce nom ridicule."[66] The change was much more probably prompted, as Scherer[67] surmised, by the presence in the original name of one of those *syllabes sales* no longer tolerated by the fine ladies who, according to Molière, *étaient plus chastes des oreilles que de tout le reste du corps*. But on this point too, Voltaire, when he branded Corneille's style in *Attila* as *raboteux,* merely demonstrated that he had not lifted himself out of the rut from the depth of which Boileau had claimed that Agamemnon was more poetic-sounding than Childebrand. When Corneille wrote as Hugolian a line as *Singibar, Gondebaut, Mérovée et Thierri* (I, ii, 179), he conclusively showed that he was a much greater poet than the author of *L'Art poétique,* who asserted:

> D'un seul nom quelquefois le son dur ou bizarre
> Rend un poème entier ou burlesque ou barbare.[68]

But the most essential element of the play, which remains obscure or grotesque until conventional ideas concerning "Cornelianism" are soundly shaken, is the truly extraordinary conception of its hero's character and personality. As long as Attila is assumed to be a thoroughgoing villain, Corneille's play remains perplexing and meaningless. But Corneille does not say anywhere that such is his notion of the Hunnish king. In his preface he lists a number of known historical facts

---

[66] *Commentaires sur Corneille* in *Oeuvres completes* (Paris: Garnier, 1877–1885), XXXII, 269.

[67] Scherer, *op. cit.*, p. 388.

[68] *L'Art poétique*, III, 243–244.

about Attila, but he remains objectively scholarly throughout, and no moral judgment can possibly be based on these facts. If we remember, however, earlier plays, such as *Le Menteur* and *Rodogune*, we may find a clue to Corneille's judgment on Attila. The strong attraction which Corneille acknowledges in his critical writings for such characters as Dorante, the "liar," or Cléopâtre, the murderess queen, must apply also to Attila, for he unmistakably belongs to the same group of ambiguously fascinating heroes, whose fascinating power has nothing to do with conventional moral values. It seems fairly safe to assume that if 1660 had not been the terminal date beyond which Corneille wrote no more *Discours* or *Examens*, he would have expressed himself about Attila somewhat as he did about Cléopâtre in his first *Discours*: "Tous ses crimes sont accompagnés d'une grandeur d'âme qui a quelque chose de si haut qu'en même temps qu'on déteste ses actions, on admire la source dont ils partent."

Corneille quite obviously attempted to portray Attila as a figure of heroic stature. His domination over all the other characters appears effortless, and even, to a certain extent, justified by the lower level or inferior tension of their passions. The only possible exception is Ildione, the "French" princess, whom he loves, who has the courage to plan his murder, and, more important, who stands above the other three prisoners of Attila in that she shares with him the devastating weapon of irony, that unmistakable attribute of the superior being. Incidentally, the obvious superiority of Ildione and Honorie over their male counterparts, Ardaric and Valamir, gives the lie to those who give Racine unquestionable precedence in the portrayal of aggressive and domineering women. Moreover, by subtly differentiating between the proud and grandiloquent Roman princess and the brave and ironical "French" one, Corneille displayed his awareness of the necessity of renewing himself and of abandoning his practice of giving birth to heroines true to the tradition of what Bayle called *la grandeur romaine*. In this respect, too, the fact that the only Roman character of the play, Honorie, is denied the privilege of irony, does not lack significance.

When, toward the end of the play, Attila addresses the other characters whom he has just placed in the most cruel quandary, he uses his most sarcastic mood, and, incidentally, Ildione is not present at the time:

> Eh bien! mes illustres amis,
> Contre mes grands rivaux quel espoir m'est permis?
> Pas un n'a-t-il pour soi la digne complaisance
> D'acquérir sa princesse en perdant qui m'offense?
> Quoi? l'amour, l'amitié, tout va d'un froid égal!
> Pas un ne m'aime assez pour haïr mon rival!
> Pas un de son objet n'a l'âme assez ravie
> Pour vouloir être heureux aux dépens d'une vie!
> Quels amis! quels amants! et quelle dureté!
>
> [V, iii, 1515–1523]

We must conclude that Corneille sides with his Hunnish hero when he has Valamir reply to this speech by an insipid retort in a righteous and somewhat pompous mood:

> A l'inhumanité joindre la raillerie,
> C'est à son dernier point porter la barbarie.
>
> [*Ibid.*,1529–1530]

Likewise, in the third act Corneille surely favored Attila over the haughty Roman princess when he had him answer Honorie's violent tirade with this disdainful and icy warning:

> Si nous nous emportons, j'irai plus loin que vous,
> Madame.
>
> [III, iv, 1068–1069]

Irony is the dominant mood of *Attila*, as it was of *Nicomède*, the superiority of Attila over Nicomède resulting from a richer and more convincing characterization. The fact that these two heroes belong at either ends of the conventional scale of moral values is not of paramount importance to Corneille.

If such considerations bring to mind some aspects of

Sartre's *Le Diable et le bon Dieu* and suggest bringing together Attila and Goetz, the temptation will be enhanced
further by a quick consideration of *Attila's* religious overtones. On this point Corneille noted in his preface: "Il est
malaisé de savoir quelle était sa religion: le surnom de *Fléau
de Dieu*, qu'il prenait lui-même, montre qu'il n'en croyait
pas plusieurs. . . . Il croyait fort aux devins, et c'était peut-
être tout ce qu'il croyait." It is a sure sign of the greatness of
Corneille's genius that, devout Catholic though he was, he
could appreciate and enjoy, indeed understand and admire,
characters of Attila's stature. For there is no doubt that he
did, as is clear from the glorious energy of the speech with
which, toward the end of the play, Attila defies his desperate
and terrorized antagonists:

> Ce dieu dont vous parlez, de temps en temps sévère,
> Ne s'arme pas toujours de toute sa colère;
> Mais quand à sa fureur il livre l'univers,
> Elle a pour chaque temps des déluges divers.
> Jadis, de toutes parts faisant regorger l'onde,
> Sous un déluge d'eaux il abîma le monde;
> Sa main tient en réserve un déluge de feux
> Pour le dernier moment de nos derniers neveux;
> Et mon bras, dont il fait aujourd'hui son tonnerre,
> D'un déluge de sang couvre pour lui la terre.
>
> [V, iii, 1573–1582]

Although Couton was technically correct in asserting that,
through this interpretation of his monster's function, Corneille
donne sa solution catholique[69] to the problem of evil, he failed
to account for Corneille's obvious fascination for his Attila as
a particular instrument of the will and wrath of God. *Attila*
is by no means a morality play, for the hero's death at the
end is emphatically not a God-sent miracle. Corneille was
careful to point out in his preface that he accepted neither
of the two accounts of Attila's death as reported by historians:

> Marcellin dit qu'elle [Ildione] le tua elle-même, et je lui
> en ai voulu donner l'idée, quoique sans effet. Tous les

---

[69] Couton, *Vieillesse*, p. 131.

autres rapportent qu'il avait accoutumé de saigner du nez, et que les vapeurs du vin et des viandes dont il se chargea fermèrent le passage à ce sang, qui, après l'avoir étouffé, sortit avec violence par tous les conduits. Je les ai suivis sur la manière de sa mort; mais j'ai cru plus à propos d'en attribuer la cause à un excès de colère qu'à un excès d'intempérance.

It is undeniable that either of these two traditional accounts of Attila's death would have been much more likely than the one Corneille invented to look like the work of Providence. It was, therefore, Corneille's considered opinion that Ildione, for all her charm and virtues, was not to be cast in the role of a French Judith, and that his Attila was to be spared an ignominious death. Bornier speculated rather paradoxically that Corneille refused to grant Attila *la fin grandiose de l'assassinat,*[70] and that Ildione, for lack of an authentic divine mission, would have been but a common murderess. Much more to the point appears Scherer's argument[71] that Corneille rationalized the available historical data concerning Attila's fatal ailment by making it a function of his anger and by submitting this anger to increasing stimulation as the play draws nearer its end.

Dort proceeds even one step further, while still reasoning according to the very logics of Corneille's notion of heroism. Corneille's Attila stands so far above the rest of humanity, not of course in moral terms, but by virtue of his energy, will-power, and will to power, that it would be absurd to have him die at the hands of his weak enemies. The only fitting death for a hero of this kind is to die a victim of himself, thus preserving till the end his heroic liberty. So, according to Dort, Corneille's way of disposing of his hero *est bien la seule fin digne d'Attila, de ce héros parvenu au bout de lui-même, qui succombe à sa propre force, à son propre afflux de sang, qui meurt engorgé, victime de sa liberté, de son propre éblouissement.*[72]

[70] Bornier, *loc. cit.,* p. 497.
[71] Scherer, *op. cit.,* p. 130.
[72] Dort, *op. cit.,* p. 107.

The same critic is also substantially correct in concluding that *Attila* is a genuine tragedy. For even if serious objection may be raised against Dort's application of Lukàcs' dialectics, according to which the play is Corneille's single tragedy, one may agree that Attila is a true tragic hero who dies a victim of himself. This would be enough to grant this play a key position in the development of Corneille's dramaturgy. If, as many critics now argue, Corneille's acknowledged masterpieces, from *Le Cid* to *Polyeucte*, are not strictly speaking tragedies, one of the reasons being that Corneille's faith in human energy led him to preserve his heroes from truly tragic fates, a play like *Attila* shows that he eventually became capable of writing tragedies. As the enthusiastic optimism of his youthful maturity waned, Corneille mustered the courage and imagination to renew himself radically; *Attila* is the evidence of this renewal, the next to last play which the poet himself called a tragedy. The last one, *Suréna*, also an authentic tragedy, is again different from any of his previous plays, including *Attila*. As Nadal perceptively wrote about *Suréna*, "La conception cornélienne de l'héroïsme et de l'amour dominé, sans être rejetée, s'y trouve menacée d'une sorte d'abandon et de discrédit."[73]

Corneille, who is traditionally presented as one of France's most moralistic and "bien-pensants" playwrights, appears, therefore, to have been the object of an amazingly effective critical hoax. Thanks, however, to the few brave and clear-minded scholars who have begun the huge task of scraping away the century-old layers which have disfigured the true face of Corneille, thanks perhaps also to the eye-opening effect of the existentialist era, a new notion of what "Cornelianism" really means is now possible. And so we perhaps find ourselves in an unprecedentedly favorable position to appreciate one of Corneille's most astounding achievements, *Attila roi des Huns*.

[73] Nadal, *op. cit.*, p. 254.

PASCAL'S SOPHISTRY AND
THE SIN OF POESY

By Jean-Jacques Demorest

Is Pascal a sophist? Voltaire wanted to believe it, Valéry as well, and recent critics have sought to establish the fact. This critical tradition, clearly Voltairian in origin yet romantic in its trappings, has proceeded artfully: extolling the writer, berating the thinker. Divide to conquer. A Solomonlike justice threatens to sever dialectic man in two. The author of the Wager is offered a dire choice: half-survive as a brilliant stylist or perish as a dangerous, beguiling impostor. In no case is a paradoxical answer tolerated.

We wonder. Is the apparent opposition between a man aloof from the grasping love of his neighbor and a man bent on saving that same neighbor, between the solitary figure and the apologist, between the cynic and the enraptured hoper— is this intense dichotomy rooted in Pascal's personality or is it a figment of our own imagination? Where does the contradiction lie? In us? In Pascal? Or in both? Did Pascal, in fact, lack rigor and constancy? Was he unfaithful to his doctrine? In short, did he betray his ideal or are we *incapables d'épouser les contraires?* Who is the sophist?

In condemning Pascal, the Voltairian tradition, best illustrated today by the Marxist Henri Lefebvre, has repeatedly scored three aspects of the *Pensées:* the Wager, the *pensée de derrière,* and the famed "Le silence éternel de ces espaces infinis m'effraie" (Brunschvicg 428). The arguments bearing on the Wager are too hackneyed and too mathematical in nature to be of much interest here. The other two, however, and particularly the *pensée de derrière*, rarely discussed, may bear further examination.

We are not so much dealing with the overt old quarrel between belief and disbelief in the present case as with a tangential quarrel over literary perfection. The problem can be put succinctly: Is poetry a sin? For strangely enough, Pascal is being accused of poetry, and those who would brand him as a sinner untrue to his tenets profess to be atheists. By implication it is suggested, and later asserted, that brilliant writing must somehow hide shallowness of content and sophistry of intent. The counts of the indictment, then, are rather subtle. Pascal's thought is not impugned directly. The first step consists in sparing no praise of the remarkable faculties of the stylist; the second step questions the motives of a man who writes too well. From there the problem of the impurity of perfection is raised, and finally it is deduced that so dazzling a prose masks the agony of a tortured and deceitful conscience. Did Spinoza or Descartes feel the urge to compose a rhapsodically beautiful prose? Surely something is amiss in a man of austere religious convictions who nurtures the cadence of imagery and studies painstakingly the art of persuasion. Lefebvre infers that had Pascal polished his style less the sincerity of his thought would be less doubtful and moribund Christianity would have gasped a little while longer—all told then, it is really fortunate that the artifacts of poetry hastened the decay of faith!

It is an easy matter to mock the champions of the Voltairian tradition. For one thing, they are from the outset at an ungraceful disadvantage, obliged to interpret a man whose very being is bound to a vision of the world which they can neither share nor comprehend. They remain at a distance and cannot penetrate his position enough to undermine him significantly. Still their accusation of sophistry carries weight, if only because it is accepted by many today—among others by Claudel and Simone Weil, who can scarcely be regarded as devotees of Ferney. In truth, our times may be dubbed the Pascalian Age, yet the impeachment of Pascal has rarely been as concentrated, imposing, and imaginative. There is some indication that Paul Valéry's concise condemnation renewed and revived a Voltairian tradition that had suffered somewhat at the hands of hot-headed romanticists. Indeed, the basic argument employed by Valéry was novel and, given the character of the accuser, nothing short of sensational: art suspected, poetry decried. Pascal incriminated for an abuse of the very qualities that should have secured him the admiring amity of the creator of *Charmes*, a fellow amateur in science and geometry. It was unexpected. Possibly Pascal owes this dolorous honor to the peculiar intellectual development of a poet who was determined at that precise moment *not* to resolve his own dialectical make-up and to use this specific confrontation as a hygienic exercise in a newly devised critical attitude: criticism *ab absurdo*, or more exactly criticism predicated on alienation, criticism based on a stanchly assumed antipathy towards the object of inquiry. Pascal proved to be an ideal opponent.

In Valéry, on the other hand, the aggressive converter encountered the most deliberately prejudiced but the most challenging adversary he had met in more than a century. The clash was as short and as lucidly cruel as Valéry's essay. Despite its forceful reverberations, which we intend to review here, it is not clear that Pascal came out the worst. For one thing, our contemporaries reading Valéry's Pythagorean arraignment are likely to judge the poet's arguments on their purely objective merits and not on the efficacy of the interior catharsis enjoyed by Valéry. Egotism has a limited posthumous appeal; its survival value is at best uncertain.

Essentially the poet is accusing Pascal of attaining unholy rhetorical ends through poetry. Or to dramatize the situation, the charge is: Impure Poetry.

The brief essay devoted to this crimination, "Variation sur une 'pensée,'"[1] is based entirely on "Le silence éternel . . ." Perhaps we should consider it as an improvisation and no more censure Valéry for his excessive rendition of the original than we would dare cavil at Mozart for the fanciful liberties he takes with a theme of Haydn's. There is a difference though: Mozart is not openly criticizing Haydn. Further-

---

[1] In *Variété*, I (Paris: © Gallimard, 1924), 139–153.

more, Valéry's *variation* has become in time the source of a great number of other aggravated variations.

The poet insists on two aspects: silence and fright. It does not even come to his mind that Pascal's *pensée* should be attributed to the unbeliever. The reason for this lack of perceptiveness is to be found in Valéry's unconscious adherence to the Voltairian tradition as elaborated and made theatrical by the romanticists. In reality, his debt to the romanticists is far greater than we first allowed.

The tone gives him away. For instance, speaking of Pascal's intelligence: "La contemplation ne manque jamais de la faire hurler à la mort. Elle me fait songer invinciblement à cet aboi insupportable qu'adressent les chiens à la lune" (p. 142). And even when he mocks the romanticists' propensity to depict a tragic, Hamletlike Pascal, Valéry's approach remains romantic. His purposeful exaggeration of Pascal's despair, solitude, and terror is patently romantic. In effect, Valéry is not writing a variation on a *pensée* of Pascal; he is merely composing a brilliant improvisation on a romantic theme.

Elsewhere in the essay his tie to Voltaire is evident, and it is in this renewal and intensification of the Voltairian tradition that Valéry's originality lies. The contention is that the *misanthrope sublime* was guilty of argumentative duplicity and rhetorical insincerity. Neither Valéry nor Voltaire fully grasp the tactical implications of writing an *Apology;* they choose to ignore the apologetical requisites of the genre and consider the *Pensées* as entirely personal reflections which Pascal somehow wishes to impose on humanity. They do not sense the strong contradiction of their own position, nor do they make any provision for the fact that the *Pensées* are an unfinished work. Valéry, nevertheless, leads the disputation to higher ground, to a poetic ground that Voltaire was not too well qualified to appreciate. He, for one, does not call Pascal a *fourbe,* finding it more telling to stigmatize the Jansenist as too much of a poet:

> Une phrase bien accordée exclut la renonciation totale.
> Une détresse qui écrit bien n'est pas si achevée
> qu'elle n'ait sauvé du naufrage quelque liberté de l'es-

prit. . . . Il y a aussi je ne sais quoi de trouble, et je ne sais quoi de facile, dans la spécialité que l'on se fait des motifs tragiques et des objets impressionnants. . . . Je ne suis pas à mon aise devant ce mélange de l'art avec la nature. Quand je vois l'écrivain reprendre et empirer la véritable sensation de l'homme, y ajouter des forces recherchées, et vouloir toutefois que l'on prenne son industrie pour son émotion, je trouve que cela est impur et ambigu. . . . Je vois trop la main de Pascal. D'ailleurs quand même les intentions seraient pures, le seul souci d'écrire, et le soin que l'on y apporte ont le même effet naturel qu'une arrière-pensée [pp. 143–144].

Finally, Valéry implies that Pascal's philosophy was static. The manner in which he dismisses the theme of the *recherche*, so central to an understanding of the *Pensées*, is rather disquieting:

Pascal avait "trouvé," mais sans doute parce qu'il ne cherchait plus. La cessation de la recherche, et la forme de cette cessation, peuvent donner le sentiment de la trouvaille. Mais il n'a jamais eu de foi dans la recherche en tant qu'elle espère dans l'imprévu [p. 152].

The next and concluding step in Valéry's demonstration brings out the real cause of irritation:

Il a tiré de soi-même le *silence éternel* que ni les hommes véritablement religieux, ni les hommes véritablement profonds n'ont jamais observé dans l'univers. Il a exagéré affreusement, grossièrement, l'opposition de la connaissance et du salut [pp. 152–153].

It is Valéry the mathematician, the amateur scientist, who is hurt to the quick. It is the scientist who is accusing Pascal of poetry. A just retribution; after all, had not Pascal himself leveled the accusation of *Poet* with a measure of contempt?

Obviously, Valéry does not care to understand Pascal. And perhaps this misunderstanding is more revealing than would be permissive agreement—that is, so long as the calculated quality of Valéry's opposition is well delineated. Such is not the case, however, with those who have taken Valéry's thesis over and, in the name of Marxism, have prosecuted the criminal investigation of Pascal's sophistry. Henri Lefebvre,[2] for one, in his exposition and general espousal of Valéry's view (I, 113–115), fails to mention that Valéry deliberately founded his criticism of Pascal on a sort of systematic egotistic malevolence, the object of which was to exercise and sharpen the critical tools while carrying on intellectual calisthenics salutary to the critic. As a matter of fact, in *Autres Rhumbs,*[3] Valéry explains his method of purposeful antipathy:

La haine habite l'adversaire, en développe les profondeurs, dissèque les plus délicates racines des desseins qu'il a dans le coeur. Nous le pénétrons mieux que nous-mêmes, et mieux qu'il ne fait soi-même. Il s'oublie et nous ne l'oublions pas. Car nous le percevons au moyen d'une blessure, et il n'est pas de sens plus cuisant, qui grandisse et précise plus fortement ce qui touche, qu'une partie blessée de l'être [p. 188].

This profession of faith in cultural sadism is perhaps more eloquent than efficacious—at least as regards Pascal.

In the case of Henri Lefebvre, however, there is no attempt to elucidate the peculiar viewpoint of Valéry. The major counts of the indictment are taken over with added virulence and with only a few corrections:

Alors le visionnaire s'épouvante. . . . Il a commencé par tuer, en pensée, l'homme; et voici que le ciel reflète impitoyablement le désert terrestre. . . . Pascal va se tirer d'affaire en prétendant que ce qu'on cherche, on l'a déjà trouvé. . . . Le cri solitaire se répand au loin dans l'espace désert qu'il ne peut remplir. Mais que nous sommes loin du sanglot balbutiant auquel parviendront les poètes avec Rimbaud, avec Lautréamont, et qu'ils auront bientôt transformé à nouveau en beau style, en littérature. Valéry, qui s'y connaissait en lit-

térature a bien senti la grande froideur du style pas-
calien. . . . Oui, mais Valéry n'a pas su voir combien
le cri angoissé de Pascal—angoissé malgré la réussite
brillante, trop brillante, du style—révèle le conflit
douloureux des deux mondes: celui de la science, celui
de la religion.[4] . . . Pascal symbolise la situation de son
temps [I, 113–115].

This brief passage is indicative of the durability of the
romantico-Voltairian tradition within the Marxist framework.
It also illustrates a contemporary tendency to allege fascination for Pascal the stylist before being led, through the
vagaries of historical research, to the "amazing" discovery of
his sophistry. For our purpose here we propose to use Lefebvre's intelligent and biased interpretation as a provocative
means of arriving at some definition of the modern incrimi-
nation of Pascal as a sophist.

The premise, grossly simplified, can be summarized as follows: Pascal is a Jansenist; Jansenism gave French classicism
its myths, poetry, pragmatism, taste, and its concern for literary perfection; in fact Jansenism is, seen from another
angle, a major element of classical stylization, itself a reflection of the bourgeoisie's bad conscience (I, 146, 132). Pascal, as much by syllogistic inference within the terms of the
argument as by observation of the real facts, was the leading
Jansenist writer; hence, the man called upon to express and
stylize his time, in other words to reduce, mummify, and lie
superbly:

> Il exprime l'humanité de son temps, et *propose* une
> image de l'homme, image illusoire et provisoire qu'il
> *impose* à force d'art [I, 150].

> L'étonnant, le stupéfiant, c'est que l'on puisse une se-
> cond prendre ce caractère stylistique pour un signe de
> vérité; au lieu de considérer aussitôt avec méfiance
> cette forme d'affirmation [I, 140].

[4] This is unfair to Valéry. See Valéry's unequivocal statement
above: "Il a exagéré affreusement, grossièrement, l'opposition de la
connaissance et du salut."

> Le trait, la force, l'éclat des formules pascaliennes tien-
> nent aussi à leur déficience idéologique [II, 238].

This last claim is undoubtedly harder to establish. What
is adduced is that philosophy too well rendered becomes
mere literature and falsehood. Lefebvre, if he deigned,
would have no difficulty, however, in mustering support for
his claim. Albert Bayet goes nearly as far: "Ses raisonnements
ne valent point. Il le sait. Mais l'important n'est pas qu'ils
vaillent, c'est qu'ils touchent."[5] The frenetical interpretation
of a Victor Delbet, too excessive to be analyzed here, goes
far beyond that of either Bayet or Lefebvre. The latter, more
moderate, still leads us to consider Pascal not as a thinker
but as an unholy artificer, a littérateur; worse yet, a Jesuit!

> Si les *Provinciales,* comme les *Pensées,* ont subi un dé-
> placement et sont devenues pour nous une oeuvre d'art,
> seules certaines conditions initiales ont permis ce dé-
> placement. . . . Pascal introduit la littérature dans la
> théorie et la métaphysique. Grandeur et décadence
> . . . Jésuitisme! Quelle distance entre la haute sincérité
> du Discours cartésien et les *Provinciales* [II, 67–68].

In this manner literature and Jesuitism, casuistry and poetry,
are closely associated. Nor does Pascal's wit enjoy the privilege of any redeeming grace; on the contrary, wit is a sign
of Christian decadence: "Il a fixé l'attitude chrétienne
théorique en l'installant dans l'absence de sérieux devant la
divine tragédie à laquelle elle feint encore de croire" (II,
70). From pleasantry to hypocrisy, a flattering progress! And
Pascal wends a crooked path that ends in sheer blackmail,
stylistic blackmail: "Ce tissu de banalités médiévales, ces
thèmes des fresques et des développements oratoires, repren-
nent une valeur à cause du style. Ici, style égale chantage"
(II, 121). Finally exposed, it will henceforth be Pascal's
dubious honor to go down in history as *le grand désenchan-
teur, spécialiste du chantage à l'éternité* (II, 135).

There is no doubt, though, that the central issue is Pascal's
sophistry and his heinous sin poetry. We do not intend to

---

[5] *Les "Pensées" de Pascal* (Paris: SFELT, 1948), p. 136.

survey the rest of Lefebvre's views nor even to refute those
that concern us when they slip, as they do occasionally, into
heavy-handed buffoonery.[6] But what, in general, can be said
in Pascal's defense?

There is no effective parry to the accusation of perfection,
but it is hoped that in time this trait of Pascal's will no longer
be considered quite so infamous. The seventeenth century
cherished a style of unnatural naturalness; we cherish one of
natural unnaturalness. This conflict between order and disorder, between a neat and a slovenly nature is too arduous to
resolve—all the more so that Pascal's style in the *Pensées*
comes closer to reconciling the two manners than any other
work we can think of.

Much can be alleged in defense of his "sophistry," nevertheless. In the first place, a certain degree of ambiguity un-
avoidably stems from Pascal's description of a "median man"
with whose condition and situation he identifies himself
totally: "C'est sortir de l'humanité que de sortir du milieu.
La grandeur de l'âme humaine consiste à savoir s'y tenir"
(Br. 378). Albeit he may risk equivocation in formulating
the discourses that express man's ambivalent position, Pascal
will not demur from his stubborn conviction that the ambiguity of man is real. It is in any case a measured risk, for his
repeated declarations of hatred for equivocation are illumined
by his acts. When Nicole and Arnauld propose a clever solution to the obligatory signing of the *formulaire,* wherein by
the use of equivocal language a good Jansenist might soothe
his conscience and blind Rome, Pascal strongly rejects the
proposed wording as *une voie moyenne, qui est abominable
devant Dieu, méprisable devant les hommes.* In his mind, the
ambiguity of man's condition is no excuse for generalized
sophistry and mediocrity; the *milieu* is less an inert point of
rest than the active center of man's racking between the two
infinites.

[6] *Sophistry* would be an even more apt definition. For instance,
we are informed soberly that the only Pascalians living today are
the *bienpensants.* Why? Because Pascal said: "Travaillons à bien
penser, voilà le principe de la morale" (II, 129; see also II, 70–71
and 96).

That incessant torture and joy of a man who partakes of two natures is expressed in motion by a contrapuntal style which even affects matters as supposedly abstract as force and justice:

La justice sans la force est impuissante; la force sans la justice est tyrannique. La justice sans force est contredite, parce qu'il y a toujours des méchants; la force sans la justice est accusée. Il faut donc mettre ensemble la justice et la force; et pour cela faire que ce qui est juste soit fort, ou que ce qui est fort soit juste.

La justice est sujette à dispute, la force est très reconnaissable et sans dispute. Ainsi on n'a pu donner la force à la justice, parce que la force contredit la justice et a dit que c'était elle qui était juste. Et ainsi ne pouvant faire que ce qui est juste fût fort, on a fait que ce qui est fort fût juste [Br. 298].

Admirable as the counterpoint may be, is it fair to assume that brilliance deters from thought; or worse, that it glitters over empty banalities? Does not in fact stylistic perfection sharpen our understanding and enliven the idea? To impose the view that philosophical truth and literary perfection are inexorably incompatible is more often than not outright guile. Beauty is not necessarily impure.

It must be recognized, however, that Pascal's utter command of style can create a galling impression of self-assurance —a circumstance all the more ironical inasmuch as one of the purposes of his seeking perfection was to arrive at a sort of primeval simplicity in which his presence would be completely sacrificed and the reader would enjoy the satisfaction of being in direct contact with the thought. This ideal, obviously not attained, implied a measure of adjustment and compromise—"L'art de persuader a un rapport nécessaire à la manière dont les hommes consentent à ce qu'on leur propose, et aux conditions des choses qu'on veut faire croire" (Esprit géométrique)—not, however, to the point of depravation: " 'Dites-nous des choses agréables et nous vous écouterons' disent les Juifs à Moïse; comme si l'agrément devait régler la créance" (loc. cit.); "Il faut de l'agréable et du réel;

mais il faut que l'agréable soit lui-même pris du vrai" (Br. 25). It would be strange indeed if a writer so aware of the psychological rules of his art, a man so intransigently suspicious of his own motives, should fall into the pitfalls of designedly deceptive reasoning.

Of course one cannot deny the existence of such a danger, particularly when Pascal and his unbeliever are locked in a fraternal dialectic combat: "S'il se vante, je l'abaisse; s'il s'abaisse, je le vante; et le contredis toujours jusqu'à ce qu'il comprenne qu'il est un monstre incompréhensible" (Br. 420). One of the major problems in the study of the *Pensées* is to determine who exactly is speaking, Pascal or the interlocutor. And what sort of a man (or of men) is that unbelieving interlocutor? There cannot fail to be, in so "impure" a genre as an apologetic dialogue, a slight degree of composition, of "sophistry." One simply does not speak to others as one speaks to oneself. It is a sign of reality and of integrity if in such a dialogue concessions to the other person do seep in. Were these concessions absent, there would be strong reasons to cry out against the author's sophistry. As matters stand, the important and debatable problem is that of the interlocutor's general identity.

The major accusations of sophistry aimed at Pascal are founded on the tenuous contention that nearly everything in the *Pensées* represents the author's beliefs or *is* the author. Maurice de Gandillac, for example, accepts the interpretation of Valéry and Lefebvre: confronted with the silence of the universe, Pascal is expressing his own fright and not that of the unbeliever.[7] To this we might reply that expressions of fright appear only in passages having an oral ring that single them out as elements of a future dialogue and probably as statements of the unbeliever.[8] We make this last inference because *all* the expressions of fright occur in passages easily ascribable to the unbeliever, but only ascribable to Pascal

[7] "Pascal et le silence du monde," in *Blaise Pascal* (Cahiers de Royaumont No. 1; Paris: Ed. de Minuit, 1956), pp. 342–385.

[8] Br. 205, 206, and par. 12, 13, and 14 of Br. 194; it should also be noted that in Br. 72 it is *l'homme* whom Pascal expects to *s'effrayer de soi-même . . . contempler en silence.*

at the price of considerable sleight of hand. Were that fearful awe really Pascal's, would it not be seen in his other works and in the numerous fragments of the *Pensées* where indubitably only he is present? Such is not the case. An accusation of sophistry based on *le silence éternel*, such as that of Valéry, loses its vigor when the texts are closely examined.

The real difficulty, the source of most misunderstandings that are not deliberate, lies in the incompleteness of the *Pensées*. It is so trite an observation, and yet . . . If we take as an example a collective work written by specialists, such as the interesting printed text of the Royaumont colloquium (see n. 7), we are appalled by the irrelevance of the erudite commentaries. Eminent historians of ideology weave fascinating and esoteric explications around Pascal. They tie him to remote figures he never read and interpret him by comparison to philosophical currents nonexistent in France between 1650 and 1660. This subtle and learned obfuscation, which at times waxes caustic, stems from a common reluctance to remember two facts: Pascal is bent on converting an unbeliever, not on expounding a metaphysical system; and the *Pensées* are not a definitive work, only notes and summary reflections. We would like to go further and suggest that the *Pensées* should not even be read as an Apology, but only as tactical projects and sketches. The author of the *Pensées* was an ardent young general surveying the forces at his command, improvising on the field; he was not a venerable marshal spinning tales of conquest during the long glowing evenings in comfortable winter quarters. In the thick of battle, he even loses a distinct notion of his identity. He is not seeking personal glorification but victory over unbelief and indifference. Eventually carried away by the storming of the objective, he subordinates his own individuality to that of the unbeliever, increases and exaggerates the unbeliever's rapid consciousness of self. The depersonalization of the author is directly proportionate to the overpersonalization of the unbeliever. Battles are dusty or muddy; there are long moments of indecision and confusion. The reader can in good faith mistake the unbeliever's cry for Pascal's, but he has little ground for censuring that cry as "sophistry" or for describing the battle as "theatrical disorder."

There are certainly other, more solid, causes of the recent charges of "sophistry"—we shall not discuss those springing from political or religious biases.[9] One possible cause, less farfetched than may first appear, is suggested vaguely by a sentence in Valéry's essay: "D'ailleurs, quand même les intentions seraient pures, le seul souci d'écrire, et le soin qu'on y apporte ont le même effet naturel qu'une arrière-pensée" (p. 144). In reality, Pascal would have agreed with Valéry, even allowing that his own intentions were not entirely pure (see Br. 150). Furthermore, his definition of the *art de persuader* is, in a way, an avowed recognition of the role the *arrière-pensée* plays in a successful rhetoric. The theme, in truth, is dear to Pascal; more colorfully, he refers to the *pensée de derrière*. Noting the frequency with which it provokes sarcastic reproaches of "Jesuitry" and "duplicity" on the part of critics, we have come to wonder whether it is not at the heart of the image of a sophistic Pascal. In any event it is central to Pascal's thought and to his being—hence, we trust, worth studying.

The *pensée de derrière* takes on various aspects and in Pascal's earlier works goes under several names. We shall try to outline its inception and evolution. Speaking with praise of Montaigne to M. de Saci, Pascal says of the essayist:

> Il conclut . . . qu'on doit prendre le vrai et le bien sur la première apparence, sans les presser . . . il agit comme les autres hommes; et tout ce qu'ils font dans la sotte pensée qu'ils suivent le vrai bien, il le fait par un autre principe [*Entretien avec M. de Saci*].

This superficial conceit and necessary deceit derive, in fact, from a recognition of man's unconscious deceit of self: "C'est une maladie naturelle à l'homme de croire qu'il possède la vérité directement . . . au lieu qu'en effet il ne connaît na-

---

[9] The general problem of Pascal's political theory is well summarized in Eric Auerbach, "La teoria politica di Pascal," *Studi francesi*, I, 1957.

turellement que le mensonge" (*Esprit géometrique*). Unable
to share the credulity of the islanders who mistake him for
their long-lost king, the castaway nevertheless acts as a king,
knowing full well that he is not: "Il cachait cette dernière
pensée, et il découvrait l'autre" (*Premier Discours sur la
condition des grands*). And Pascal, addressing himself more
directly yet to the young son of the duc de Luynes, the future duc de Chevreuse, admonishes him: "Vous devez avoir,
comme cet homme dont nous avons parlé, une double pensée . . . une pensée plus cachée mais plus véritable" (*loc.
cit.*). Here truth is concealed, no longer out of a type of arrogant indifference towards others, but on the contrary out
of humility and wisdom. The seeking out of truth is based
on a refusal of society's values and on a deliberate effort of
introspection: "Nous haïssons la vérité, on nous la cache;
nous voulons être flattés, on nous flatte: nous aimons à être
trompés, on nous trompe" (Br. 100). And the end is accomplished when Pascal, or the unbeliever, finally states: "J'aurai
aussi mes pensées de derrière la tête" (Br. 310).

What is the origin of the *pensée de derrière* in Pascal?
What is its significance? We shall have to find our own answer; none of Pascal's sympathizers or accusers treat the subject directly. We might, nevertheless, apply a general statement of Lefebvre's to this specific case; it would probably
be the sort of response our question would elicit from Pascal's
detractors:

> Au XVIIe, le malaise inexplicable, le déchirement se-
> cret, aboutirent à une nuance tout à fait particulière
> du tragique: un sentiment profond et discret, le senti-
> ment d'une blessure secrète et inguérissable, la con-
> science d'une douleur un peu honteuse que "l'honnête
> homme" dissimulait sous la politesse, sous l'étiquette,
> sous le style [I, 92].

There is a fascination about such a sweeping prejudice en-
compassing all of history. The weakness, of course, lies in any
system's inability to provide for the exceptional personality.
And are we sure that man's psyche is determined by social

forces, rather than vice versa? We shall have to pursue cautiously our analysis of the *pensée de derrière*.

The very notion implies a certain secretiveness, more akin to humility or to muzzled pride, as we saw above, than to deceit. The beginning of the *Entretien avec M. de Saci* may offer a clue, Pascal is commending the view Epictetus holds of man: "Il veut qu'il soit humble, qu'il cache ses bonnes résolutions, surtout dans le commencement et qu'il les accomplisse en secret; rien ne les ruine davantage que de les produire." This secretiveness, indicative of a personality and perhaps of a philosophy, appears even in small matters: "Je me moque de ceux qui disent que le temps me dure à moi, et que j'en juge par fantaisie: ils ne savent pas que je juge par ma montre" (Br. 5).

The notion of a concealed truth and a universally respected falsehood may account for the inclination towards what Pascal's detractors dub sophistry: "Lorsqu'on ne sait pas la vérité d'une chose, il est bon qu'il y ait une erreur commune qui fixe l'esprit des hommes" (Br. 18). Pascal, though, was acutely aware of the danger and relied upon his own *esprit de finesse* to guide him: "Il faut de l'agréable et du réel; mais il faut que cet agréable soit lui-même pris du vrai" (Br. 25).

Cacher, recéler, serrer (in the sense of "set aside," "hide") recur frequently in his vocabulary, often in banal circumstances that are nevertheless revealing of the man: "Les choses qui nous tiennent le plus, comme de cacher son peu de bien, ce n'est souvent presque rien: c'est un néant que notre imagination grossit en montagne" (Br. 85). The constant in the vocabulary reminds us of Pascal's own secretive acts of charity and penance: the hidden *Mémorial* sewn in his doublet, the immediate assistance to the young girl met near Saint-Sulpice, the working family taken into his lodgings, his love of poverty, the belt of spikes which he concealed under his shirt; and other acts which have remained unknown:

Les belles actions cachées sont les plus estimables . . .
mais enfin elles n'ont pas été tout à fait cachées,
puisqu'elles ont été sues; et quoi qu'on ait fait ce qu'on
a pu pour les cacher, ce peu par où elles ont paru gâte

tout; car c'est là le plus beau, de les avoir voulu cacher [Br. 159].[10]

This inclination towards withdrawal and a deepening inner experience played an obvious role in Pascal's religious life, and perhaps sprang from it. As a matter of fact, the *Instruction* by Singlin, which, it is related, determined Pascal's ultimate conversion, is constructed around the idea that Christian perfection should remain *inconnue et secrète aux hommes*.[11] Moreover, this inner deepening is characterized, logically enough, by a degree of indifferent docility to the exterior world, social or political. In Pascal's view the advantages abandoned are of little value compared to the priceless inner freedom of spirit acquired—and in a sense the Wager is centered on this uneven barter. The same process applies to faith itself, and the ultimate consequence is a new and higher aspect of the *pensée de derrière:*

Il faut que l'extérieur soit joint à l'intérieur pour obtenir de Dieu; c'est-à-dire que l'on se mette à genoux, prie des lèvres, etc. . . . . Attendre de cet extérieur le secours est être superstitieux, ne vouloir pas le joindre à l'intérieur est être superbe [Br. 250].

Les autres religions, comme les païennes, sont plus populaires, car elles sont en extérieur; mais elles ne sont pas pour les gens habiles. Une religion purement intellectuelle serait plus proportionnée aux habiles; mais elle ne servirait pas au peuple. La seule religion chrétienne est proportionnée à tous, étant mêlée d'extérieur et d'intérieur. Elle élève le peuple à l'intérieur, et abaisse les superbes à l'extérieur; et n'est pas parfaite sans les deux, car il faut que le peuple entende l'esprit de la lettre, et que les habiles soumettent leur esprit à la lettre [Br. 251].

[10] See also what he says about confession in Br. 100. From evidence in the *Mémorial* and from what we know of him, there is reason to believe that he was not at first a docile confesser ready to bare either his hidden thoughts or his hidden virtues.

[11] See Pascal, *Oeuvres complètes* ("Collection des grands écrivains de la France"; Paris: Hachette, 1910), IV, 9.

The gist of our interpretation is that the *pensée de derrière* is founded more upon religious conviction than upon purely political expediency or obscure class frustrations. In a perspective such as ours, then, the above example of submissiveness to the letter, and by extension, to the state and to the corrupt temporality of our physical being, is in essence a preliminary act of faith, an introductory exercise in humility.[12] In any case, it seems undeniable that the *pensée de derrière* is closely linked to the conception of a hidden God:[13]

> Toutes choses couvrent quelque mystère; toutes choses sont des voiles qui couvrent Dieu. Les Chrétiens doivent le reconnaître en tout [IVth letter to the Roannez].

> L'Ecriture . . . dit au contraire que Dieu est un Dieu caché [Br. 242].

> Au lieu de vous plaindre de ce que Dieu s'est caché, vous lui rendrez grâces de ce qu'il s'est tant découvert [Br. 288].

> Toute religion qui ne dit pas que Dieu est caché n'est pas véritable [Br. 585].

There is no scarcity of such examples; but the link between faith in a hidden God and the nearly religious necessity of practicing the *pensée de derrière* is better elucidated in fragment 337, where it is considered in the various stages leading to Christian perfection:

[12] Théodule Spoerri's paper, "Les Pensées 'de derrière la tête' de Pascal" (pp. 386–429, in the Cahiers de Royaumont [see n. 6]), despite the title, scarcely mentions the subject we are discussing. Spoerri does imply, however, that the *pensée de derrière* served Pascal as an ethical brake against an instinctive pride and he associates it with the inclination towards *abaissement*. Spoerri, nevertheless, devotes little attention to the matter and does not pretend to determine its role in Pascal's thought.

[13] Lucien Goldmann's lengthy sociological and Marxist study, *Le Dieu caché* (Paris: Gallimard, 1955), treats the subject of the *Deus absconditus* with deft dialectical acrobatics; it does not, however, analyze the topic that concerns us here. It should be noted that Léon Brunschvicg, in his many commentaries on the hidden God, really laid the foundations of Goldmann's study.

Raison des effets.—Gradation. Le peuple honore les personnes de grande naissance. Les demi-habiles les méprisent, disant que la naissance n'est pas un avantage de la personne, mais du hasard. Les habiles les honorent, non par la pensée du peuple, mais par la pensée de derrière. Les dévots qui ont plus de zèle que de science les méprisent, malgré cette considération qui les fait honorer par les habiles, parce qu'ils en jugent par une nouvelle lumière que la piété leur donne. Mais les chrétiens parfaits les honorent par une autre lumière supérieure.

Here, quite clearly, the *pensée de derrière* does not represent the light of charity, but the median *order* characteristic of the *habiles*. Hence it would belong to the order of reason and be only a mundane, intellectual reflection of the *lumière supérieure;* yet in many passages, Pascal, a believer, a man who aspires to the higher, spiritual perception, ascribes the *pensée de derrière* to himself. This slight ambiguity, perhaps exaggerated by our own commentary, derives naturally from the fact that man by his very condition, no matter how perfect, must partake of the two lower orders. In a way the *pensée de derrière* leads to the order of charity; it is a perspective in which the *contraires* co-exist and it is cognizance of the contrasting forces. If it were purely rational it would be communicable, but in fact it scarcely is. It is both the secret of the *habile* and the treasure of the saint. After all, the power of thought is hidden within the frailty of the *roseau pensant*. At times the reader gathers the impression that the capacity to develop a *pensée de derrière* is truly a God-given privilege and that the hidden message it withholds is a view of the world seen in God's eyes or a nearly rational disclosure of divine judgment and grace. The terms used by the unbeliever during the dialogue of the Wager are rather revealing: "Mais encore n'y a-t-il point moyen de voir le dessous du jeu?—Oui, l'Ecriture, et le reste."

Undoubtedly the *pensée de derrière* is a faculty that contributes to isolation of the individual. Still it is not to be discarded: "Il faut avoir une pensée de derrière et juger de tout par là, en parlant cependant comme le peuple" (Br. 336). Duplicity? No, its practice is old and respected; Plato observed it: "Le plus sage législateur disait que pour le bien des hommes, il faut souvent les piper" (Br. 294). Pascal also speaks of Plato and Aristotle *acting as if* their political treatises were solemn and serious things, whereas in fact they were writing laws for a lunatic humanity (Br. 331). The cruelty of the perception afforded by the *pensée de derrière* is so naked that Pascal could scarcely imagine exposing and teaching it to all men; and one wonders at the rare qualities of the young man to whom such verities were dealt:

> Mais si vous étiez duc sans être honnête homme, je vous ferais encore justice: car en vous rendant les devoirs extérieurs que l'ordre des hommes a attachés à votre naissance, je ne manquerais pas d'avoir pour vous le mépris intérieur que mériterait la bassesse de votre esprit [*Second Discours sur la condition des grands*].

The question has an interesting scientific facet. In the course of a dialogue with a fictitious supporter of the theory of a finite universe, Pascal's retort brings the point home: "Il ne faut pas dire qu'il y a ce qu'on ne voit pas.—Il faut donc dire comme les autres, mais ne pas penser comme eux" (Br. 266). Here the patience and prudence which Pascal demonstrated as a scientist are brought out succinctly. He defers breaking with public opinion until he has at hand positive experimental evidence to back his intuition of the existence of infinite matter, time, and space; and in the meantime he will still recognize the validity of scientific laws of which he is no longer sure. In effect, he illustrated this strict observance of a pragmatic form of the *pensée de derrière* during the protracted experiments on vacuum and the weight of air. By the same token we can, perhaps, attribute his contradictory opinion of the Copernican system to the *pensée de derrière*, which appears once again as an earnest scientific scruple and not as sophistry.

Thus the *pensée de derrière* informs the attitude of the

savant, of the political thinker, and of the Christian. In fact it is a sign of universality: "Les gens universels ne sont appelés ni poètes, ni géomètres, etc. . . . mais ils sont tout cela et juges de tous ceux-là. On ne les devine point" (Br. 34). Pascal normally refers to these universal beings—here possessing an inner secret—as *honnêtes hommes*. They at least sought belief and probably were believers. We have reason to expect that the *honnête homme* will practice some form of the *pensée de derrière la tête* in proportion to his faith. In truth, is not the *pensée de derrière* simply an expression of Christian irony, with all of the wounded detachment that it implies? Is it not the spontaneous reaction of a man of wit who seems to view this world from elsewhere with a mixture of restive compassion, amused irritation, and secretive conviction?

Every time one studies Pascal, more new issues are raised than questions solved. The most elusive problem remains not that of Pascal's improbable sophistry but of our own integrity as critics. Sympathy for an author is no substitute for intelligence; but, with regard to Valéry and Lefebvre, intelligence is not a very satisfactory substitute for sympathy either. Gide states that cultivated men read works they do not take to instinctively. Read, yes; but, criticize?

Most of the difficulties—injustices and tortured eulogies—arise from the incompletion of the *Pensées* and from the fact that Pascal, by temperament as an individual, by necessity as an apologist, is a brilliant improviser. He belongs to the race of Mozart and Napoleon, and perhaps of Stendhal. If he is anti-Cartesian it is precisely because he sensed that Cartesianism was capable of leading French thought to mad extremes. He is in many ways a reactionary, a man who reacts excessively to excess.

In the case of his supposed sophistry, time is the culprit or the savior. It has split him in two: the thinker, the stylist. Voltaire, Valéry, Lefebvre, are not entirely at fault. In some ways, instead of aggravating the cleavage, the latter have added a dimension to Pascal and have helped reintegrate him dialectically by renewing a dialogue between Voltaire and himself which is the richest and the longest of the *Dialogues des vivants*.

Time is the Solomon; we are but an awed and divided jury. Nevertheless, an ironic and definitive verdict of "Poète et non honnête homme" does not quite appear in the offing.

HUMAN NATURE AND INSTITUTIONS
IN MOLIERE'S PLOTS

By James Doolittle

Plot in any play implies conflict of some kind. In Molière the conflict invariably takes place between human nature and something else. The something else is always recognizable because it is always logical, always rationally consistent with itself. For Harpagon, for example, a dollar is worth 100 cents, no more, no less; the sum of the enemas and other medicaments of *Le Malade imaginaire* adds up to medical beatitude; to call M. Jourdain *Monseigneur* or *votre grandeur* is to send him to his conception of paradise as surely as Orgon expects to get there by renouncing his humanity and aping the pious system of words and gestures of his friend Tartuffe.

If these very logical characters receive their comeuppance, it is not for lack of logical procedure on their part. On the contrary, their logic is impeccable; the trouble is that they start from a false premise, the premise, in every case, that human nature is a reasonable or logical phenomenon. That Molière did not think human nature a logical phenomenon is abundantly demonstrated by every play in his theatre.

To define Molière's concept of human nature is not part of my purpose here. It is part of my purpose, however, to repeat that for Molière the notion of human nature carries with it an inseparable attribute which we may call "dignity," and that for him dignity can neither be attained to nor preserved by logical means. One may go a step further and suggest that a Molière character who rigidly adheres to systematically logical procedure in his thoughts and behavior is thereby annulling his dignity and making himself ridiculous. Such is the situation of every comic hero, every victim of Molière's laughter, that is, in the canon of his plays. Reason, twenty-four-hour-a-day rationality, is incompatible with human nature, human dignity, and he who guides his every word and move thereby sooner or later finds himself the butt of human ridicule, deprived of his dignity.

Molière's victims are rationalists; they are logicians who proceed faultlessly from a fallacious premise through one or three or five acts to their ultimate discomfiture, of which in many cases they are made aware, and of which in all cases the audience is made aware. Orgon is freed of Tartuffe, M. Jourdain becomes a *mamamouchi,* Argan receives his medical degree, Harpagon gets his cherished money back. These characters are presumably happy when they leave the stage; the fact remains that in the eyes of the audience they are still fools or dupes or scoundrels, and it is the audience that matters. And then there are others who are not so happy at their final exit: Arnolphe, Alceste, George Dandin, Pourceaugnac. Each of these has been brought face to face with the failure of his logic as a means to success and happiness; and though the extent to which the lesson has been learned by any one of them may be debatable, the fact is that, be he happy or not, wiser or not, we have seen the desires and ambitions of each of these characters frustrated because he would not allow its due to the illogical phenomenon of human nature.

My principal concern here is with the premises upon which Molière's victims base their logic. These premises fall into two categories. Conveniently enough, these categories occupy two nearly equal chronological divisions of Molière's Paris career. From 1659 until his death in 1673 he produced thirty-one plays. The mid-point of this career is marked by the presentation, in successive years, of three masterpieces: *Tartuffe, Dom Juan, Le Misanthrope.* It is *Dom Juan,* produced in 1665, which, as I see it, stands at the beginning of the second phase of Molière's dramatic practice.

The first phase is perhaps best exemplified by *L'Ecole des femmes,* whose conduct I should like to summarize as follows:

Arnolphe intends to marry his ward Agnès. He has imposed upon her a regime of ignorance and isolation from society which results from his conviction that only thus can he guarantee her fidelity to him and avoid the ignominy of becoming a cuckold, a condition which he dreads above all others. The activities of young Horace prove that Arnolphe's idea of the peculiar dangers of social contact is sound, as far is it goes, and it is so far altogether logical that he should seek to prevent them. He is moreover kept fully apprised in advance of every step that Horace proposes to take in seducing Agnès, and his actions in each case are quite rationally calculated in accordance with the demands of the moment. Despite these extraordinary advantages, Arnolphe fails, and we must attribute his failure to the fact that his efforts, reasonable as they are, ignore certain realities of human nature, including his own, and are exerted against these realities in an attempt, conscious or otherwise, to subvert, indeed to destroy, the civilized personal dignity of his opponents.

Considered superficially or logically, there is nothing intrinsically wrong about either Arnolphe's objective or his methods. Generally speaking, a faithful wife seems to be a good thing to have, and it is a common notion that one's reason is the best instrument for the solution of one's problems. Arnolphe's downfall occurs because his reasoning is based upon a faulty or partial premise, and also because his objective is in fact not the fulfillment of his dignity (which would require his respect for the dignity of Agnès as well) but the satisfaction of his vanity, of his desire to show that he is different from and superior to other people.

This scheme of things, this way of conducting a play, occurs in all of Molière's plays. In all of them the essential situation consists of objectives conceived in and rendered desirable by passions, these objectives being pursued by means which are rationally devised and employed with rigid logic. The initial premise may be, and usually is, ill-judged, ill-chosen, or at odds with human nature, and hence doomed to failure. That the objectives sought may be, and often are, eminently desirable from any dispassionate point of view does not alter the fact that it is because of their passions that the characters look upon them as being desirable, or, to put it perhaps more accurately, that the stated objectives—a faithful wife, scientific eminence, a pious character, the practice in society of complete sincerity, and so forth—are so many pretexts or masks disguising a vain, egotistical desire to show oneself to be better than other men, superior to one's own humanity or to humanity in general.

We observe that, while this scheme is common to all the plays of Molière, it is utilized in two different ways, one of them in the plays presented before *Dom Juan*, the other in the remainder.[1] Before *Dom Juan*, the objectives and the means of the principal characters are such as would be appropriate to virtually anyone in comparable circumstances. Arnolphe's desire not to be a cuckold is shared, at least theoretically, by any prospective or actual husband, including Arnolphe's friend Chrysalde; Arnolphe is distinguished from these others, not by the nature of his desire, but by its intensity. The social ambition of the *précieuses* Cathos and Madelon is neither reprehensible nor in any way different from that of numerous young ladies in any time; it is not the ambition of Molière's *précieuses* which is ridiculous, but rather their misunderstanding of the nature of its fulfillment. The jealousy of Dom Garcie de Navarre is particularized only by the courtly heroic tradition which governs its expression; his princess Elvire behaves, not like a coquette, but simply like any civilized lady who is unwilling to be dominated by a boor. And so on. *Dom Juan*, in short, is preceded on the list by a baker's dozen of plays, outstanding among them *Les Précieuses ridicules*, *L'Ecole des femmes*, *Tartuffe*, and also the gloomy failure *Dom Garcie de Navarre*. In the details of form, plot, and conduct, these four plays differ a good deal, to be sure, from one another. At the same time the rights and wrongs of the matter, in every case, are amply clear to the audience and to most of the characters as well; there is not the slightest difficulty in distinguishing the fools from the

---

[1] There is one exception, *L'Amour peintre*.

sensible people. As in our horse opera, one can always tell
the good guys from the bad guys, except that, *Tartuffe* apart,
there are no villains, morally speaking, before *Dom Juan*.
Indeed, Molière goes out of his way to inform us in these
plays that his fools are decent people, their foolishness notwithstanding.

The name role of *Tartuffe* introduces a genuine villain.
But he is not a genuine human being. Tartuffe is not a man;
he exhibits no inconsistency with himself; he is all black. He
is not a character but a puppet or mask—a mask beautifully
and subtly contrived, to be sure, but inhuman precisely because he so perfectly embodies pious gestures for impious
purposes. It is not in *Tartuffe* but in *Dom Juan* that the humanity of the hypocrite is made manifest, that the causes,
human and other, which can turn an imperfect man into the
perfect criminal that Tartuffe is are illustrated and set in
place, to form the matrix, so to speak, in which such criminal
perfection may be conceived.

Dom Juan provides, I believe, the key to Molière's subsequent practice. As a creation of comic character, Dom Juan
is scarcely less enigmatic than Célimène or Alceste; since,
however, his actions and words are uttered upon a much
larger variety of subjects than those of his predecessors, it is
possible to perceive with somewhat greater clarity a consistent
pattern underlying them.

Whatever else Dom Juan may be, he is always and everywhere a nonconformist; thus his independence is expressed
almost exclusively in terms of a willful violation of institutional conventions. No other Molière play contains such a
variety of institutional conventions. No other Molière cast
contains representatives of so many classes and professions.
Peasant, commoner, lackey, merchant, hermit, brother, wife,
ghost, statue; the claims of religion, law, science, rank; of the
honor of soldier and nobleman, of filial duty, reason, passion,
heaven, earth, hell—all of these enter into the fabric of this
remarkable play. Dom Juan's constant effort is to assert his
independence of all of them. His constant desire is to flout
authority of whatever kind, less for any profit that he may
thereby obtain than for the sheer joy of flouting authority.

In marrying his Elvire, for example, Dom Juan has not only adapted the trappings of marriage to his own peculiar purpose; he has also violated the sanctity of a convent and induced Elvire to abjure her duty to her monastic condition, her family, and her fiancé (whether the fiancé is divine or human is a question which Molière leaves unanswered). Before the play is over, Elvire has called Dom Juan to account on the basis of duties by turns marital, chivalric, and religious, each time to the vast amusement of her unrepentant husband, who entertains himself also by mocking, deadpan, the heroic efforts of Elvire's noble brothers. Each of his conquests, accomplished or intended, must be made in the face of institutional obstacles. These women are protected not only by their share of natural modesty but much more formidably by contractual engagements. Dom Juan is delighted by feminine beauty, to be sure, but feminine beauty considered as an object, not of contemplation or worship, but of action, as something to be conquered.

What is true of his view of the love of women characterizes also his attitude toward other social relationships, toward religious and scientific institutions. He exhibits, with complete frankness, the utmost scorn for the attitudes, the gestures, and the jargon whose use is presumed to show that the user adheres faithfully to these institutions. Dom Juan has only contempt for those people who knowingly or unknowingly accept the consecrated word and gesture for the reality of an action originating in belief. For him, only the man whose exterior represents exactly that man's inner conviction seems worthy of respect. The only such character in this play is the poor hermit; all the others utilize appearances, not as expressions of their inner truth, but as disguises for it. In each case Dom Juan unerringly penetrates the hypocritical disguise, and for so doing he is of course punished by death and damnation, the sentence being executed by the most completely conventional and respectable character of all—the statue.

Dom Juan is not a particularly funny character; we do not laugh at him. But we do laugh with him. His function is to penetrate the disguises of his interlocutors and to laugh at the incongruity between the mask and the reality of each of them. Thus, although he is not a comical character, he functions precisely as does a comedian, a creator of comedy, a Molière. Dom Juan is amused, pursued, oppressed, and finally destroyed by the acolytes of institutional respectability. And this, with variations only in degree, is the situation, at least potentially, in nearly every subsequent play. Here the success and happiness of the heroes are menaced less by individual characters themselves than by characters, and events also, representing one or more of the institutions of society, science, and religion.

Tartuffe is the first play to introduce the words and gestures, the external aspect, of an unmistakably identifiable and very respectable institution as constituting a menace to the dignity of decent human nature. But the basic design of *Tartuffe* is identical with that of most of the earlier plays: there is a single character whose mistakenly conceived obsession threatens the desires and the well-being of his fellow characters, all of whom are cognizant of his error. And the error is always an error of judgment, not one of moral delinquency.

With *Dom Juan* two important alterations appear. The first is the presentation of characters who are guilty of varying degrees of moral corruption. The second is the employment of established institutions as corrupting agents. By this I do not mean institutional appearances, as used by Tartuffe; I mean the substance underlying the appearances—the institutions themselves. Thus in the plays beginning with *Dom Juan* it is often difficult to distinguish with certainty between right and wrong, between the good guys and the bad guys. Dom Juan, for instance, is no model of virtue by any standard, but then the purity of his antagonists is doubtful also. The moral dilemmas arising in *Le Misanthrope* are simply insoluble. *George Dandin* presents the most completely villainous cast in Molière, yet there is a good deal to be said in defense of both the hero and his wife. The Bourgeois and Pourceaugnac are both victimized by scoundrels more intelligent than they, but it is their own snobbery and greed which make this possible.

The corruption of all these characters originates and is expressed in terms of one or more of the institutions that I have mentioned. Science is represented either by pedantry or, more often, by medicine. Religion, after the bitter experience of *Tartuffe*, appears only in *Dom Juan* and, safely disguised as astrology, in *Les Amants magnifiques*. The institution most frequently utilized is a social one, the convention of distinction of rank.

Of the latter, perhaps the most striking examples occur in *George Dandin* and *Amphitryon*.[2] Molière's treatment of the story in the latter differs in at least one important way from earlier versions. His text is shot through with episodes and comments emphasizing the absolute authority of the divinities Jupiter and Mercury over the men whose rights they usurp and whose dearest and most legitimate desires they poison with jealousy and shame—and this simply in order to amuse themselves. Jupiter leaves behind him, as a sort of gratuity or tip for his hours of pleasure, the seed which will one day become the hero Hercules. The cuckolded Amphitryon, from Plautus to Rotrou, pronounces himself respectfully grateful for the honor thus done him. Not so Molière's hero, who says exactly nothing about it, while the slave Sosie remarks first that *le Seigneur Jupiter sait dorer la pilule*, and then concludes some twenty lines later with a speech that sounds very strange in an entertainment composed for seventeenth-century royalty. He cuts short the felicitations of Amphitryon's officers as being embarrassing; Jupiter, he says,

>   nous fait beaucoup d'honneur,
> Et sa bonté sans doute est pour nous sans seconde;
>   Il nous promet l'infaillible bonheur
>   D'une fortune en mille biens féconde,
> Et chez nous il doit naître un fils d'un très-grand coeur:
>   Tout cela va le mieux du monde;

---

[2] Cf. *Psyché*, whose Venus resents her divine son's passion for a mortal; *Mélicerte*, where again the notion of rank and fortune threatens disaster to the lovers.

Mais enfin coupons aux discours,
Et que chacun chez soi doucement se retire.
Sur telles affaires, toujours
Le meilleur est de ne rien dire.
[1934-1943]

The speech is full of resignation, but the resignation is sarcastic.

We notice that even the all-powerful king of the gods is compelled to assume a correct form, in this case that of Amphitryon, just as Dom Juan for the same purpose assumes the form and title of husband. The god and the high-ranking nobleman, for all their authority, malice, and cynicism, must nonetheless be subservient to the ultimate authority of conventional form. The power that they wield with ruthless effectiveness originates, not in themselves as god or man, but in the institutions whose masks they put on.

The view of institutions as oppressors of human dignity may be clarified once more by some comparisons between plays occurring before and after the critical moment represented by *Dom Juan*. Certain of the later plays are developments or *reprises* of earlier ones. Thus, for example, *Les Précieuses ridicules* is echoed and elaborated in *Les Femmes savantes; Dom Garcie de Navarre* has its counterpart in *Le Misanthrope; La Princesse d'Elide* comes to full bloom in *Les Amants magnifiques*. In these pairings the distinction between the earlier member and the later one is the same: none of the conflicting elements in the earlier one are specifically institutional, whereas in the later one the institution has become the indispensable element.

For instance, both Euryale of *La Princesse d'Elide* and Sostrate of *Les Amants magnifiques* are in love with their princesses. Sostrate is opposed far less by his lady than by his inferiority in rank; to this obstacle, furthermore, Molière adds another more formidable one in the hostility of the astrologer Anaxarque. There is no hint anywhere in *La Princesse d'Elide* of dishonesty or other corruption; Anaxarque, on the other hand, sets the whole weight of his combined religious and scientific authority against Sostrate because each of Sostrate's rivals, both of them princes by the way, has sought to procure the astrologer's favor by bribery.

The *précieuses* Cathos and Madelon speak and act according to their mistaken notion of the ways of the kind of society to which they aspire to be admitted. The *femmes savantes*, on the contrary, emulate with exactness the speech, behavior, and tastes of a well-defined and limited group, that of the pedants. Mascarille and Jodelet are frankly pretending to be what they are not; Trissotin and Vadius are genuinely the pedants that they claim to be. The only vice of the *précieuses* is stupidity; in *Les Femmes savantes*, by contrast, Trissotin, Armande, Bélise, and Philaminte are all guilty of self-interested dissimulation, of hypocrisy.

Dom Garcie de Navarre and his princess Elvire are virtuous heroes in the Cornelian tradition. Dom Garcie is cursed with a streak of jealousy which Elvire does nothing whatever to provoke, as Dom Garcie himself acknowledges. Alceste is jealous too, of course; but his jealousy is first of all justified to some extent by the behavior of Célimène; secondly, it is only one of a number of traits in an extraordinarily complex character whose fundamental component is a domineering egotism disguised as a virtuous concern for sincerity. Alceste is doubtless unaware of his hypocrisy; one may say that in him hypocrisy is sublimated into the misanthropy which manifests itself in the constant denigration of all things which are not itself; and among these things the most prominent are the institutional gestures of polite social conduct. It is true that the vice of Alceste, like that of Dom Garcie, originates within himself; unlike that of Dom Garcie, it is deliberately fostered and inflamed by the behavior of others, behavior for which Alceste is not responsible. I should say that in the earlier play Dom Garcie is manifestly wrong and his fellow characters manifestly right; in *Le Misanthrope* Alceste and his society together are simultaneously right and wrong. While one can agree that Alceste carries his opinions and his actions too far, one cannot so easily declare that his announced principles are wrong, that his misanthropy is his fault alone and not justified to a considerable extent by the conventional conduct of the society in which he lives. Célimène too is vastly different from Dom Garcie's Elvire, who is utterly right from start to finish, correct, frank, loving, and very dull. As to Célimène, who can say? One of the most enigmatic of characters, she is also one of the most charming.

From this comparison it should be clear that, in the later member of each pair of plays, Molière utilized institutional customs and concerns which do not occur at all in the earlier member. And he uses them to threaten or actually to destroy the personal dignity, happiness, or well-being of most of the individuals involved. Institutional conventions, the logical application of their codified rules and regulations, are set in opposition to human happiness and dignity.

Previous to *Dom Juan*, society, its principles, customs, beliefs, usages, are viewed as the proper criteria for good judgment and right conduct. This notion, abundantly obvious in the earlier plays themselves, is carried over into the great critical pieces: *La Critique de l'Ecole des femmes* and *L'Impromptu de Versailles*, in which the judgments of cultivated (and hence institutionalized) people overwhelmingly prevail against the narrow opinions of rule-mongering pedants, a few prudes, and one's jealous professional rivals. What happens after *Tartuffe* is not precisely a reversal; rather the authority of all socially respectable institutions is cast with that of the prudes and the pedants into the scales against the expression and maintenance of what, for Molière as for any other authentic artist, must be the indispensable subject and final justification for his art, the illogical phenomenon which also justifies human existence, namely, human dignity.

It would, I think, be moronic to regard Molière in any sense as a revolutionary. There is nowhere in his theatre the slightest suggestion that existing institutions should be altered or eliminated; but there is everywhere, and especially after *Dom Juan*, the implication that any man who deserves the title of man must be the master and not the servant of institutions. This is not to say that I would make of Molière a systematic thinker or philosopher, social or otherwise. Molière was an artist, and thus by definition independent of institution and system and intellectualism alike. Like Pascal, he seems to have believed that reason is indeed something, but it is not everything. Like Pascal, he was aware that it takes no more than a buzzing fly to dethrone man from his reasonable lordship of this world. Unlike Pascal, Molière came to see in the systematic observance of institutional gestures not the means to wisdom but the annihilation of dignity.

FUTILITY AND SELF-DECEPTION IN
LE MISANTHROPE

By *Judd D. Hubert*

Dramatically Alceste is so impressive a character that even those critics who regard him as a figure of fun rather than a hero barely resist the temptation of putting him on a pedestal as though his sincere and apparently righteous behavior could have little in common with the frivolous futility of Célimène and her flock of admirers. Actually, the misanthrope shares with the society he so strongly condemns at least one serious fault—vanity, to which he adds the sin of self-deception.

BLINDNESS AND LUCIDITY

In previous plays Molière had exploited the humor of psychological and intellectual blindness, e.g., Orgon's cecity to the obviousness of Tartuffe's hypocrisy; but, until *Le Misanthrope*, he had not systematically attempted to combine within a single character lucidity with blindness. Some two years before *Le Misanthrope*'s first performance La Rochefoucauld had dramatized the ceaseless struggle of incompatible traits for the possession of man's will, but it is quite a different matter for a playwright to breathe life into a being capable of the sharpness and frankness of a Dorine as well as of the obtuseness of an Orgon.

Blindness to one's shortcomings often takes the form of complacency.[1] In this respect Acaste's self-portrait is truly a

---

[1] The words *complaisance* or *complaisant* reappear frequently in the course of the play.

masterpiece—a much more devastating piece of satire than
Célimène's most withering sketches. Acaste, in damning himself with faint praise, prides himself only on externals: his
noisy admiration for the latest literary craze, his sartorial elegance, his winning smile. He boasts of a single *affaire*, thus
demonstrating his physical courage if not his usefulness to
the state. His friend and rival, Clitandre, voices his approval
of this self-portrait, as though agreeing that Acaste has every
right to be satisfied with his lot and with his accomplishments.
Each marquis so little questions his own merits that he feels
certain of obtaining Célimène's affection. The other suitors,
Oronte and Alceste himself, express the same unwarranted
confidence in the coquette's preference—a delusion which
tends to put the high-minded misanthrope on the same foot-
ing as the *petits marquis* and the poetaster.

Against the pervasiveness of complacency, several of the
characters stress the need for self-awareness. Clitandre, in
concluding his remarks about Cléonte, asks rhetorically:

N'a-t-il point quelque ami qui pût, sur ses manières,
D'un charitable avis lui prêter les lumières?

[569–570]

Clitandre and most of his acquaintances evidently lack this
type of friend. Not that advice, whether charitable or cruel,
would in any way modify their conduct; Acaste will interpret
Célimène's strictures as proofs of her fickleness and lack of
sincerity rather than as valid criticisms of his own behavior:

Et je vous ferai voir que les petits marquis
Ont, pour se consoler, des coeurs du plus haut prix.

[1697–1698]

Previously, Célimène, in unmasking Arsinoé, had stated with
obvious insincerity the usefulness of self-awareness:

On doit se regarder soi-même un fort long temps,
Avant que de songer à condamner les gens.

[951–952]

And friendly frankness would be most beneficial, because

> On détruiroit par là, traitant de bonne foi,
> Ce grand aveuglement où chacun est pour soi.
> [967–968]

Now, one cannot accuse the sharp-eyed Célimène or the prying Arsinoé of blinding themselves to their own faults. Both deserve, of course, to be publicly exposed, but neither really requires self-revelation, for the hypocrite is consciously and consistently performing a part, while the coquette is breathlessly playing a perilous game for her own diversion. The young widow's barbed prediction that upon reaching Arsinoé's advanced stage in life she too might consent to play the part of prude for want of a worthier pastime, shows unusual insight: the coquette of today can hardly avoid becoming the hypocrite of tomorrow. All in all, obtuseness, at least in Le Misanthrope, remains essentially a masculine prerogative. Awareness of the excruciating deficiencies of others would, however, be universal were it not for Eliante's constant efforts to see the sunny side of her various acquaintances: she esteems, and almost loves, Alceste for his frankness and sincerity, and she alone does not paint, or even enjoy, satirical portraits. At the conclusion of the comedy she will marry Philinte; thus is tolerance rewarded.

Carping awareness of the imperfections of others most frequently takes the form of the satirical portrait: one after the other the faults and vices of the milieu are made public. At the end, scarcely anyone has anything to hide, and the arch-painter of them all, Célimène, is exposed, transformed into a reasonably definitive portrait. The petits marquis threaten:

> Il suffit: nous allons l'un et l'autre en tous lieux
> Montrer de votre coeur le portrait glorieux.
> [1693–1694]

The very first scene of the play had already contained a portrait, that of Alceste's hypocritical party: "Au travers de son masque on voit à plein le traître" (125). The victims of Célimène's etchings are by no means evildoers but merely *fâcheux*—pretentious bores whose presence she tries to avoid. Alfred Simon has pointed out the numerous analogies between *Les Fâcheux* and *Le Misanthrope*, whose plot consists of Alceste's repeated attempts to discover the true feelings of Célimène, attempts that are interrupted by various sorts of extraneous events: a lawsuit, a sonnet, Arsinoé, other suitors, and even Philinte.[2] Alceste appears as a spectacular bore in the eyes of his rivals as well as in the letter of Célimène. As in *Les Fâcheux*, a person will become a nuisance and arouse laughter merely by making an appearance at an inauspicious moment. As these repeated interruptions are merely annoying and as the portraits themselves serve mainly to assess the nuisance value of a given character without ever delving into moral issues, the type of existence thus depicted appears as a mixture of idleness and futility. In this respect the most striking portrait is that of the *grand flandrin de Vicomte* whom Célimène has watched *trois quarts d'heure durant, cracher dans un puits pour faire des ronds*. Molière here unmasks the spitten image of futility. These portraits tend to be revealing in three different ways, sometimes simultaneously: as consciously depicting the faults of the "victim," as unwittingly pointing out the deficiencies of a given social group and thereby exposing the painter. In this manner *Le Misanthrope* gives a complete picture of seventeenth-century salon society while containing a thorough study of an *atrabilaire amoureux*. But the character study itself provides an insight into the true nature of this corrupt society, condemned for its futility, its idleness, and its general uselessness. These weaknesses will appear all the more ridiculous if we see them in the perspective of Colbertism, which stressed practicality and efficiency—deeds rather than words.

As we have already suggested, the various characters unintentionally reveal much more about themselves and their way of life than they had anticipated, particularly when they attempt to expose the deficiencies of their friends. Unmasking, as Arsinoé and later on Célimène will discover to

[2] Alfred Simon, *Molière par lui-même* (Paris: Ed. du Seuil, 1957), p. 119.

their sorrow, can work both ways. As a comic device, it closely approximates the old trick of the *voleur volé*, with effects ever so much more subtle and sometimes more devastating. But what about poor Alceste, who objects to Célimène's *médisances* and who paints satirical portraits only under emotional stress? True, he condemns the entire race of man, but in the light of the highest and soundest moral principles. As a result, critics, and particularly philosophers, have been ashamed to laugh at him: "Et enfin il faut bien l'avouer,—quoiqu'il en coûte un peu de le dire,—que nous ne rions pas seulement des défauts de nos semblables, mais aussi, quelquefois, de leurs qualités." And in the next paragraph, Bergson adds: "C'est donc la raideur d'Alceste qui nous fait rire, quoique cette raideur soit ici honnêteté. Quiconque s'isole s'expose au ridicule, parce que le comique est fait, en grande partie, de cet isolement même."[3] But must we let Alceste isolate himself from the rest of humanity, as though morality itself might perish with him? Will he not prove to be much more ridiculous if we can convict him of the same vices he condemns in others?

THE CASE AGAINST ALCESTE

Apart from Jean-Jacques Rousseau, few critics would deny that Alceste has serious faults. As Professor Jasinski and, more recently, P. J. Yarrow have pointed out, not only is he unreasonable, tactless, and childish in his outbursts, but he is vain and egotistic to boot.[4] When Philinte admonishes him: "Mais on entend les gens, au moins, sans se fâcher" (4), he retorts, like a sullen boy: "Moi, je veux me fâcher, et ne veux point entendre." The absurd Argante, in *Les Fourberies*, will sound precisely the same note:

SCAPIN: Mon Dieu! je vous connois, vous êtes bon naturellement.

[3] H. Bergson, *Le Rire* (Paris: P.U.F., 1947), pp. 105–106.
[4] R. Jasinski, *Molière et le misanthrope* (Paris: Colin, 1951), pp. 136 ff.; P. J. Yarrow, "A Reconsideration of Alceste," *French Studies*, Oct., 1959, pp. 314–331.

ARGANTE: Je ne suis point bon, et je suis méchant quand je
          veux.

[I, 4]

Such petulance so early in the play should warn the audience not to regard Alceste as a sterling champion of moral
principles in a corrupt world.

His vanity, which usually takes the form of egocentricity,
appears everywhere. In the first scene, he exclaims:

Non, non, il n'est point d'âme un peu bien située
Qui veuille d'une estime ainsi prostituée;
Et la plus glorieuse a des régals peu chers,
Dès qu'on voit qu'on nous mêle avec tout l'univers.

[53–56]

A few lines later, he expresses still more clearly his sense of
superiority: "Je veux qu'on me distingue" (63). Throughout
the play, he exaggerates, if not his merits, at least the value
of his opinions, of his feelings, and of everything else that
concerns him. His self-centeredness manifests itself only too
clearly in his tactless proposal to Eliante, whose attitude
toward humanity is diametrically opposed to his own. He
actually believes that his personal revenge should matter so
much to the world that Eliante will be overjoyed to marry
him and subordinate her entire existence to his momentary
spite. His tactlessness results no doubt from an overwhelming *dépit amoureux*.

He grossly exaggerates the importance of his trial, which
he probably regards as a momentous battle in his war with
the universe:

je veux qu'il demeure à la postérité
Comme une marque insigne, un fameux témoignage
De la méchanceté des hommes de notre âge.

[1544–1546]

His vanity thus transforms an ordinary legal matter, involving a goodly sum of money, into a historical event, comparable at the very least to the condemnation of a Mont-
morency or a Fouquet.

Célimène, in coldly adding Alceste to her list of bores, seems to question the authenticity of his misanthropy:

> Le sentiment d'autrui n'est jamais pour lui plaire;
> Il prend toujours en main l'opinion contraire,
> Et penseroit paroître un homme du commun,
> Si l'on voyoit qu'il fût de l'avis de quelqu'un.
> L'honneur de contredire a pour lui tant de charmes,
> Qu'il prend contre lui-même assez souvent les armes;
> Et ses vrais sentiments sont combattus par lui,
> Aussitôt qu'il les voit dans la bouche d'autrui.
>
> [673–680]

Alceste's attitude toward Arsinoé appears to confirm Célimène's judgment. When the prude accuses the court of having neglected a man of his tremendous merits, he immediately retorts:

> Moi, Madame! Et sur quoi pourrois-je en rien prétendre?
> Quel service à l'Etat est-ce qu'on m'a vu rendre?
> Qu'ai-je fait, s'il vous plaît, de si brillant de soi,
> Pour me plaindre à la cour qu'on ne fait rien pour moi?
>
> [1052–1056]

This rejoinder reveals Alceste's eagerness to contradict even those people—and there are many of them, including, at first, Oronte—who appreciate his merits. Paradoxically he condescends to uphold the court—the only time in the entire course of the comedy when he rises to the defense of human behavior:

> Elle auroit fort à faire, et ses soins seroient grands
> D'avoir à déterrer le mérite des gens.
>
> [1063–1064]

Under normal circumstances, the mere idea of the court's callous indifference to merit would have aroused his wrath.

His retort to Arsinoé is important in still another respect. By admitting that he has not rendered any real services to the state, he puts himself in about the same position as the complacent Acaste. A few years later Wycherley will create in the sea captain Manly a misanthrope of more heroic dimen-

sions than poor Alceste, who, in spite of his lofty language, is
no more than a pillar of high society. He can spend the entire day in Célimène's cosy salon, idling away the hours, as
indolently as Acaste, who exclaims: "Rien ne m'appelle
ailleurs de toute la journée" (738), or Clitandre, who echoes:

> Moi, pourvu que je puisse être au petit couché,
> Je n'ai point d'autre affaire où je sois attaché.
>
> [739–740]

The male characters, almost without exception, are domesticated oppressors leading a life of luxurious futility while
seeking means to gratify their ego: Acaste, by his addiction
to fashion; Oronte, by writing innocuous verse; Alceste, the
noblest of the lot, through sterile misanthropy. They remind
us of La Bruyère's Narcisse, who, we are told, *se lève le
matin pour se coucher le soir.*

Because of his vanity and inaction, we cannot regard
Alceste as an upholder of heroic virtue in a degenerate society any more than we could consider Sganarelle as a champion of religion against the atheistic Don Juan. Intent only on
covering up the emptiness of his existence, he never suspects
that he might accomplish something more useful than to stay
in Paris courting a coquette or to retire in a huff to his coun-
tryseat. His final exit confirms this barren attitude: he will
seek

> un endroit écarté
> Où d'être homme d'honneur on ait la liberté.

And perhaps Philinte will persuade him to stay, for in his
désert he might not find any petty noblemen or hypocritical
intriguers on whom to vent his spleen. The evil world of
Paris provides him with a distraction, in the Pascalian sense
of the term. By playing the part of misanthrope, he can dis-
sociate himself from the world he condemns while continuing
to partake in its activities.[5]

[5] See W. G. Moore, *Molière, a New Criticism* (Oxford: Clarendon Press, 1949), p. 124: Alceste "is ridiculous because he forgets
that he is part of the picture."

From the very first scene, Alceste opposes himself to the rest of humanity:

> mon dessein
> Est de rompre en visière à tout le genre humain.
> [95–96]

Philinte mockingly feigns concern for the human race after his friend's long tirade against mankind and his hypocritical party: "faisons un peu grâce à la nature humaine" (146), as though the misanthrope's impotent and hardly genuine hatred might consign man to eternal damnation. By setting himself up as a champion, as a knight-errant jousting against teeming millions, Alceste behaves in a manner reminiscent of Corneille's more cowardly Matamore, who boasted that with a single glance he could pulverize an entire army. But Alceste's jousting remains purely moral, and he somehow finds it more convenient to choose as opponent the human race in all its vagueness than to join battle against a specific evil. Although Molière nowhere suggests that his misanthrope is a coward, he subtly indicates the hollowness of his heroism. Alceste's love for Célimène, which he persists in regarding as the only chink in his armor, in no way diminishes his sense of moral superiority. Did not Samson yield to his passion for Delilah and Hercules submit to the whims of Omphale?

In spite of the questionable nature of his misanthropy, Alceste, who is potentially a hero, completely dominates the fops whose life he shares, both by his dream of a more honest world and by the intensity of his feelings. Moreover, he is potentially a tragic figure, beset with trivialities instead of evils. Finally, he bases his existence on a false premise: the identification of an insignificant fragment of humanity with the entire race of man. And this false, unstated premise explains the strange dilemma which imprisons him: the choice between Célimène's salon and isolation. In the glaring disproportion between so absurd a premise and feelings so intense, Alceste resembles Arnolphe who strove to put himself above destiny itself in planning a perfect marriage. He differs from Arnolphe in the fact that his absurdity, far from

involving only himself, embraces the society of which he is
an unwilling member.

ALCESTE AND DON GARCIE DE NAVARRE

Alceste's absurdity will stand out more clearly if we compare him to Don Garcie, with whom he shares two or three
speeches. Critics agree that Molière, in transferring these
passages from one play to another, was trying to salvage a
few poetic gems from an unsuccessful work. But critics have
not explained why Don Garcie's words do not seem out of
character when spoken by the misanthrope. The prince, a
pathologically jealous man of action who lacks confidence in
his merits, can have little in common with the sedentary,
self-deceiving Alceste, who, until Arsinoé arouses his suspicions, persists in trusting a notorious coquette. Both Don
Garcie and Alceste movingly express their despair and indignation at betrayal by the woman they love:

Voilà ce que marquoient les troubles de mon âme;
Ce n'étoit pas en vain que s'alarmoit ma flamme;
Par ces fréquents soupçons, qu'on trouvoit odieux,
Je cherchois le malheur qu'ont rencontré mes yeux;
Et, malgré tous vos soins et votre adresse à feindre,
Mon astre me disoit ce que j'avois à craindre.
Mais ne présumez pas que, sans être vengé,
Je souffre le dépit de me voir outragé.
Je sais que sur les voeux on n'a point de puissance,
Que l'amour veut partout naître sans dépendance,
Que jamais par la force on n'entra dans un coeur,
Et que toute âme est libre à nommer son vainqueur.
Aussi ne trouverois-je aucun sujet de plainte,
Si pour moi votre bouche avoit parlé sans feinte.

. . . . . .

Mon coeur n'auroit eu droit de s'en prendre qu'au sort.
Mais d'un aveu trompeur voir ma flamme applaudie,
C'est une trahison, c'est une perfidie,
Qui ne sauroit trouver de trop grands châtiments,
Et je puis tout permettre à mes ressentiments.

. . . . . .

Je ne suis plus à moi, je suis tout à la rage.
[*Le Misanthrope*, 1289–1310; *Don Garcie*, 1276–1297]

The intensity of this reaction is not unexpected on the part of the prince or the misanthrope. But even a cursory examination of the text shows that this speech does not quite fit Alceste's present predicament. He has no right to speak of the coquette's dependency upon him, or to mention his *astre*, or even to refer to past or future violence—to *châtiments*, whereas Don Garcie (granted his suspicions) is justifiably referring to the power he holds over Done Elvire. The point is that Molière wished to put in the mouth of his misanthrope the most intensely dramatic speech available, abounding in heroic and even tragic overtones. That the words did not quite fit the hero's situation probably suited the playwright's purpose, for the discrepancy between speech and action drives home the fact that Alceste is really living in an imaginary world, quite unrelated at times to his surroundings. Thus the chief value of his intensely dramatic speech stems from its irrelevance. It reveals Alceste in his true light as a mock-heroic character who vainly attempts to transform the banalities of Parisian salons into momentous, anachronistic adventures. His misguided efforts serve also a satirical purpose, for they show that the society in which he was born precludes all heroic values.[6]

Alceste's lawsuit fulfills a purpose rather similar to Mauregat's usurpation in *Don Garcie*: it provides the misanthrope with an ordeal; it ironically represents the triumph of injustice, of evil. And his fierce quarrel with Oronte over the sonnet, which nearly results in a duel, can be compared to the rivalry between Don Garcie and Don Alphonse, who almost join in single combat. Obviously both the trial and the quarrel represent a considerable comedown from the swashbuckling, if slightly comic, world of the *Prince jaloux*—a world in which Alceste, by temperament, really belongs. In facing these paltry obstacles, in courting a silly young

---

[6] Alceste is a burlesque hero, in the same sense that Boileau's *Lutrin* is a burlesque poem. By his attitude and by his language the misanthrope is trying to transform the trivial events which take place in a coquette's salon into heroic and even tragic happenings.

widow, the misanthrope behaves as though the fate of kingdoms must hang in the balance. And throughout the comedy this behavior is characterized by misplaced intensity, by confusion between trivialities and absolutes. Oronte's sonnet suddenly becomes a matter of principle and must be judged according to absolute standards. Significantly Oronte insists that it took him only fifteen minutes to write the poem, whereas Alceste retorts: "Le temps ne fait rien à l'affaire" (314), for the sonnet must be good or bad absolutely, and attenuating circumstances, such as time or poetic intent, simply do not count. He asserts, for the same reasons, that the result of his lawsuit must depend, not on his own or on his friends' exertions on his behalf, but on *la raison, mon bon droit, l'équité* (187) or, in other words, on pure essences, as if human justice could be concerned only with absolutes, as if a judge could perceive, unassisted, the justice of a given cause, as though there could never be two sides to an issue.

Alceste is even more out of place in Célimène's salon, with his moral and aesthetic absolutes, than a medieval knight-errant in the Spain of Philip III. Although he persists in dwelling in an imaginary realm, he does not, like Don Quixote or even Mascarille, recreate the world to suit his fancy, for he has nothing of the creator or of the poet in his makeup. Rather he seeks to impose absolute standards where they do not belong. Instead of striving to modify the world and thereby increase his own merit, he perpetually interposes between outside reality and his inner being a scheme of values and a system of feelings that cannot possibly be relevant to a given situation. And he is continually suffering from the inevitable discrepancy between essences that cannot be realized and a reality for which he refuses to accept any responsibility whatever. Absolutes thus absolve Alceste from action or, rather, provide him with a seemingly valid excuse for inaction.

THE COUNTERFEITERS

If the foregoing interpretation of Alceste's motives and situation be correct, then *Le Misanthrope* should be regarded as a comedy of values rather than as a mere character study or a play about manners. In opposing his principle-ridden misanthrope to a scheming, but devitalized, society, Molière is dramatizing, among other things, the divorce, inherent in every man, between so-called ethical laws and actual practice. As the old Latin saw puts it: "Video meliora proboque, deteriora sequor." And Molière complicates the inevitable conflict between ethical absolutes and behavior by equating monetary with moral values, business with human emotions.[7]

Throughout the comedy human relations are usually reduced to some form of commerce. Acaste's parting shot to Célimène humorously associates love with value:

> Et je vous ferai voir que les petits marquis
> Ont, pour se consoler, des coeurs du plus haut prix.
> [1697–1698]

Oronte concludes in a similar manner when he says to Alceste:

> Monsieur, je ne fais plus d'obstacle à votre flamme,
> Et vous pouvez conclure affaire avec Madame.
> [1707–1708]

Alceste follows the general trend of this final scene in squelching Arsinoé:

> Mon coeur a beau vous voir prendre ici sa querelle,
> Il n'est point en état de payer ce grand zèle.
> [1719–1720]

And Arsinoé pays him back in kind:

> Le rebut de Madame est une marchandise
> Dont on auroit grand tort d'être si fort éprise.
> [1727–1728]

[7] The ironical comparison between love and money completely dominates Corneille's *Le Menteur;* a similar comparison between friendship and money can be found everywhere in Shakespeare's tragedy about a misanthrope, *Timon of Athens.* It would seem that poets spontaneously reach the conclusion that lucre represents the most debased as well as the most superficial form of exchange known to man or to woman.

Already in the first scene Philinte had excused in monetary
terms his enthusiastic greeting of a nodding acquaintance:

> Lorsqu'un homme vous vient embrasser avec joie,
> Il faut bien le payer de la même monnoie,
> Répondre, comme on peut, à ses empressements,
> Et rendre offre pour offre, et serments pour serments.
>
> [37–40]

Human relations thus strike him as a system of barter and
exchange, in which gestures and grimaces take the place of
currency. Alceste, true to his nature, refuses to accept this
type of tender, which he regards as counterfeit:

> on devroit châtier, sans pitié,
> Ce commerce honteux de semblants d'amitié.
>
> [67–68]

The misanthrope would like to replace this "commerce hon-
teux" of meaningless gestures by a total exchange in which
both parties to a friendship would give themselves without
any reservation. The petty commerce of commonplace relations makes him furious, for he considers friendship and, of
course, love as absolutes, which the cursed superficiality of
mankind puts beyond his reach. In his frustration he perpetually attacks the words and gestures of others; and he
succeeds only in opposing them with words and gestures of
his own making, which are no less futile and hardly more
significant. At odds with humanity, he tends to use mer-
cenary comparisons as a means of separating himself from
the rest of the world. When Oronte showers him with compliments and protestations of friendship, Alceste warns him:

> nous pourrions avoir telles complexions,
> Que tous deux du marché nous nous repentirions.
>
> [283–284]

It remains, however, for Acaste to bring out most clearly
the relationship between love and money, more or less as a
corollary to his complacent self-portrait:

Mais les gens de mon air, Marquis, ne sont pas faits
Pour aimer à crédit, et faire tous les frais.
Quelque rare que soit le mérite des belles,
Je pense, Dieu merci! qu'on vaut son prix comme elles,
Que pour se faire honneur d'un coeur comme le mien,
Ce n'est pas la raison qu'il ne leur coûte rien,
Et qu'au moins, à tout mettre en de justes balances,
Il faut qu'à frais communs se fassent les avances.

[815–822]

In other words: *donnant donnant* or *les affaires sont les affaires* in love as elsewhere. The device of Eros will no longer be the bow and arrow but the scales of blind justice and of the corner grocery. Acaste knows, or thinks he knows, his own value; but so do most of the other characters in the comedy. Esteem, the greatest single cause and sole justification of passion in seventeenth-century tragedy, becomes ridiculous as soon as it is metamorphosed into self-esteem by such people as Acaste, Oronte, or even Alceste himself. No wonder Célimène enjoys cheating them!

The coquette and the prude bring to bear a veritable arsenal of financial terms in their great battle of words. Célimène hammers away at Arsinoé's hypocrisy:

Elle est à bien prier exacte au dernier point;
Mais elle bat ses gens, et ne les paye point.

[939–940]

Words, even in the form of orisons, are less costly than cash. In a later retort the prude describes Célimène's flirtations in terms of a commercial enterprise. Referring to lovers, she asserts:

Qu'on n'acquiert point leurs coeurs sans de grandes avances,
Qu'aucun pour nos beaux yeux n'est notre soupirant,
Et qu'il faut acheter tous les soins qu'on nous rend.

[1014–1016]

The type of love she describes can have little to do with passion, for on both sides of the ledger it is based on the coldest calculations.

Alceste's misanthropy is closely tied in with the idea of money: "je veux me tirer du commerce des hommes" (1486), particularly in regard to his lawsuit:

> Ce sont vingt mille francs qu'il m'en pourra coûter;
> Mais, pour vingt mille francs, j'aurai droit de pester
> Contre l'iniquité de la nature humaine,
> Et de nourrir pour elle une immortelle haine.
>
> [1547-1550]

The laughable contrast between twenty thousand francs and immortal hatred sums up the entire play. Alceste parts with real money as readily as the other characters spend their counterfeit cash. It is as though money could somehow give a solid valuation to the empty precepts which he takes for moral worth, to the withdrawal which he substitutes for action.

His ultimatum to Célimène to choose between him and Paris shows that he would like to end all his dealings with the world. Ironically the coquette responds by making her first genuine offer, her hand; but she refuses to follow Alceste into his *désert*. In short, she agrees to meet him halfway: "Il faut qu'à frais communs se fassent les avances," to quote, once again, Acaste. Alceste, who sees human relations in terms of a total, unstinted gift, without the least suggestion of compromise, must reject her:

> Puisque vous n'êtes point, en des liens si doux,
> Pour trouver tout en moi, comme moi tout en vous,
> Allez, je vous refuse, et ce sensible outrage
> De vos indignes fers pour jamais me dégage.
>
> [1781-1784]

And the word *dégager* typifies Alceste's general attitudes toward the commerce of the world.

THE SONNET

In all his undertakings Alceste confuses concepts with actions, words with reality, attitudes with heroism. By his imagined exclusion from the world he plays the part of hero;

and he wishes to take Célimène with him, not only because he loves her according to his fashion, but in order to become entirely self-sufficient in his private universe. He is so full of himself that he cannot judge the outside world (including Célimène) with any degree of objectivity. He criticizes Oronte's sonnet in the light of his own obsessions. Compared with similar *précieux* productions of the period, this poem is almost a masterpiece:

> L'espoir, il est vrai, nous soulage,
> Et nous berce un temps notre ennui;
> Mais, Philis, le triste avantage,
> Lorsque rien ne marche après lui!
> Vous eûtes de la complaisance;
> Mais vous en deviez moins avoir,
> Et ne vous pas mettre en dépense
> Pour ne me donner que l'espoir.
> S'il faut qu'une attente éternelle
> Pousse à bout l'ardeur de mon zèle,
> Le trépas sera mon recours.
> Vos soins ne m'en peuvent distraire:
> Belle Philis, on désespère,
> Alors qu'on espère toujours.
>
> [315-332]

This sonnet fits perfectly into the plot and metaphorical structure of the play. Alceste has probably guessed that, under the name of Philis, Oronte is addressing Célimène. Moreover, he is expressing the wish of all the suitors, including Alceste: the young widow should reveal her true feelings and not make them wait any more. Finally, the poem contains key words: *complaisance*, which the misanthrope detests above all others, as well as the antithetical *donner* and *dépense*. In short, the sonnet refers to the commerce of love with its system of half-promises and empty exchanges. The famous *chute*:

> Belle Philis, on désespère
> Alors qu'on espère toujours

is not quite as trite as it sounds, for *désespère* does not really mean "despair," but signifies merely that the suitor, namely Oronte, if forced to wait much longer, might possibly give up hope and try his luck elsewhere. The apparently conventional recourse to *trépas* contains a strong suspicion of irony. The sonnet can thus be interpreted as a witty statement of intention, quite devoid of passion. And the clever Oronte regards it perhaps as just another gambit in his playful pursuit of Célimène. As such, it cannot fail to arouse the wrath of Alceste, who refuses to see love as a parlor game:

> Si le Roi m'avoit donné
> Paris, sa grand'ville,
> Et qu'il me fallût quitter
> L'amour de ma mie,
> Je dirois au roi Henri:
> "Reprenez votre Paris:
> J'aime mieux ma mie, au gué!
> J'aime mieux ma mie."

The misanthrope's archaic song foreshadows his ultimatum of the *dénouement*. It reveals his desire to escape to a century when men were men, and it expresses his refusal of the world—of the king's gift, namely Paris. The two poems, however, have an important concept in common—*donner*. In the sonnet Philis gives nothing but promises, while in the lyric, in which the very idea of exchange is rejected, the hypothetical gift of Paris conveys the impression that the lover has already secured the affection of his *mie*.

Thus the two rivals quarrel over words. The worldly superficiality of the sonneteer clashes with the wishful escapism of the misanthrope. Here as elsewhere in the comedy Molière is amusing the audience with the interplay between antithetical forms of the unreal: Oronte's world lacks depth and substance, whereas Alceste's private universe lacks existence and being. In a society so devitalized, the only plausible attitude remains that of Eliante: you must recreate the outside world in the image of your more generous emotions and supply it with the values that it may lack. But here Molière twisted Lucretius' satirical comments on man's blindness to suit his purpose. Moreover, he introduces a concept that was missing in the original Latin, that of naming. The true lover transforms the person he adores not directly but by discovering nice words with which to describe her worst features. Lovers, according to Eliante,

> comptent les défauts pour des perfections,
> Et savent y donner de favorables noms.
>
> [715–716]

For instance,

> La malpropre sur soi, de peu d'attraits chargée,
> Est mise sous le nom de beauté négligée.
>
> [721–722]

Molière, or at least Eliante, has at last found a useful function for the imagination. Prompted by emotion, and with the help of names and words, it can attempt to conciliate the ideal with the real.

"LES YEUX DE CESAR": THE LANGUAGE OF VISION IN *BRITANNICUS*

By Jules Brody

Immediately after the murder of Britannicus, Racine has Burrhus convey to the other characters and to the audience this vivid picture of the death scene:

> La moitié s'épouvante et sort avec des cris;
> Mais ceux qui de la cour ont un plus long usage
> Sur les yeux de César composent leur visage.
> Cependant sur son lit il demeure penché;
> D'aucun étonnement il ne paraît touché.
>
> [1634–1638]

This is an important moment for Néron. He has committed his first crime, an act designed to implement the several purposes he has pursued throughout the play. With the demise of Britannicus he is relieved of a potentially dangerous political opponent who was at the same time an irritating obstacle to his passion for Junie. This act has also dealt a crippling blow to the prestige and aims of Agrippine. That Néron dared to dispose so summarily of her protégé is proof to her that her son has come into his own and that the days of her influence are at an end. At the moment which Burrhus describes, Néron has just crossed the threshold to unlimited power: frightened or servile courtiers, a defenseless virgin, a once-domineering mother, all, so he has the right to believe, are now at his mercy. But Burrhus is shocked less by Néron's act itself than by a certain change that seems to have taken place in his young master's very expression.

Burrhus has been deeply shaken by the dramatic contrast between those horror-stricken, screaming witnesses to the murder and the total indifference of Néron, mirrored and magnified in the composed, impassive faces of those in his entourage who have lived in closest intimacy with violence and evil.

The elements of Burrhus' report are found in Tacitus: "Trepidatur a circumsedentibus: diffugiunt imprudentes; at quibus altior intellectus, resistunt defixi, et Neronem intuentes" (XIII, 16). At Racine's hands, however, this tersely factual narrative has come alive. The scene has been re-written with a fresh emphasis, around a new focus barely suggested by the historical account. To Tacitus' *diffugiunt imprudentes* Racine has added *des cris,* sound effects which have already been heard offstage (at 1609) and which were no doubt intended to be recalled by the tone of voice of the actor portraying Burrhus. More significant, however, is the refinement brought by the dramatist to the picture we are given of Néron himself. The manner in which Racine has amplified *Neronem intuentes* directs attention to the facial expression of the full-blown *monstre,* to the blank, calloused, indifferent stare, which is presumably meant to be taken as the external sign of an inner psychological evolution.

Agrippine, too, shows awareness that things are no longer as they were with Néron. In V, 6, she calls him to account with a characteristically hollow imperiousness ("Arrêtez, Néron: j'ai deux mots à vous dire" [1648]),[1] only to be answered for the first time that we know of in the sarcastic, contemptuously ironic tones which, until now, Néron has reserved for all but his mother. It may easily be supposed that he hears her famous curse and prediction (1672–1694) with the same bemused remoteness and disdain which good directors will imagine on the face of Molière's Dom Juan during his father's sermon. This, at least, is what the self-assured brevity of Néron's reply ("Narcisse, suivez-moi" [1694])— his last words in the play—seems to suggest. But Agrippine, like Burrhus in the scene directly preceding, professes to have

[1] Cf. 917, 1115, 1583.

read in Néron's eyes much more than was contained in his words:

> Burrhus, avez-vous vu quels regards furieux
> Néron en me quittant m'a laissés pour adieux?
> C'en est fait: le cruel n'a plus rien qui l'arrête;
> Le coup qu'on m'a prédit va tomber sur ma tête.
>
> [1697–1700]

Néron's *regards furieux* (not "angry" or even, necessarily, "wild," but *furieux* in the older sense of "distraught," "wandering," with more than a hint of madness) have told her that his emancipation has carried him beyond crimes of passion or state to utter contempt for the ties of nature.

Agrippine is right. Néron has come a long way. Burrhus' "D'aucun étonnement il ne paraît touché" (1638) brings sharply back to mind the earlier picture of a nervous, intimidated, indecisive Néron who would all but fall to pieces in the overwhelming presence of his mother: "Mon Génie étonné tremble devant le sien" (506). His recently acquired firmness and self-sufficiency, however, have been bought, as Agrippine will finally realize, at the price of the little humanity he had left. In his reply to Agrippine, Burrhus cannot banish from his mind a haunting image of the "new" Néron. He is drawn once again, recapitulating both his own earlier remarks and those of Agrippine, to dwell on the terrifying transformation he has read in *les yeux de César*:

> Son crime seul n'est pas ce qui me désespère;
> Sa jalousie a pu l'armer contre son frère;
> Mais s'il vous faut, Madame, expliquer ma douleur,
> Néron l'a vu mourir sans changer de couleur.
> Ses yeux indifférents ont déjà la constance
> D'un tyran dans le crime endurci dès l'enfance.
>
> [1707–1712]

In these final scenes Racine seems clearly to be urging our attention toward what Néron *looks* like, in both the transitive and intransitive senses of the English verb. And he does this a little less discreetly than is his custom—three times over a space of seventy lines. The reason for this insistence? It may, of course, be the merest accident, or, again, simply one of a poet's ways of suggesting to directors and actors how to stage the final, pivotal encounter between Néron, his mother, and his tutor. But it should also be observed that the action of *Britannicus* is taken up very largely with moments of seeing, gazing, spying, and meeting. In addition, the tangential acts of fleeing, hiding, probing, and searching appear, even after a casual reading, to have been given unusual prominence. In fact, if the play's gist had to be summed up in a few words it could be said that *Britannicus* depicts the struggle between an old woman, who persists in looking at her emperor with the eyes of an authoritarian parent, and a young man who would devour the world around him in one rapacious glance but who lacks the strength, still, to look his mother in the eye.

In I, 1, Agrippine bitterly recalls the good old days, a time when she ruled Néron and, through him, the state:

> Lorsqu'il se reposait sur moi de tout l'Etat,
> Que mon ordre au palais assemblait le sénat,
> Et que derrière un voile, invisible et présente,
> J'étais de ce grands corps l'âme toute-puissante.
>
> [93–96]

In *Britannicus* this *voile* is as much a metaphor as it is the literal curtain from behind which the historical Agrippina would overhear the Senate's deliberations. As far as Racine's heroine is concerned, her concealment had not been merely a habitual act of eavesdropping but, rather, a characteristic attitude. She had once been the ubiquitous unobserved observer in what Professor Lapp has called "a drama of watcher and watched."[2] And the drama proper begins with her awareness that very real, opaque *voiles* have gradually been lowered between her and her son and the affairs of the state.

Of Agrippine more must be said later. Her problem, moreover, stems directly from the conduct of Néron himself, who, from the very outset, even in violent rebellion, seems to have patterned his aims and psychological habits after those of the

---

[2] *Aspects of Racinian Tragedy* (Toronto: University of Toronto Press, 1955), p. 8. See also pp. 138–142 on the notion of "presence" in *Britannicus*.

mother whom he fears and despises. In I, 2, Agrippine makes her first fruitless effort to see her son face to face—she will not succeed until IV, 2. "César pour quelque temps s'est soustrait à nos yeux" (134) is Burrhus' reply to her urging. In this line Néron's tutor is saying more than he knows. He is actually describing an elaborate *modus operandi*, a way of running things and manipulating people from behind the scenes, of which Agrippine had made an art and which Néron has taken over from her along with her power. Later in the play he will make this boast to Britannicus:

> Rome ne porte point ses regards curieux
> Jusque dans des secrets que je cache à ses yeux.
> [1049–1050]

The obverse of this statement, however, would constitute a fair description of Néron's own situation in the play. The freedom of observation which is denied the *regards curieux* of Rome emerges early as the distinguishing characteristic of Rome's master. The chief thing we learn from Néron's first appearance on stage (II, 1) is that, the night before, a *désir curieux* (385) had fastened his avid *regard* on Junie. And before the act is over, the audience will be allowed to see him, rehearsing this very posture, peering from behind a palace pillar into the souls of Junie and her lover.

These famous scenes of spying, far from being the mere anthology pieces they often pass for, assume their full significance when thought of as fitting into a pattern as large, perhaps, as the tragedy itself. In I, 4, the scene directly preceding Néron's first entrance, his piercing glance is felt to operate as perspicaciously as if he were actually there in the flesh. I am surrounded, Britannicus confides to Narcisse, by

> les témoins assidus,
> Qui choisis par Néron pour ce commerce infâme,
> Trafiquent avec lui des secrets de mon âme
> . . . . .
> Il prévoit mes desseins, il entend mes discours;
> Comme toi, dans mon coeur il sait ce qui se passe.
> [330–335]

The efficacy of these tactics can be measured by the fact that it is to none other than Néron's lieutenant that he announces his awareness of being watched. Ironically enough, the cunning eyes of Narcisse to which Brittanicus has entrusted his safety are but an extension of *les yeux de César*:

> Tes yeux, sur ma conduite incessamment ouverts,
> M'ont sauvé jusqu'ici de mille écueils couverts.
>
> [345–346][3]

These eyes—truly *invisibles et présents*—reach into every corner of the sharply confined space in which the tragedy unfolds. Their aim is everywhere to intimidate, control, and impose a frightened silence. Under the weight of Néron's vicarious stare all communication between Britannicus and his allies is muffled. "Examine leurs yeux," he enjoins Narcisse, "observe leurs discours" (349). He has the impression —but it cannot be more than an impression—that a faction at court is in sympathy with his cause: "Chacun semble des yeux approuver mon courroux" (721). Such is the climate of constraint created by Néron that no one dares, literally, look his fellow in the eye. When glances do happen to meet, they are so carefully guarded that one is never quite sure just what their message is.

This cryptic ocular dialogue between Britannicus and his allies, however schematically suggested, prefigures and sets the climate for the great spying scene in the following act. Here, Néron—this time *actually* though invisibly present— will so project his tyrannical glance as to dim the very lights of love which, heretofore, in keeping with *précieux* conceit, Britannicus was accustomed to see glowing in Junie's eyes. This dramatic moment, however, must be viewed with full awareness of the function and effect of the language of vision which permeates the scenes directly preceding it.

Néron comes on stage for the first time at the beginning of Act II. Almost immediately Narcisse is made to draw atten-

---

[3] Cf. F. W. Lindsay, "Néron and Narcisse: A Duality Resolved," *Modern Language Quarterly*, XI (1950), 169–179.

tion to the look on his master's face, the expression in his eyes:

> Que présage à mes yeux cette tristesse obscure,
> Et ces sombres regards errants à l'aventure?
>
> [379–380]

In one of his most revealing speeches Néron explains why he looks the way he does. He has seen Junie:

> excité d'un désir curieux,
> Cette nuit je l'ai vue arriver en ces lieux,
> Triste, levant au ciel ses yeux mouillés de larmes,
> Qui brillaient au travers des flambeaux et des armes:
> Belle, sans ornements, dans le simple appareil
> D'une beauté qu'on vient d'arracher au sommeil.
> Que veux-tu? Je ne sais si cette négligence,
> Les ombres, les flambeaux, les cris et le silence,
> Et le farouche aspect de ses fiers ravisseurs
> Relevaient de ses yeux les timides douceurs.
> Quoi qu'il en soit, ravi d'une si belle vue,
> J'ai voulu lui parler, et ma voix s'est perdue
>
> . . . . .
>
> De son image en vain j'ai voulu me distraire:
> Trop présente à mes yeux, je croyais lui parler;
> J'aimais jusqu'à ses pleurs que je faisais couler.
>
> [385–396 and 400–403]

In the terms of a time-worn conceit the eye is gateway to the heart.[4] Néron has beheld the lady and now "loves" her. But so does Britannicus. His imagined vision of Junie's abduction, however, is far different in texture and focus from the one which enthralled Néron:

> De mille affreux soldats Junie environnée
> S'est vue en ce palais indignement traînée.
> Hélas! de quelle horreur ses timides esprits
> A ce nouveau spectacle auront été surpris?
>
> [291–294]

---

[4] For a brilliant discussion in this connection of Racine's language of vision, see J. Starobinski, "Racine et la poétique du regard," *Nouvelle Nouvelle Revue française*, V (1957), 246–263.

Britannicus, viewing the scene through the eyes of Junie, re-lives her terror at the unaccustomed spectacle of ugliness and violence. His hyperbolic *mille* lends point to the pitiful vul-nerability of her *timides esprits* in the presence of Néron's *affreux soldats*. It is curious, but surely no accident, that Néron should have been struck by this same confrontation between weak and strong, the beautiful and the terrible. In fact, he is twice drawn in the space of ten lines (cf. 387–388: *larmes–armes;* 393–394: *Farouche aspect–timides douceurs*) to stress the visual contrast between Junie and her captors. Lines 389–391, suggesting as they do an indeterminate de-gree of undress and without doubt the most discreetly sen-suous in all Racine, add a prurient, almost obscene note to Néron's description and imply, on his part, a quasi-Baude-lairian attraction to a victim: "J'aimais jusqu'à ses pleurs que je faisais couler" (402).

A scene which in Britannicus had evoked the deepest compassion becomes for Néron a source of titillation. His eyes, much like Phèdre's, seem endowed with a native capac-ity for soiling and denaturing the object on which they fasten. Nothing stimulates the exercise of vice more powerfully than virtue. A painful though tacit reminder of lost purity and, at the same time, perfect prey for new conquest, Junie, though arousing what in all but a growing *monstre* would be the most generous of sentiments, must inevitably bring out the worst in Néron. Ironically the very innocence of *la modeste Junie* (423) emerges as her most powerful allure-ment:

> c'est cette vertu, si nouvelle à la cour,
> Dont la persévérance irrite mon amour.
>
> [417–418]

In still another way the novelty and rareness of this *vertu* represents to Néron a challenge to his power. It irks him that she alone of all Roman ladies should somehow have evaded the sweep of his all-encompassing eye. Narcisse, shrewd psychologist that he is, reads his master's mind:

NARCISSE: Quoi, Seigneur? croira-t-on
               Qu'elle ait pu si longtemps se cacher à Néron?

NÉRON: Tu le sais bien, Narcisse; et soit que sa colère
               M'imputât le malheur qui lui ravit son frère;
               Soit que son coeur, jaloux d'une austère fierté,
               Enviât à nos yeux sa naissante beauté;
               Fidèle à sa douleur, et *dans l'ombre enfermée*
               Elle se dérobait même à sa renommée.
                                                    [409–416]

For Néron it is as much a psychological as a political need to
take in at a glance, himself inscrutable, all that transpires
around him. His ostensibly playful chiding of Junie, when
finally the two of them come face to face, is in reality grimly
serious:

               Quoi? Madame, est-ce donc une légère offense
               De m'avoir si longtemps *caché* votre présence?
               Ces trésors dont le ciel voulut vous embellir,
               Les avez-vous reçus pour les *ensevelir?*
               L'heureux Britannicus verra-t-il sans alarmes
               Croître, *loin de nos yeux,* son amour et vos charmes?
                                                    [539–544]

Néron is jealous, but not only of Britannicus. He is jealous
also of a newly claimed power, as much personal as political,
which he has reason to believe none too secure. Néron suffers the fears of every rebel or usurper. Unsure whether he
will be able to keep what he has taken, he builds for the
world to see an image of himself more imposing and grandiose
than would one who stood on firmer ground. In open rebellion against his mother's dearest wishes he has decided to
bestow his own royal person on Junie:

               Oui, pour vous faire un choix où vous puissiez souscrire,
               J'ai parcouru des yeux la cour, Rome et l'Empire.
                                                    [575–576]

In the second line of this couplet Néron strikes the pose
which he desperately seeks to maintain and, at the same

time, sums up with an uncanny succinctness the urge underlying his conduct up to this point in the play. The carefully
placed pauses after *la cour*, *Rome* and *l'Empire*, along with
the fact that each place named in this series takes us progres-
sively into more remote and extensive regions, illustrates
rhythmically and graphically the sweeping force of *par-
courir des yeux*. Néron would view himself as a towering,
inaccessible beacon casting its probing beams into reaches
hidden from the sight of ordinary mortals.

In II, 6, Néron materially *becomes* this unseen, allseeing
force. Here, before the spectator's very eyes, language,
psychology, and action fuse to make dramatic poetry. The
unsuspected presence of Néron on the stage will add powerful resonances to the words of Junie and Britannicus.
Néron's final warning to Junie prefigures the cruel irony of
the scene that is to follow: "Madame, en le voyant, songez
que je vous voi" (690). Pinned under Néron's glance she
will be able to think of nothing else:

> Vous êtes en des lieux tout pleins de sa puissance.
> Ces murs mêmes, Seigneur, peuvent avoir des yeux;
> Et jamais l'Empereur n'est absent de ces lieux.
>
> [712–714]

To Britannicus this is but political comment; to Junie it is a
horrible reality; to us it is poetry. "To say that walls have ears
is not poetic, except when they really do."[5] This kind of poetry, however, owes its depth to its oneness with action.
Britannicus registers for us the actual effect of Néron's eyes
on those who are caught within their compass:

> Quoi? même vos regards ont appris à se taire?
> Que vois-je? Vous craignez de rencontrer mes yeux?
>
> [736–737]

This is the glance that paralyzes, cripples, wilts its object.
Early in the play Junie is said to have wished she had never
been brought into contact with Néron, coveting above all

5 W. G. Moore, *Racine: Britannicus* (London: Arnold, 1960),
p. 35.

l'heureuse liberté de ne le voir jamais (233). At that moment this was perfunctory talk. When she did lay eyes on him, however, she sensed immediately what it meant to see and be seen by Néron. Before she could utter a word, his first lines to her were made to reflect for the spectator's benefit the instinctive horror inspired in her by the mere sight of him:

> Vous vous troublez, Madame, et changez de visage.
> Lisez-vous dans mes yeux quelque triste présage?
>
> [527–528]

There was indeed a *triste présage* to be read in those eyes. And in the interview with Britannicus which we have been discussing, Junie has cause to appreciate what capacity for evil that first glance of Néron's had portended. She now knows that to be seen by Néron is to be dominated, dehumanized, and, ultimately, destroyed. This new awareness surely informs the warning which, echoing Agrippine ("Vous, si vous m'en croyez, évitez ses regards" [926]), she addresses to Britannicus at the end of Act III: "Allez, encore un coup, cachez-vous à ses yeux" (1017).

It is something more than poetic justice that Néron should himself be beset by apprehensions similar to those he inspires in others. For it is a fact that throughout the greater portion of the drama he is fleeing a power as menacing and terrible to him as any he holds over Junie and Britannicus. This power is Agrippine, or, more exactly, a way she has of looking at him which he finds unbearable. Shortly after setting forth the amorous ambitions to which his nocturnal vision of Junie had given rise, he confesses to Narcisse that one formidable obstacle stands in the way of their fulfillment—his mother.

> Eloigné de ses yeux, j'ordonne, je menace,
> J'écoute vos conseils, j'ose les approuver;
> Je m'excite contre elle, et tâche à la braver.
> Mais (je t'expose ici mon âme toute nue)
> Sitôt que mon malheur me ramène à sa vue,
> Soit que je n'ose encor démentir *le pouvoir*
> *De ces yeux où j'ai lu si longtemps mon devoir;*

> Soit qu'à tant de bienfaits ma mémoire fidèle
> Lui soumette en secret tout ce que je tiens d'elle,
> Mais enfin mes efforts ne me servent de rien:
> Mon Génie étonné tremble devant le sien.
>
> [496–506]

In the eyes of Agrippine, Néron reads the same threat of tyranny and humiliation which those whom he seeks to control
read in his own. (Cf. to Junie: "Lisez-vous dans mes yeux
quelque triste présage?" [528]) Despite his passion for Junie
and the latitude of action which imperial greatness affords
him, he is frozen in his tracks at the mere thought of a certain forbidding look that he has so often read in his mother's
eyes:

> Mon amour inquiet déjà se l'imagine
> Qui m'amène Octavie, et d'un oeil enflammé
> Atteste les saints droits d'un noeud qu'elle a formé.
>   • • • • •
> De quel front soutenir ce fâcheux entretien?
>
> [484–486 and 489]

When finally he brings himself to take a step toward self-
assertion and banish Pallas (notice, however, the immature,
nervous quality of his commands: "qu'il s'éloigne, qu'il
parte:/Je le veux, je l'ordonne" [368–369]), his first concern
after the accomplished fact is as much for how Agrippine
looked as for what she said:

>   de quel oeil
> Ma mère a-t-elle vu confondre son orgueil?
>
> [761–762]

Nor is Agrippine unaware of the nature and source of the
power which she had until but recently wielded over her son.
She fears not that Néron may fall into evil ways—her com-
punctions are neither maternal nor moral—but that other eyes
may usurp a role that had always been hers. To Burrhus:

> Ne saurait-il rien voir qu'il n'emprunte vos yeux?
> Pour se conduire, enfin, n'a-t-il pas ses aïeux?
>
> [161–162]

A similar apprehension underlies her concern over Néron's passion for Junie:

> Elle aura le pouvoir d'épouse et de maîtresse.
> . . . . .
> Tout deviendra le prix d'un seul de ses regards.
> [888–890]

Throughout the first three acts Agrippine's sole interest is to come face to face with a son who, for reasons which we understand, has been strenuously avoiding her. All would be well if only she could once again bring Néron beneath *le pouvoir de* [*ses*] *yeux* (501): "Ah! lui-même à mes yeux puisse-t-il se montrer!" (874). When in IV, 2, this much-hoped-for meeting does take place, Agrippine seems, for the moment at least, to have retrieved her lost power. Paramount among the conditions she lays down for future relations between herself and her son is that he be always accessible to her: "Que vous me permettiez de vous voir à toute heure" (1292). His decision whether or not to accede to her demand seems to turn on a single, pivotal word. Trust Narcisse to find it:

NARCISSE: Agrippine, Seigneur, se l'était bien promis:
    Elle a repris sur vous son souverain empire.

NÉRON: Quoi donc? Qu'a-t-elle dit? Et que voulez-vous dire?

NARCISSE: Elle s'en est vantée assez publiquement.

NÈRON: De quoi?

NARCISSE: Qu'elle n'avait qu'à vous *voir* un moment . . .
           [1414–1418]

This hurts. And Narcisse knew that it would. Néron's reaction was predictable: "Mais, Narcisse, dis-moi, que veux-tu que je fasse" (1422)? From this point forward Néron is a free agent—as free to do evil as his mother had ever been before him.

 The next and last time that Néron appears before us (V, 6) he is a changed person. Gone are his earlier fears and hesitations. Agrippine has been defied, Britannicus dispatched. There is no doubt now that Néron is irretrievably committed to the life of cruelty and crime for which history has made him famous. And it is highly significant that at this capital juncture in his career he is able for the first time, literally, to look his mother in the eye—to meet, with what Agrippine will call a *regard furieux* (1697), that crippling glance of hers which had never failed before to stop him short.

It is worth reading once again this climactic couplet in Burrhus' epilogue to Néron's transformation:

> Ses yeux indifférents ont déjà la constance
> D'un tyran dans le crime endurci dès l'enfance.
>
> [1711–1712]

It may not be an exaggeration to suggest that the "new" Néron is able to stare his mother down precisely because his eyes, true mirrors of his soul, have become as *constants* and *indifférents* as her own. For Néron repudiates his mother's influence only the better to follow in her footsteps. Like Agrippine, and no doubt from her, he has learned to covet, connive, and trade in human life for the sake of personal aggrandizement (cf. 1119 ff.). In her blindness she may lay the blame elsewhere for what she calls Néron's "ingratitude," but in reality it is she who made him what he is. I am guilty, she tells him, of many crimes—"des crimes pour vous commis à votre vue" (1267). He is in more ways than one her *fils* and her *ouvrage* (1108). As Néron approaches for their final interview it is with no small irony that she is made to say: "Le voici. Vous verrez si c'est moi qui l'inspire" (1647).

It is both logically and morally satisfying that the offspring of this aging *monstre* should resemble her so closely. But this fact also has esthetic implications. In the final analysis, the tragic interest of *Britannicus* centers on Agrippine's realization that Néron has become everything that we know she has been. In the very first speech of the play she is made to sense what the future holds in store: "Je sens que je deviens importune à mon tour" (14). By the end of the fifth act this intuition has grown into a certainty:

Je prévois que tes coups viendront jusqu'à ta mère.
Dans le fond de ton coeur je sais que tu me hais.
[1676–1677]

Le coup qu'on m'a prédit va tomber sur ma tête.
[1700]

Although without remorse or regret, Agrippine at long last understands how inevitable it is that she should suffer at the hands of Néron the same fate as those who had stood in her way. Until this moment, however, it is her dearest illusion that things may turn out otherwise.

In this play Racine focuses attention on two ostensibly divergent lines of action which in the end prove to have been leading in the same direction. Superficially viewed, *Britannicus* can appear to be a mere character study of a growing *monstre*. In his second preface, however, Racine tells us that he was intensely interested in *la disgrâce d'Agrippine*. Indeed, as vital to the play's movement as Néron's becoming a *monstre* is Agrippine's refusal to believe that she has borne and nurtured one. And her every effort is spent to belie and stifle her early feeling that this, after all, may be the case. Her position, of course, is deeply ironical. Closing her eyes to the dreadful, though imposing, suspicion that her son may be inherently vicious and that events can now follow but one course, with customary relentlessness she sets about ascertaining what hidden causes may underlie his insubordinate behavior. In one of those bald Racinian lines which have the effect of recapitulating in twelve syllables whole characters and situations, Agrippine states to her confidante what her purpose will be throughout the play: "Surprenons, s'il se peut, les secrets de son âme" (127). It will be Agrippine's misfortune to succeed in this endeavor.

From like causes like effects. One *monstre* will produce another, only to be destroyed by it as it exploits its inherent propensities. Viewed in this light, *Britannicus* seems to trace what one critic has called, with respect to Racine's last play, a tragic cycle.[6] And were it only for this symmetrical, almost

---

[6] E. E. Williams, "*Athalie*: The Tragic Cycle and the Tragedy of Joas," *Romanic Review*, XXVIII (1937), 36–45. See also J. D.

rhythmical pattern of action, the play would be, at least by classical standards, an artistically successful work. But here, as in the other great Racinian tragedies, structure is but one element in an elaborate and unified dramaturgy. What the main characters in *Britannicus* think and do is reflected as well in what they say and how they look. On the level of psychology and action the cycle is complete with Agrippine's illumination. Stylistically and scenically, however, we are permitted very early in the play to anticipate this moment of insight. Having been reminded incessantly of Néron's surreptitious peering, probing, and spying, we finally behold him at a given moment as he transfixes Junie and Britannicus under the same tyrannical glance which Agrippine, in her prime, had so often leveled at him. For us at this point the inner movement of the play has come full circle. We have seen Néron become another Agrippine.

Here, as always, Racine allows the spectator to enjoy the tragic perspective considerably before his protagonist. And when in that fateful scene Néron's *yeux indifférents* meet the eyes of Agrippine, we are afforded the profound satisfaction of hearing and seeing her grasp a fundamental truth that is already ours. The cycle is now complete—this time for protagonist and spectator alike. The play, however, has not yet ended. The last scene of Act V provides a telling epilogue to the supreme moment of indifferent constancy which Néron has achieved. Before the final curtain we learn that Junie has escaped and that Néron has gone mad:

> Il marche sans dessein; ses yeux mal assurés
> N'osent lever au ciel leurs regards égarés.
>
> [1757–1758]

The *monstre* has matured and, like his progenitor, has begun to decline. Néron's *regard,* a moment before hard and intrepid, enjoys its triumph for the briefest moment. Reinforcing the sense of unity, balance, symmetry, and order which his play is meant to procure us, Racine indicates here that the cycle has recommenced its relentless pattern.

Hubert's penetrating study of tragic heredity in *Britannicus* in his *Essai d'exégèse racinienne* (Paris: Nizet, 1956), pp. 102–118.

ARIOSTO AND LA FONTAINE:
A LITERARY AFFINITY

By John C. Lapp

Orlando Furioso ranks without doubt among the most fertile of the many books, ancient and foreign, that nurtured French Renaissance and classical literature, not merely enriching it with specific source materials, but, like some wondrous *terra infinita,* even overshadowing the real world or coexisting with it. Its influence ranged through every genre, beyond poetry and beyond the boundaries of centuries.[1]

What was it that drew such disparate writers to the *Furioso,* for that lengthy epic is by far the most popular of Ariosto's works? What maintained Ariosto's popularity in France throughout the sixteenth and seventeenth centuries despite the fact that he served both Montaigne and Boileau as an illustration of how *not* to write? The primary appeal lay in his infinite variety, his power of invention. As C. S. Lewis, who does not hesitate to rank him with Homer, admirably puts it,

> His actors range from archangels to horses, his scene from Cathay to the Hebrides. In every stanza there is something new: battles in all their detail, strange lands with their laws, customs, history, and geography, storm and sunshine, mountains, islands, rivers, monsters, anec-

[1] Cf. Alice Cameron, *The Influence of Ariosto's Epic and Lyric Poetry on Ronsard and His Group* (Baltimore: Johns Hopkins Press, 1930); A. Cioranescu, *L'Arioste en France* (Paris: Les Presses Modernes, 1939), 2 vols. It is a pleasure to thank Professor Alan Gilbert for his valuable suggestions.

dotes, conversations—there seems no end to it. He tells us
what his people ate, he describes the architecture of
their palaces; when you tire of one adventure he plunges
you into another with something so ludicrous or questionable in its exordium you feel you must read just one
more.[2]

Such diversity had its critics, of course. Montaigne complained of him that *on le voit . . . voleter et sauteler de conte
en conte comme de branche en branche, ne se fiant à ses
aisles que pour une bien courte traverse, et prendre pied à
chaque bout de champ, de peur que l'haleine et la force luy
faille*.[3] But Jean de La Fontaine, the poet who boasted *di-
versité c'est ma devise*, could scarcely have failed to be won
by Ariosto. Indeed two other self-descriptive phrases of his
sound like a poetic paraphrase of Montaigne's characterization of the Italian poet:

> Je suis chose légère, et vole à tout sujet
> Je vais de fleur en fleur et d'objet en objet.[4]

In La Fontaine's lifetime the vogue of Ariosto was wide-
spread. The *Furioso* inspired poems, plays, operas, and that
most spectacular offspring of all, the royal divertissement *Les
Plaisirs de l'île enchantée*, in which Louis XIV played the
amorous Ruggiero and Louise de La Vallière the enchantress
Alcina—perhaps unaware or unconcerned that in the poem
Alcina is actually a withered hag whose beauty is the product
of magic. Among the Italian poet's admirers was Racine, who
praised him frequently in his letters, on one occasion comparing him to Homer, thus anticipating Mr. Lewis.[5] La Fontaine

[2] C. S. Lewis, *The Allegory of Love* (Oxford: Clarendon Press,
1936), pp. 301–333.
[3] *Essais*, ed. Villey (Paris: Alcan, 1923), II, x, 111.
[4] "Discours à Mme de la Sablière." In the "Epître à Huet" he
wrote: "Je chéris l'Arioste et j'estime le Tasse" (*Oeuvres complètes*,
ed. Pilon, Groos, Schiffrin, and Clarac [Ed. de la Pléiade; Paris:
Gallimard, 1959], II, 647; 649). All quotations are from this edition, with these abbreviations: Vol. I, *Fables, Contes et Nouvelles:
FCN*; Vol. II, *Oeuvres diverses: OD*.
[5] See G. May, *D'Ovide à Racine* (Paris: Presses Universitaires de
France, 1949), pp. 98–101; V. Lugli, *Il prodigio di La Fontaine*

must have agreed, since in the opera *Daphné* he placed the
bust of Ariosto in the palace of Apollo alongside those of
Homer, Anacreon, Pindar, Virgil, Horace, Ovid, Tasso, and
Malherbe.

References to Ariosto's poem sprang readily to our poet's
mind. For the opera *Roland* by Lully and Quinault, he turned
a gracious dedicatory ode, comparing Angelica to Helen of
Troy and urging the king,

> Plaignez le paladin que mon art vous présente
> Son malheur fut d'aimer; quelle âme en est exempte?
>   [*OD*, 621–622]

In the amusing *ballade*, "Je me plais aux livres d'amour," he
seems to be speaking through the lips of the prude who in-
advertently admits her pleasure in love stories and, in particular, in the *Furioso*:

> J'ai lu maître Louis mille fois en ma vie;
> Et même quelquefois j'entre en tentation
> Lorsque l'Ermite trouve Angélique endormie,
>   [*OD*, 586]

a reference to the amusing passage about an old hermit who
tries in vain to rape the sleeping heroine and whose lament
recalls the plaintive *O che sciagura* of *Candide*.[6]

But for the best evidence of an affinity between La Fontaine and Ariosto one must turn to the *Contes*. The first glance
reveals that his most incidental allusions to the *Furioso* have
nothing extraneous about them; they invariably have a function. Take, for example, "Les Aveux indiscrets." It is rather
startling to encounter, in this rather prosy, matter-of-fact tale
of a husband who symbolized his cuckoldry by wearing a sad-
dle, a reference to Orlando:

(Milan: Principato, 1939), pp. 121–131; P. Wadsworth, *Young La
Fontaine* (Evanston, Ill.: Northwestern University Press, 1951), pp.
145–151.
  [6] Other incidental references: in *Psyche*, Angelica has her place
in the palace of Cupid alongside Armida, Cleopatra, and Helen of
Troy (*OD*, 143), and Chancellor Séguier's finery is compared to
that of Medoro (*OD*, 510).

> Quand Roland sut les plaisirs et la gloire
> Que dans la grotte avait eus son rival,
> D'un coup de poing il tua son cheval.

The episode La Fontaine recalls so exactly is Orlando's discovery of the triumphant message his rival Medoro inscribed
above the entrance to the cave and on the surrounding trees
after making love to Angelica. Mad with grief, the paladin
kills Medoro's horse with one blow and drags Angelica's mare
away by the tail. And La Fontaine asks,

> Pouvait-il pas, traînant la pauvre bête,
> Mettre de plus la selle sur son dos;
> Puis s'en aller, tout du haut de sa tête,
> Faire crier et redire aux échos:
> "Je suis bâté . . ."?

Here La Fontaine treats his source in the same way as Ariosto
approached the romances of chivalry; the hero of the *Furioso*
is made to seem as ludicrous as the talkative Damon of the
conte.

The incongruity of Orlando's appearance in such a context
is typical of Ariosto. For his variety did not consist merely of
multiplying scenes, incidents, and characters; it frequently
produced an intentionally ironic counterpoint. He achieved
this in a number of ways, all of them pertinent to our study of
La Fontaine. First of all, he deliberately stresses his position as
an omnipresent author. He is forever commenting on his narrative, his characters, his art; plucking the reader by the
sleeve, often in the midst of the most violent action. He will
pause to declare variety one of his chief methods of creating
interest:

> Cosi mi par, che la mia istoria, quanto
> Or qui or là piú variata sia
> Meno a chi l'udirá noiosa fia.
>
> [XIII, 80]

In this particular instance he is justifying the way he abruptly
changes scenes or interrupts one action to describe another.
Such asides may be addressed to various persons: the court of

Ferrara, to which he is presenting his story; the reader; or one
of his own characters, both fictional and real. The levels of
action and of setting are legion, but there are also different
levels of time: the present, the historic past of Italy, the legendary past of the epic itself. Nor does the poem progress in
an orderly chronological fashion: it frequently interrupts its
flow like an old-time serial movie, halting one action just before its climax to take up another. And Ariosto constantly
reaches back into his story, reminding his reader of earlier
events and the characters' roles in them.

To intervene in this way is to produce various effects of
suspension and distance. The reader is invited to take a de-
tached viewpoint, to inspect and judge for himself. When
Ariosto comments, in a variety of tones, upon his characters,
he produces a precariously balanced relationship between author, characters, and reader which he delights in tipping this
way and that. One of the best examples is his remark when
his heroine, the pure Angelica, has declared

> che'l fior virginal cosí avea salvo,
> Como se lo portó del materno alvo.

The author concludes gently:

> Forse era ver, ma non peró credibile
> A chi del senso suo fosse signore;
> Ma parve facilmente a lui possibile,
> Ch'era perduto in via più grave errore.
>
> [I, 56]

Remember that this is the heroine, who for the story's basic
interest must remain virginal until she yields to Medoro!

Yet Ariosto is far from being a misogynist. For example,
when Rodomonte denounces the female sex, the author tells
us he must have lost his mind:

> Et certo da ragion si dispartiva;
> Che per uno o per due che trovi ree,
> Che cento buone sien creder si dee.
>
> [XXVII, 122]

In the *Furioso* man and woman can be equally heroic, despicable, or ridiculous. Three insertions, or novella, treat specifically of feminine unchastity, the story of Giocondo (XXVII, 1–74), and two tales illustrating the triumph of cupidity over virtue (XLII, 70–XLIII, 143). The ambiguity of Ariosto's attitude toward woman appears not so much in their content, which is clearly antifeminist, but in the way he presents them. The story of Giocondo, the first that La Fontaine adapted, is a case in point. The author carefully prepares us through the mood of Rodomonte, who before the story begins is furious at being rejected by Doralice. His blanket denunciation of woman swiftly narrows to the single theme of infidelity. On arriving at an inn, he asks the guests if any of them believe their wives faithful. All assure him that they do. But the innkeeper offers to tell tales that prove no chaste woman ever existed. Whereupon the Saracen demands to hear one that "will fit his opinion." Not content with showing the bias of both narrator and listener, when the story ends Ariosto brings forward an old man who defends womankind, thus effectively countering, by its framing, the antifeminist content of the tale.

Further ironic contrasts develop from shifts between fantasy and realism. This interplay occurs both in the structure and the descriptive technique of the *Furioso*. The "realistic" story of Giocondo, for example, follows upon the intervention of archangels and the goddess of Discord in the Saracen camp. In describing the Hippogriff, the magician's winged horse, Ariosto takes pains to tell us that this new Pegasus is not a magical, but a real creature, borne by an ass to a griffin. Though rare, he adds, such beasts may be found on the other side of the frozen seas. So he seasons the magical element by the witty intrusion of pseudozoology.

There is no dearth of such examples—for instance, the contrast between realistic and magic hindrances to love when Ruggiero, in his amorous haste, tries to remove his armor and knots up two laces for every one he unties. When he is finally ready to embrace Angelica, however, she pops the magic ring into her mouth and disappears into thin air (X, 114–XI, 9).

Such blending may be one aspect of what Croce has called Ariosto's universal harmony.[7]

A final device which produces an effect of ironic detachment I shall call, for the purposes of this discussion, the pose of the subservient narrator. Turpin, the feigned chronicler of the *Furioso*, serves to justify certain of Ariosto's more ludicrous flights:

> Il buon Turpin, che sa che dice il vero
> E lascia creder poi quel ch'a l'uom piace.
> [XXVI, 23]

He shelters behind Turpin to excuse the antifeminism of the story of Giocondo by urging women not to read it. He had only set it down because Turpin did so and not through any ill will toward them:

> Ch'io v'ami, oltre mia lingua che l'ha espresso
> Che mai non fu di celebrarvi avara,
> N'ho fatto mille prove; e v'ho dimostro
> Ch'io son né potrei esser se non vostro.
> [XXVIII, 2][8]

But all the protests in the world could not disguise the theme of the Giocondo tale, woman's weakness and sensuality, and it was probably inevitable that La Fontaine should adapt precisely the three novellas on that theme, which was also the theme of the *Contes*. The first, "Joconde," had previously been translated into French five times; of the other two, "La Coupe enchantée" had been adapted once (by Deimier), but "Le Petit Chien qui secoue de l'argent et des pierreries" never before. In the Italian original all three stories are complete insertions; that is, they do not, as Ariosto's other tales do, include characters who participate in the main action of the epic. Each is told to a paladin who has, at that particular moment at least, cause to despair of woman's fidelity. In the case of "Giocondo," this was the fiery Rodomonte, king of

---

[7] See B. Croce, *Ariosto, Shakespeare e Corneille* (Bari: Laterza, 1929), p. 20.

[8] See also *Orlando Furioso*, XXX, 49, and XXXIII, 85.

Algiers, who was furious with all women because he had been forsaken by Doralice for Mandricardo. The other two tales are heard by the despondent Rinaldo, who has learned of Angelica's infidelity.

1. "JOCONDE"

Here is a summary of the story as Ariosto tells it, the main lines of which La Fontaine follows. Giocondo, the hero, renowned for his beauty, is summoned to the court of Astolfo, king of Lombardy, a famous *coureur* who has heard of Giocondo and is curious to see whether he might prove a worthy rival. The hero, shortly after setting out, realizes he has forgotten his wife's parting gift and returns unexpectedly to find her in the arms of another man. He takes no action but departs, disconsolate, for Astolfo's court. There he languishes, pale and sickly, until by chance he discovers the queen herself in dalliance vile with an ugly dwarf, a discovery which quite restores his humor and good looks. When he tells the king, the two husbands decide to set out on a journey of seduction in order to avenge themselves on the female sex. In the final episode they share the favors of an innkeeper's daughter who manages to entertain them and a third lover, all in the same bed. When they discover this crowning example of feminine infidelity, they good-humoredly resign themselves to the fact that women are all alike and return, full of tolerance, to their wives.

In discussing La Fontaine's version of this story, Alexandre Cioranescu errs, I believe, in finding the chief difference between the two writers to be the Italian's realism and the Frenchman's fantasy. Superficially defining realism as mere attention to detail in such matters as the careful identification of characters, the use of proper names, or exact physical and topographical description, he claims that the French version lacks realism, explaining, somewhat tautologically, that La Fontaine *aime mieux l'indécis, l'atmosphère de pure fantaisie qui caractérise les contes.*[9] I would reproach him not so much for such a gross misstatement concerning the *Contes,* but for

[9] Cioranescu, *op. cit.,* p. 63.

failing to see that each author could command both realism and fantasy at will.

Actually, La Fontaine employs or suppresses detail in his own way, and to a special purpose. In his version he establishes the contrast, familiar in French classical literature from Guez de Balzac to Mme de La Fayette, between court and countryside. Thus, when he tells us, not that Joconde lives in Rome, as Ariosto notes in the original, but in the country *loin du commerce et du monde,* he is not shirking a detail but suggesting an opposition between court and country life. Such an opposition appears in the farewell speech of Joconde's wife, a lyrical passage which replaces a few lines of indirect discourse in the original:

> As-tu bien l'âme assez cruelle
> Pour préférer à ma constante amour
>   Les faveurs de la cour?
> Tu sais qu'à peine elles durent un jour;
> Qu'on les conserve avec inquiétude,
>   Pour les perdre avec désespoir.
>   Si tu te lasses de me voir,
> Songe au moins qu'en ta solitude
>   Le repos règne jour et nuit;
>   Que les ruisseaux n'y font du bruit
> Qu'afin de t'inviter à fermer la paupière.
> Crois-moi, ne quitte point les hôtes de tes bois,
> Ces fertiles vallons, ces ombrages si cois.

Such reflective moments help to provide, in the brief framework of the *conte,* some of the depth and variety Ariosto achieved through the scope and movement of the entire epic.

Further details not present in the Italian stress aristocratic values. So in the French version Joconde smarts at his disgrace because his betrayer is not of his class:

> Encore si c'était un blondin
> Je me consolerais d'un si sensible outrage;
> Mais un gros lourdaud de valet!
> C'est à quoi j'ai le plus de regret.

Ariosto merely notes that Giocondo recognized in his wife's arms his servant whom he had befriended as a youth.

In the *Furioso*, Giocondo's failure to take vengeance on the lovers is an effect of his deep love. Boileau, in his "Dissertation sur 'Joconde,'" berated the Italian poet for intruding such a serious note in a comic tale, and concluded in favor of La Fontaine: "Un mari qui se résout à souffrir discrètement les plaisirs de sa femme, comme l'a dépeint M. de La Fontaine, n'a rien que de plaisant et d'agréable, et c'est le sujet ordinaire de nos comédies."[10] But it is apparent from the "Joconde" and the other two *contes* that La Fontaine's conjugal philosophy is quite the opposite. It is not the complaisant, but the jealous husband he finds comical, in accord with the aristocratic morality which considered marital jealousy or proprietariness essentially a bourgeois trait, a manifestation of middle-class rapacity and acquisitiveness. Molière shared La Fontaine's attitude. From *La Jalousie du Barbouillé* on down through *L'Ecole des femmes* and *Amphitryon*, not only cuckoldry but the fear of it evoked hearty laughter; such a fear revealed the bourgeois's basic sense of inferiority, his fundamental fear of woman.[11] In the Italian poem, before telling the king his shocking news, Giocondo makes Astolfo swear a sacred oath not to take vengeance (XXVIII, 40). Despite this, when the king witnesses his own betrayal, he reacts so violently that only the thought of the oath restrains him. La Fontaine's Astolphe, on the other hand, shows the blasé detachment of the aristocrat:

> Il fut comme accablé de ce cruel outrage.
> Mais bientôt il le prit en homme de courage
> En galant homme, et, pour le faire court,
> En véritable homme de cour.

By other "realistic" details, absent in Ariosto, La Fontaine emphasizes rank and hierarchy. It has already been pointed

[10] Boileau, *Oeuvres complètes* (Ed. des Grands Ecrivains), IV, 15.

[11] Cf. P. Bénichou, *Morales du grand siècle* (Paris: Gallimard, 1948), pp. 178–195, for a thorough study of Molière's attitude. Bénichou does not discuss La Fontaine.

out that the king and Joconde's decision to keep a list of their conquests is an innovation in the French version, but it has not been noticed that this list was kept *according to rank.* By the time the wanderers' eyes fall upon the innkeeper's daughter their long list ranges from aldermen's to governor's wives. And while in the original the two men conduct their campaign on a basis of perfect equality, in La Fontaine the king demands his royal prerogative to be the first to enjoy the favors of their last bedmate.

This final and most ludicrous conquest develops, in the Italian version, out of Astolfo's belief that a woman might prove faithful to two men if never to one alone. La Fontaine presents it as a result of his disenchantment with ladies of quality. "Laissons-là la qualité," proclaims Astolphe, denouncing the rigors of courtly love:

> Sous les cotillons des grisettes
> Peut loger autant de beauté
> Que sous les jupes des coquettes.
> D'ailleurs il n'y faut point faire tant de façon,
> Etre en continuel soupçon,
> Dépendre d'une humeur fière, brusque ou volage:
> Chez les dames de haut parage
> Ces choses sont à craindre et bien d'autres encor.
> Une grisette est un trésor,
> Car, sans se donner de la peine,
> Et sans qu'aux bals on la promène,
> On en vient aisément à bout;
> On lui dit ce qu'on veut, bien souvent rien du tout.

Curiously, despite this clearly expressed preference, which once again depends for its point on class distinction, Cioranescu tells us that in the French poem the adventurers *tirent au sort à qui aura la fortune de la courtiser le premier, après quoi ils commencent à lui faire la cour selon toutes les règles de la galanterie, avec des compliments, des danses et des rendez-vous.* But La Fontaine tells us that she yields her favors with alacrity, in exchange for a ring:

> A cet objet si précieux
> Son coeur fit peu de résistance:
> Le marché se conclut.

Cioranescu compounds his error by adding that the Fiam-
metta of the French version is *une jeune vierge qu'il faut
conquérir à force d'assiduités et de promesses.* The fact is that
La Fontaine derives one of his most original effects from the
two friends' naïve belief in the wench's virginity. The irony
in this situation affects the erotic element in the story. Cioranescu declares that La Fontaine went farther than his
predecessor: "L'imitateur s'emploie autant qu'il peut à com-
pléter ce que le modèle ne faisait que suggérer et à mettre les
points sur les *i* avec une ironie et une sincérité toutes gau-
loises," although he adds, in apparent contradiction, "il est
curieux de constater que là où le tableau du modèle devient
trop osé, l'imitateur français recule."[12] Actually, rather than
suppressing Ariosto's crudity of detail, La Fontaine uses a
method he described later in "Le Tableau," a conte inspired
by one of Aretino's more licentious works:

> Nuls traits à découvert n'auront ici de place;
> Tout y sera voilé, mais de gaze, et si bien
> Que je crois qu'on n'en perdra rien.

Thus, while he preserves the erotic episode of three men in
bed with one girl, La Fontaine displaces it from the position
of central interest it held in the Italian version by his stress on
the gallants' foolish belief in her virginity. Joconde states his
opinion with almost ludicrous intensity:

> Je la tiens pucelle sans faute,
> Et si pucelle qu'il n'est rien
> De plus puceau que cette belle:
> Sa poupée en sait autant qu'elle.

When the two draw lots to determine which will teach her *la
première leçon du plaisir amoureux,* La Fontaine comments
dryly:

[12] Cioranescu, *loc. cit.*

> De la chape à l'évêque, hélas, ils se battaient
> Les bonnes gens qu'ils étaient!

And to the recital of the night's event, he adds a 14-line comment on the naïveté of Joconde, *qui crut avoir rompu la glace*. He further "veils" the Ariostian coarseness with comic allegories such as *maître Pucelage*, who *joua des mieux son personnage*.

He achieves a further "veiling" by heightening the effects of illusion, so prevalent in the *Furioso* as a whole. To the conclusion he adds a speech by Astolphe suggesting magic as a cause of infidelity and the influence of *quelque astre malin* on errant husbands and wives:

> D'ailleurs tout l'univers est plein
> De maudits enchanteurs, qui des corps et des âmes
> Font tout ce qu'il leur plaît: savons-nous si ces gens,
> Comme ils sont traîtres et méchants,
> Et toujours ennemis soit de l'un, soit de l'autre,
> N'ont point ensorcelé mon épouse et la vôtre?
> Et si par quelque étrange cas
> Nous n'avons point cru voir chose qui n'était pas?

Such a universe of enchantment and illusion is also that of the *Orlando Furioso*.

But despite the indulgence of this conclusion La Fontaine will not go as far as the Renaissance optimist in his defense of woman. He expresses his skepticism through various interventions similar to those in the *Furioso*, assuming an omniscience, an awareness, surpassing those of his gullible readers:

> Vous autres, bonnes gens, eussiez cru que la dame
> Une heure après eût rendu l'âme;
> Moi, qui sais ce que c'est que l'esprit d'une femme,
> Je m'en serais à bon droit défié.

In typically Ariostian fashion he parries imagined objections at the number and rapidity of the two gallants' conquests:

> J'entends déjà maint esprit fort
> M'objecter que la vraisemblance
> N'est pas en ceci tout à fait.

But he concludes, all that matters is my adherence to Ariosto:

> Je le rends comme on me la donne;
> Et l'Arioste ne ment pas.

In this last line we recognize the device we have called the pose of the subservient narrator. La Fontaine pretends to efface himself before his Italian master, as Ariosto had done before Turpin. By this means he boldly justifies distortions which suit his particular purpose, or even omissions. In the French version, as Joconde leaves for the court of Astolphe, his wife delivers her long and tearful farewell, whereupon, writes La Fontaine:

> L'histoire ne dit point ni de quelle manière
> Joconde put partir, ni ce qu'il répondit,
>   Ni ce qu'il fit, ni ce qu'il dit;
> Je m'en tais donc aussi de crainte de pis faire.

This is simply not true. Actually Giocondo's reply takes almost a whole stanza and is full of sadness at the prospect of his parting.[13] But through the device of the subservient narrator La Fontaine has been able to voice his doubts about the durability of conjugal love:

> Marié depuis peu;
> Content, je n'en sais rien.

These lines embody an essential element of French classic art which the poet employs with consummate skill: the eloquence of the *unsaid*, the unexpressed, the *je ne sais quoi*. Joconde, among La Fontaine's first published works, is already a masterpiece, ranging in its subtlety and suggestion far beyond its model.

2. "LA COUPE ENCHANTEE"

The episode in Ariosto extends through 101 stanzas (XLII, 70–XLIII, 67). Rinaldo, crossing the Po as evening approaches, meets a courteous stranger who asks if he is mar-

[13] "Deh, vita mia, non piagnere . . ." (XXVIII, 13). See also *FCN*, 565.

ried and, upon receiving an affirmative answer, invites him to spend the night in his palace. After a sumptuous meal his host urges him to drink from a gold cup; if his wife is faithful he will be able to drink all the wine, but if she is unchaste, every drop will spill. After a moment's thought, Rinaldo refuses:

Ben sarrebbe folle
Chi quel che non vorria trovar cercasse.

Whereupon his host, in tears, begins his story. He had married the daughter of an elderly man and inherited all his possessions, including the palace, after his death. But his wedded bliss was interrupted when a sorceress fell in love with him and, on being rebuffed, dared him to try his wife's chastity. She gave him the magic goblet, he drank, and all was well. But, urged the magician, he must leave for a time and make the test again when he returned. He refused, and she next offered to change his appearance so that he might test his wife's virtue in the guise of one of her admirers. This he did, and when his wife was on the point of yielding, revealed the trick. Furious at his distrust, she left him for the suitor he had impersonated. Since that time he has been urging travelers to make the test, seeking consolation in the numbers whose draft of wine is spilled by the magic cup.

La Fontaine prefaces his version with a 78-line prologue in praise of cuckoldry, a dazzling virtuoso's creation, reminiscent of the *Paradossi*, such as those of Landi, but apparently based on a few lines from Rabelais's *Tiers Livre*, in the course of which he pushes to its ultimate extreme the *morale aristocratique* he had made a basic element of "Joconde." A similar prologue, addressed to the reader, begins Canto XLIII of the *Furioso*, but its theme is the curse of avarice, of which the husband in the story is a victim, since his wife yields at the promise of money and jewels. La Fontaine's Damon suffers only because he succumbs to the *morale bourgeoise*, which brings about his betrayal through suspicion.

This theme pervades "La Coupe enchantée." No longer is the poet content with mild statements such as the following concerning Joconde's inaction:

> Et mon avis est qu'il fit bien;
> Le moins de bruit que l'on peut faire
> En telle affaire
> Est le plus sûr de la moitié.

The lengthy prologue presents with almost savage irony what La Fontaine calls *ma thèse:* "Cocuage est un bien." There are numerous resemblances between this remarkable passage and Chrysalde's speech in *L'Ecole des femmes* (IV, 8). We find in both the suggestion that the jealous husband is ridiculous because he conceives of honor only in these terms, that to be cuckolded should be thought of as an "accident," a trick of fate, and that in short, as Chrysalde puts it,

> le cocuage
> Sous des traits moins affreux aisément s'envisage.

But Molière's character, as one would expect, advises moderation. As much to be deplored as Arnolphe's intransigence is the complaisance of

> ces gens un peu trop débonnaires
> Qui tirent vanité de ces sortes d'affaires.

La Fontaine, in unequivocally associating himself with this one of the two *extrémités* against which Chrysalde cautions, seems to take a more uncompromising stand against bourgeois morality than even Molière.

His interventions are now no longer merely ironic asides; he makes it clear that he has a thesis and on occasion leaves his story to point the moral at some length, carefully indicating the juncture at which he picks up the narrative again by some such phrase as *Venons à notre histoire,* or *Vous allez entendre comment.* He preaches directly at the reader, who halfway through the Prologue, like Diderot's anonymous interlocutor, retorts in protest: "Oui, mais l'honneur est une étrange affaire!" provoking the heated rejoinder:

> Qui vous soutient que non? ai-je dit le contraire?
> Et bien! l'honneur! l'honneur! je n'entends que ce mot.

Various additions to the original express skepticism about

marriage, which is one ingredient of the *morale aristocratique*. Unlike his source, the author of "La Jeune Veuve" tells us, for example, that the wife's father had adamantly forsworn marriage. When his mistress died in childbirth, writes La Fontaine, his grief was the more sincere because it was not that of a widower:

> Le pauvre homme en pleurs
> Se plaignit, gémit, soupira,
> Non comme qui perdrait sa femme,
> Tel deuil n'est bien souvent que changement d'habits,
> Mais comme qui perdrait tous ses meilleurs amis.

The subservient narrator reappears in a comment on Damon's resistance to the sorceress' advances when the French poet artfully declares some of the more preposterous phenomena in the *Furioso* to be more believable than a faithful husband:

> Où sont-ils ces maris? Le race en est cessée,
> Et même je ne sais si jamais on en vit.
> L'histoire en cet endroit est, selon ma pensée,
> Un peu sujette à contredit.
> L'Hippogriffe n'a rien qui me choque l'esprit,
> Non plus que la Lance enchantée.
> Mais ceci, c'est un point qui d'abord me surprit.

This surprise relegates marital fidelity to the realm of the unknown. At least it has no place in the aristocratic norm. The suggestion is obvious: it is a bourgeois virtue, as the sorceress argues when trying to tempt Damon:

> Je vous croyais plus fin,
> Et ne vous tenais pas homme de mariage.
> Laissez les bons bourgeois se plaire en leur ménage:
> C'est pour eux seuls qu'Hymen fit les plaisirs permis.

But the suggestion falls on deaf ears; only jealousy, through her suggestion that a friend, Eraste, has betrayed him, succeeds in transforming his trust into suspicion.

Such transformations occur on several levels. They may be

intellectual, such as the remarkable *tour de force* of the Prologue, which in skillful steps transforms the abhorrent concept of cuckoldry to a dream of comfort and delight. The process involves the creation, through dialectic, of an illusion, or, rather, the replacement of one illusion, one *songe*, by another:

> Ses songes sont toujours que l'on le fait cocu;
> Pourvu qu'il songe, c'est l'affaire.

Inexorably the author moves from *cocuage n'est point un mal* to *cocuage est un bien,* and, in the final demonstration, transforms his imaginary interlocutor into a complacent and complaisant Menelaus, ready even to believe that gallantry has beautified his wife:

> Elle n'en vaut que mieux, n'en a que plus d'appas.
> Ménélas rencontra des charmes dans Hélène
> Qu'avant d'être à Pâris la belle n'avait pas.

The sorceress' magic philters fail to sway Damon, but through insinuation she creates illusions that seem just as occult. The *songe* she produces by hinting at an affair between Caliste and Eraste is almost hallucinatory. A rapid line suggests the stroke of a wand: "Ce discours porta coup, et fit songer notre homme." The vision at once appears; there is no preparatory verb; instantly the tableau of a faithless Caliste appears before him:

> Une épouse fringante, et jeune, et dans son feu . . .
> Un personnage expert aux choses de l'amour . . .
>   la donzelle
> Montre à demi son sein, sort du lit un bras blanc,
> Se tourne, s'inquiète . . .

the illusion is complete:

>   Damon a dans l'esprit
> Que tout cela s'est fait. . . .
> Sur ce beau fondement le pauvre homme bâtit
>   Maint ombrage et mainte chimère.

Physical metamorphoses follow these intellectual transformations. Damon rubs his wrist with the magic *eau de la métamorphose* and in a trice becomes Eraste and puts his wife to the test. Just as she is about to yield, he becomes himself again, to confound her with still another *métamorphose*.

These transitions take place with a rapidity which also characterizes La Fontaine's narrative technique. He tells the story of Caliste's life, from birth to marriage, with a dazzling combination of verbs of action and descriptive images. To do this 44-line passage justice it would be necessary to quote it entire. We must be content with five remarkable lines in which the poet takes her from infancy to womanhood:

> La fille crût, se fit: on pouvait déjà voir
> > Hausser et baisser son mouchoir.
> Le temps coule: on n'est pas sitôt à la bavette
> Qu'on trotte, qu'on raisonne: on devient grandelette,
> Puis grande tout à fait; et puis le serviteur.

With what skill La Fontaine supports the dry narrative past definites *crût* and *se fit* with the charming concrete and dynamic image of the maiden's breast swelling beneath the modest shield of her neckerchief! The impersonal verbs of the following three lines suggest that Caliste's rapid flowering is a universal truth, thus preserving the *exemplary* nature of her story.

It is evident that La Fontaine played far freer with his model here than in "Joconde": the convent upbringing of Caliste, the imprisonment of the errant wife by the husband, the *armée royale* of cuckolds, each with his military designation, the final reconciliation of Damon and Caliste, all represent changes from the original. He skillfully reverses Ariosto's structure, which placed Rinaldo's refusal to test his wife before the host's narration. Renaud's rejection of the magic goblet effectively ends Damon's campaign and the story itself. La Fontaine agrees with Ariosto that avarice is so potent a force women may be pardoned for yielding to it, but adds the cynical suggestion that money invariably triumphs over love. Caliste is courted more for her money than for her other attributes:

> Sa sagesse, son bien, le bruit de ses beautés,
> Mais le bien plus que tout y fit mettre la presse.

Wealth will always win against mere youth and beauty:

> Soyez beau, bien disant, ayez perruque blonde,
>   N'omettez un seul petit point;
> Un financier viendra qui sur votre moustache
> Enlèvera la belle; et dès le premier jour
>   Il fera présent du panache;
> Vous languirez encore après un an d'amour.

And finally, Caliste's jailer remains adamant only because she has no money with which to bribe him:

> Comme on ne lui laissait argent ni pierrerie
> Le geôlier fut fidèle.

To "La Coupe enchantée" La Fontaine could certainly apply these words of his preface to the *Deuxième Partie* of the *Contes,* published in 1666: "Il retranche, il amplifie, il change les incidents et les circonstances, quelquefois le principal événement et la suite; enfin, ce n'est plus la même chose, c'est proprement une nouvelle nouvelle." Yet this aesthetic independence is typical of Ariosto himself. The story of the magic cup provided our *conteur* with a vehicle for the expression of his own ideas on woman, marriage, and man's will to self-delusion.

3. "LE PETIT CHIEN QUI SECOUE DE L'ARGENT ET DES PIERRERIES"

After his night's repose Rinaldo continues on his journey down the Po, and as he rests, the boatman tells him still another story, running through 72 *ottavi* (XLIII, 72–143), which demonstrates the power of gold over virtue. The tale of the magic dog might have been subtitled "La Précaution inutile," since this time the jealous husband, called away on a mission to Rome, showers his wife with riches precisely in order to forestall the inevitable effect of lovers' bribes. As we might expect, there is a suitor, the penniless Adonio, who is befriended by the fairy Manto (the scene is in Mantua) after having saved her from being killed by a peasant as she lay helpless in the form of a snake. Manto promises Adonio to help him win the beautiful but virtuous Argia. To this end, she transforms him into a pilgrim and herself into a white dog, which not only does remarkable tricks but with one shake can produce gold coins and jewels. Argia yields to the pilgrim in exchange for his dog. When the husband, Anselmo, returns, an astrologer tells him of Argia's fall from virtue, and he dispatches a servant to kill her. The magic dog makes her disappear in the nick of time. When Anselmo goes to the spot, he finds a magnificent palace, at the door of which an ugly Moor bids him enter. All this will be his, says the Moor, if . . .

> E gli fa la medesima richiesta
> Ch'avea già Adonio alla sua moglie fatta.
> [139]

Out of cupidity Anselmo agrees to this monstrous proposal, whereupon Argia appears and demands that he grant her pardon, since his guilt is equal to hers. As in the other two *contes*, reconciliation results, "E sempre poi fu l'uno all'altro caro."

"Le Petit Chien" is a more complex tale than "La Coupe enchantée," and here La Fontaine follows his model even more closely than in *Joconde*. Interventions are reduced to a minimum. To the power of *avarizia*, which inspired in Ariosto four eloquent stanzas, La Fontaine devotes fifteen introductory lines, in the course of which he somewhat attenuates the skepticism which had run so strongly through "La Coupe enchantée." Whereas in the latter he had asked,

> Et quelle affaire ne fait point
> Ce bienheureux métal, l'argent, maître du monde?

in "Le Petit Chien" he makes a distinction:

> La clef du coffre-fort et des coeurs, c'est la même.
> Que si ce n'est celle des coeurs,
> C'est du moins celle des faveurs.

In this indulgent tone, so different from that of "La Coupe
enchantée," he comments gently on the love affair between
Argie and Atis (the Adonio of Ariosto):

> Chacun s'en aperçut; car d'enfermer sous l'ombre
>   Une telle aise, le moyen?
>   Jeunes gens font-ils jamais rien
>   Que le plus aveugle ne voie?

We saw earlier that Ariosto, in mingling realism and fantasy, frequently dwelt on the realistic qualities of strange or
magical phenomena. Ariosto explained Adonio's intercession
in favor of the snake by the odd coincidence that he was a
descendant of Cadmus, whose arms he bore. La Fontaine
rounds out this explanation by adding that Cadmus became
a serpent in his old age.[14] But then he "naturalizes" the
hero's action by an aside reminiscent of the *Fables*:

> Il est à remarquer que notre paladin
> N'avait pas cette horreur commune au genre humain
> Contre la gent reptile et toute son espèce.

He gives the magic dog a name, Favori, and at the point in
the story where it must warn Argie of her danger, he inter-
venes to address the reader:

> Si vous me demandez comme un chien avertit,
>   Je crois que par la jupe il tire;
>   Il se plaint, il jappe, il soupire,
> Il en veut à chacun: pour peu qu'on ait d'esprit,
>   On entend bien ce qu'il veut dire.

After this brief description of a real dog warning his mistress,
the magical tale begins again with the phrase, *Favori fit bien
plus . . .*

Although the author makes his presence felt in this way,
critical interventions are conspicuously lacking in "Le Petit
Chien," with the exception of the 20-line conclusion. Once
more we hear the voice of an imaginary critic:

---

[14] Ovid, *Metamorphoses,* IV, 563–603.

"Que devint le palais?" dira quelque critique.
—Le palais? que m'importe? il devint ce qu'il put.
A moi ces questions! suis-je homme qui se pique
D'être si régulier? Le palais disparut.

Although Ariosto does not tell what became of the magic palace, such disappearances are frequent elsewhere in the *Furioso*.[15] The dialogue continues, with the poet bursting out, "Censeur, tu m'importunes," but finally answering his critic's further questions concerning the dog and the lover by explaining that Atis used the magic animal in other conquests.

This is a skillful way of tying up Ariosto's loose ends while still maintaining the impression of freedom from any superimposed pattern of aesthetic logic; in differing from his predecessor, La Fontaine follows him in spirit. The same tendency to complete his source appears in his treatment of the metamorphoses in which this tale is so rich. Where Ariosto tells us simply that Argia disappeared when threatened with death, La Fontaine has the fairy envelop her in a cloud. The compliant judge is transformed into a page boy, retaining only his beard! The final scene when Argie turns the tables on Anselme becomes a kind of magic show, as at her command the Moor changes into the dog, which dances and sheds jewels in profusion.

Another modification recalls the bucolic scenes in "Joconde." Ariosto's rejected lover simply absents himself seven years. La Fontaine's Atis takes refuge in a *désert*, giving rise to this remarkable evocation of pastoral silence:

Le Silence y faisait sa demeure ordinaire,
    Hors quelque oiseau qu'on entendait,
    Et quelque écho qui répondait.
    Là le bonheur et la misère
Ne se distinguaient point, égaux en dignité
Chez les loups qu'hébergeoit ce lieu peu fréquenté.

But perhaps the most striking feature of "Le Petit Chien" is its dramatic quality. La Fontaine seems to be moving closer to the dramatic form, increasing the amount of dialogue un-

15 On palaces, see *OF*, II, 42; XXII, 17; XXIII, 9; XLIII, 14.

til, of the 525 lines in the poem, 222 are in direct quotation.
There are, in addition, several lines in *style indirect libre*,
such as the following:

> Il devait demeurer dans Rome
> Six mois, et plus encor; que savait-il combien?
> Tant d'honneur pouvait nuire au conjugal lien:
> Longue ambassade et long voyage
> Aboutissent à cocuage.

In an earlier version of "La Coupe enchantée" La Fontaine
had included a long passage of dialogue in dramatic form, a
kind of play within the play, which he later deleted.[16] He
now inserts a similar passage, precisely at the point where
the Moor makes his indecent proposal to Anselme:

LE MORE: Tu connais l'échanson du monarque des dieux?

ANSELME: Ganymède?

LE MORE: Celui-là même.
       Prends que je sois Jupin.

The dramatic form brings the speakers into the foreground,
yet the poet "veils" the scabrous by having them make
oblique allusions and hesitant replies.

Further dramatic expansion appears in Atis' lyric monologue, in which he resolves to return to his love, beginning

> Adieu, ruisseaux, ombrages frais,
> Chants amoureux de Philomèle . . .

and in the prominence La Fontaine gives to the role of the
nurse who persuades Argie to accept Atis' offer. She becomes
the typical go-between of Roman comedy, expostulating at
length with her reluctant mistress. Her arguments repeat and
expand those of the Prologue to "La Coupe enchantée." Here,
as in Molière, it is the maidservant who bluntly asserts
woman's right to love freely:

> Pour qui ménagez-vous les trésors de l'amour?
> Pour celui qui, je crois, ne s'en servira guère.

[16] *FCN*, pp. 831–832.

In her hour of triumph over the *barbon* Anselme, Argie exclaims:

> Ne le soyez donc point; plus on veut nous contraindre,
> Moins on doit s'assurer de nous.

These lines echo those of Léonor's servant Lisette, in *L'Ecole des maris:*

> Et si par un mari je me voyais contrainte,
> J'aurais fort grande pente à confirmer sa crainte.
>   [I, 2]

Thus "Le Petit Chien" ends, as had the other two tales, on a note of reconciliation, each partner agreeing to keep his share of the bargain, the wife to remain faithful and the husband to resist suspicion henceforth. Ariosto's Anselmo was more blameworthy than his spouse, but the more skeptical La Fontaine tends towards Montaigne's conclusion: "Le fourgon se moque de la poêle."

4. THE IMPLICATIONS OF AFFINITY

The three novella La Fontaine adapted from Ariosto exhausted the meager supply. Perhaps it was for this reason that he turned to Boccaccio, of whom he wrote,

> ce divin esprit
> Plus que pas un me donne de pratique.

Many of Boccaccio's straightforward, realistic stories of sensual man and woman illustrate a perpetual war of the sexes in which the weapons of both sides are invariably deceit and subterfuge, in which native cunning triumphs. To this reader at least La Fontaine's versions of them are far less rewarding than those imitated from Ariosto. Perhaps this is because, in adapting Boccaccio, La Fontaine almost invariably follows his model closely without those flights of fancy and changes of tone that characterize his versions of Ariosto.

Indeed *variété c'est ma devise* scarcely seems applicable to La Fontaine's Boccaccian tales. One reason for this, at least on the formal level, is immediately evident. All but two of the

eighteen *contes* from Boccaccio are in decasyllabics. Now La
Fontaine the fable writer is by common consent a master of
prosody, but his decasyllabic has brought him no glory.
Pierre Clarac simply dismisses it as *le décasyllabe de Maître
Clément*.[17] Valéry supported his low opinion of the *Contes*
in general by quoting from "Belphégor" a single decasyllabic
which is certainly banal enough taken out of context.[18]
While I believe that, despite these strictures, La Fontaine's
decasyllabic far surpasses Marot's, it is true that his genius
as a prosodist shines clearest in *vers libres*. Yet he deliberately chose the ten-syllable line for the broad and earthy
tales from Marguerite de Navarre, Rabelais, and *Les Cent
Nouvelles nouvelles*, as well as Boccaccio, suggesting, in the
"Avertissement" to the *Première Partie*, that he considered
it the most appropriate line for the subject matter.[19] Of the
sixty-seven *contes*, all but eighteen are in this form. Of these,
eleven *contes* are in *vers libres*, three imitated from Ariosto
and two from Boccaccio, one of which, "La Fiancée du roi
de Garbe," departs radically from its model. The other six
are either without clearly identifiable sources or extremely
free adaptations.

La Fontaine's *contes* from Ariosto are all in *vers libres*,
which he seems to have decided was the form that would
best convey the particular quality of the author of the
Furioso. Moreover, he used it in all the *contes* in which, like
the Italian poet he was tempted to digress, to blend fantasy
and reality, to intrude his own personality by conjecture, allu-
sion, and change of pace. One of these is "Les Oies de frère
Philippe," imitated from Boccaccio. We recall Ariosto's preface to the story of Giocondo, with its declaration of good will
toward womankind. A similar, if less impassioned denial of
misogyny is the long preamble in which La Fontaine pays

[17] P. Clarac, *La Fontaine* (Paris: Boivin, 1950), p. 60.
[18] Paul Valéry, *Variétés*, in *Oeuvres* (Ed. de la Pléiade; Paris:
Gallimard, 1957), p. 85. For a fuller rebuttal of Valéry, see my
article "The Esthetics of Negligence: La Fontaine's *Contes*," in
L'Espirit Créateur, Winter, 1964.
[19] *FCN*, p. 343.

homage to women, denying that he believes them to be liberal with their favors:

> Le monde ne vous connaît guères,
> S'il croit que les faveurs sont chez vous familières.

Like Ariosto he pleads his devotion to the fair sex, but adds a
melancholy personal note in conclusion:

> J'ai servi des beautés de toutes les façons;
> Qu'ai-je gagné? Très peu de chose.

Another *conte* from Boccaccio takes on an Ariostian quality
throughout. This is "La Fiancée du roi de Garbe," of which
La Fontaine makes an adventure story. Of course a myriad
of sources could have suggested many of the details we find
in it, but read in the context of the affinity we have been discussing, the story seems full of the flavor of Ariosto.

It tells how Alaciel, affianced to the king of Garbo, has
eight lovers before finally arriving in his kingdom. After she
sets sail with her first lover, Hispal, her ship is attacked by
pirates led by a ferocious giant, Grifonio, whose name recalls
that of Orlando's son Grifone, and whom Hispal, exactly like
the heroes of the *Furioso*, slices in two. Like Ruggiero, Hispal
swims from reef to reef until he reaches shore, and shortly
thereafter, like Medoro, celebrates his conquest of his mistress by inscribing his triumph on the surrounding trees. Occasionally in the *Furioso* wandering knights discover sleeping
beauties in woodland glades. When a paladin comes upon
Alaciel in such a pose, La Fontaine describes the scene with
Ariostian skepticism about the heroines of romance:

> Un jour, entre autres, que la belle
> Dans un bois dormait à l'écart,
> Il s'y rencontra par hasard
> Un chevalier errant, grand chercheur d'aventures,
> De ces sortes de gens que sur des palefrois
> Les belles suivaient autrefois,
> Et passaient pour chastes et pures.

Certainly both in tone and in form, this *conte* seems clearly to reflect the affinity between the two poets. Philip Wadsworth, in a brilliant analysis, finds "La Fiancée du roi de Garbe" "profoundly original, a triumph of fancy, of cynicism, of irony."[20] I would add that these qualities set it in the tradition of Ariosto.

The discovery of affinities, of a place in a tradition, is of course no proof of excellence. Yet the most cursory examination of any one of them demonstrates the error of such judgments as Clarac's brusque characterization of the *Contes* as "monotones polissonneries." One must, I believe, consider their eroticism as an aesthetic factor which La Fontaine dealt with as an artist. As to their poetry, could Valéry, who said he could not bear their *son rustique et faux*, their *vers d'une facilité répugnante*, have really read them?[21] Could he have known "Joconde," with its mastery of *vers libres*?

In discussing the two authors I have tried to show that their relationship went beyond that of adapter and source, that in imitating Ariosto La Fontaine most resembles him in his aesthetic independence. If this be granted, we may even surmise that his use of *vers libres* for Ariosto's tales and others of different inspiration was his way of achieving metrically the freedom of the Italian poet, whose structural and contextual liberty he could not enjoy. At the very least, we may finally assert that the spirit of Ariosto helps to explain why, in the *Contes* as well as in the *Fables*, we have a work of lasting variety and genius.

[20] *Young La Fontaine*, pp. 163–166.

[21] Clarac, *op. cit.*, p. 62; Valéry, *loc. cit.* Unfortunately a recent work on La Fontaine, Margaret Guiton's *La Fontaine, Poet and Counterpoet* (New Brunswick, N.J.: Rutgers University Press, 1961), while admirable on the *Fables*, dismisses the *Contes* in three brief paragraphs as "suggestive," "indecent," and written in an "archly pseudoarchaic manner" (pp. 17–18).

L'ART POETIQUE: "LONG-TEMPS PLAIRE, ET JAMAIS NE LASSER"

By Nathan Edelman

For Boileau, the only possibilities open to the poet are signal success or utter failure. There is no in-between, no graded scale or measurable percentage of poetic accomplishment:

> Il n'est point de degrez du mediocre au pire.
> Qui dit froid Ecrivain dit detestable Auteur.[1]

A poem is either a joy, or a scandal, and no bickering over details of literary doctrine will settle the matter, or can ever be much to the point.

It is the poet-satirist that animates the critic in Boileau. To portray him as a drill master, an advocate of the three R's—Rules, Regimentation, Regularity—would be grossly to disfigure him; as we have been shown often enough by now, he is not a bureaucrat or technocrat of literature. If his style waxes imperative, to the point of sounding dogmatic to us at times, this comes from the certitude of a strong personal faith in his experience of beauty and art, but not out of any concern with official regulations. It is revealing that he can never be discovered to inveigh against his numerous victims for infractions of formal, technical rules.[2] But it would be equally

---

[1] L'Art poétique, IV, 32–33. All quotations follow the spelling and punctuation of the Charles-H. Boudhors edition of Boileau's Oeuvres complètes (7 vols., unnumbered; Paris: Les Belles Lettres, 1934–1943).

[2] As we are aptly reminded by E. B. O. Borgerhoff, The Freedom of French Classicism (Princeton: Princeton University Press, 1950), p. 212.

misleading to represent him, more flatteringly, as a high theorist intent on unraveling the nature of poetry by a searching
process of analysis, and equipped to pursue such a philo-
sophic inquiry, up to the last answerable question. He had
no disposition for such a task. His aptitude for understanding
was that of a poet, and his account of poetry itself was chiefly
a poetic figuration of the subject, even or especially in the
long, elaborate *Art poétique*.

It reads like a representation or enactment of what happens between an author and his reader. It is not a portrait
of the poet alone, held statically under focus. Boileau would
have been at a loss to comprehend poetry as expression sufficient to itself, or as the poet's private concern. He sees it as
quite manifestly and essentially a phenomenon of direct and
felicitous communication. He requires, as he puts it in one of
his most beautiful lines, that the poet, within us, leave of his
work a long remembrance—that all he utters "de son ouvrage
en nous laisse un long souvenir" (III, 158). Repeatedly he
addresses to the poet a question or challenge by which he
binds the artist to his reader as to an indispensable recipient
and companion in "l'acte des Muses." Would you be cherished, he asks at the outset, "Voulez-vous du public mériter
les amours" (I, 69)? Would you, he asks again, endear the
opulent creations of your imagination to your readers?—
"Voulez-vous faire aimer vos riches fictions" (IV, 86)? Would
you offer such tragedies as will cast a lasting spell on all of
Paris?

> Voulez-vous sur la scene étaler des ouvrages,
> Où tout Paris en foule apporte ses suffrages,
> Et qui toûjours plus beaux, plus ils sont regardez,
> Soient au bout de vingt ans encor redemandez?
>   [III, 11–14]

"Voulez-vous," he urges, "long-temps plaire (long attract and
captivate), et jamais ne lasser (never breed lassitude)" (III,
245)?

These are the two requirements, which are but one, and
which he illustrates with a multitude of descriptions, scenes,
skits, and thumbnail sketches, all dwelling on the one picture

of delight and lassitude, predominantly a picture of motion along a course. Among the smaller genres, for example, the eclogue, which gathers its engaging though humble lore and its quality of style from the rustic scene, has its own path to find, clear of both platitude and pomposity, and "Entre ces deux exeès la route est difficile," requiring "et la force et la grace" of a Theocritus or a Virgil (II, 1–37). The ode, "Elevant jusqu'au Ciel son vol ambitieux," knows no constraint: "Son stile impetueux souvent marche au hazard," artfully showing "un beau desordre"—this is no expedition for those timorous rhymesters whose

> esprit phlegmatique
> Garde dans ses fureurs un ordre didactique.
> [II, 58–81]

Along the road of tragedy, one of the major genres, where Boileau expects that "la passion émue (aroused)/Aille chercher le coeur," he requires that the exposition without strain open and clear the way at once ("applanisse l'entrée"), and that all along the poet move swiftly from marvel to marvel:

> Il faut . . .
> Qu'il coure dans ses vers de merveille en merveille.
> [III, 151–156]

For "Ainsi la Tragedie agit, marche, et s'explique" (unfolds) (III, 159). Epic poetry, in its vast account of a long enterprise, sustains its narration with more grandeur still. The poet, without keeping to an "ordre methodique," but without straying over lengthy byways ("Il ne s'égare point en de trop longs détours"), moves on and drives forward: "tout marche et se suit." Each verse, each word, speeds on to the final outcome—"court à l'évenement" (III, 160–334).

This metaphoric language becomes indispensable to Boileau, at almost every turn of *L'Art poétique*. Even the lowly "vaudeville," that malicious offspring of satire, turns into a jolly tale bearer, busily on the move; led on by the melody to which it is sung ("conduit par le chant"), this poem scurries from mouth to mouth, and grows larger as it goes—"Passe de bouche en bouche, et s'accroist en marchant" (II, 181–184). We see one poem after another "marcher," "passer," "courir," or even fly upon its course, now in a swift, overpowering onrush and now like

> un ruisseau, qui sur la molle arene
> Dans un pré plein de fleurs lentement se promene.
> [I, 166–167]

Whatever the course, or the apparent ease of the traveler, "la route est difficile." It is something of a miracle road on which journeying and arriving are synchronized into one act. The perfection to be reached is *la raison*—but *raison* as Boileau understood it: not ratiocination but, in Descartes's language, a "puissance," a swift, intuitive power of *l'esprit*. Instantaneous, like sensation, it bears another familiar name: *le bon sens*, the *good* sense, the sense that is right and infallible. Transferred to the aesthetic realm, for Boileau *raison* —*bon sens* remains a species of sensitive energy, a prompt and live sense of rightness. That is the desired goal, yet it is also the necessary guide. In making its discoveries *raison* exercises upon itself its own critical power of judgment and, therefore, of control. Not that Boileau can ever arrive at a systematic statement of these operations of *raison*. With an ambiguity that is perhaps unavoidable and even necessary in these matters, he offered this striking mixed metaphor:

> Tout doit tendre au Bon sens: mais pour y parvenir
> Le chemin est glissant et penible à tenir.
> Pour peu qu'on s'en écarte, aussi-tost l'on se noye.
> La Raison, pour marcher, n'a souvent qu'une voye.
> [I, 45–48]

There is but one road. It leads to *le bon sens;* all must tend toward that goal. Yet this *bon sens* is at the same time the *raison* that goes forward, along the very road of which it is the fixed end. This concurrence of discovery and searching is suggested by the ambiguity of the word *sens* itself, which can mean direction as well as insight: most authors, says Boileau, eager to be original and

emportez d'une fougue insensée,
Toujours loin du droit sens vont chercher leur pensée,
[I, 39–42]

which suggests both that they miss the right sense and that they stray from the right direction.[3]

The road not only represents an uncommon course, on which discovering and searching are telescoped; it also merges the reader's course with that of the poet. Pictures of felicitously flowing, speeding, or soaring motions are pictures of the reader's as well as of the poet's sustained and elated act of discovery. The poet and the reader are endowed with the same *raison–bon sens*, an essential attribute of all human beings. Boileau, it is true, never states this Cartesian assumption in so many words, and is even accused at times of setting up his own taste as a norm of *raison;* but an assumption of universality would still be implicit in his very self-assurance. If there is an infallible human *bon sens* in both, the reader and the poet cannot but be similarly affected by the finished poem.

And yet, despite the vaunted universality of *raison,* Boileau is forever being scandalized by the number of frigid and insipid *sots* that he finds in Paris and beyond. Are they devoid of *raison* and unhuman? Or is it that our native *raison* in them remains dormant, or obstructed? However that may be, they are the bane of Boileau's existence, for the apathy, boredom, and lassitude that they breed. The ineptitude and lethargy of their soul lie heavy on a reader's spirit, and oppress him beyond endurance; it is on such fiascos of poetry that Boileau, a satirist at heart, dwells with special relish and verve.

He opens *L'Art poétique* by sketching at once images of futile and frustrated motion, which will illuminate what he means later by *raison–bon sens.* In vain does an author propose to reach the peak of Mount Parnassus if he is not a born

[3] For a more detailed analysis of these terms and, in general, for the most comprehensive and searching discussion of Boileau's literary doctrine, see Jules Brody, *Boileau and Longinus* (Geneva: E. Droz, 1958). For a capital survey of French classical doctrine in its various stages and tendencies, see Borgerhoff, *op. cit.*

poet. "Dans son génie étroit" (within his narrow endow-
ments), he remains a captive, "il est toujours captif." Winged
Pegasus restively balks at carrying such a rider. He is condemned to immobility, or to aimless, pointless agitation, like
those who burning with a reckless zeal sally forth on "la
carriere épineuse" and fruitlessly, upon verses, labor and
waste away; or like that would-be epic poet (Saint-Amant)
who impudently goes and sings the triumphant Exodus of
the Hebrews and, chasing across the desert after Moses, in
his rush drowns himself in the sea, along with Pharaoh—
"court avec Pharaon se noyer dans les mers"; or like that
windbag (Scudéry) who, should he come upon a palace,
needs must take me through the whole estate and show me
around the whole edifice—to reach the end, I skip twenty
leaves of the book, and even then "je me sauve à peine au
travers du jardin."

Paralysis, sluggishness, or debility are common afflictions
of a motionless spirit, whose "vers plats et grossiers" always
hug the ground "et rampent tristement" (II, 19–20). In epic
poetry, if the author does not, like Virgil, readily and steadily
take hold of us with a force "qui surprend, frappe, saisit, attache," then

> le vers tombe en langueur,
> La Poësie est morte, ou rampe sans vigueur
> [III, 160–192]

—his dragging verse is without savor, without warmth, without life. Frigidity especially, with the hardness of ice, con-
geals all energies, as in those verses of Motin, a weary poet
chilled to the bone, who leaves us numbed with cold—"ces
vers où Motin se morfond et nous glace" (IV, 40). The bom-
bast of "les grands mots," those big, bloated words, induces
another variety of stiffness, which makes an author stumble
and grotesquely take a hard fall, as in the case of Ronsard,
"ce Poëte trébuché de si haut" (I, 124–129); the most vivid
example, more acceptable to modern readers partial to Ronsard, is a caricature, sketched outside L'Art poétique, of Jean
Chapelain's pretentious, gawky verses, hoisted upon a pair of
pompous big words as on a pair of stilts:

> ces vers et sans force et sans graces,
> Montez sur deux grands mots, comme sur deux échasses.
> [*Satire IV*, 97–98]

Frozen or stilted verse will not transport us far. But neither will mere agitation. Drowning (or shipwreck at times), seen from a comic angle as a disaster which swiftly brings to nought, with ludicrous finality, a reckless expenditure of energy, is an image which the satirist Boileau particularly fancies. The drowning poet has failed lamentably to steer his course unerringly among *excès—excès*, it is to be noted, are not just faults of overabundance but, more generally and fundamentally, vices of deviation from *le droit sens*.[4] For the live and the quick, there is often but one road to vital discovery and, "Pour peu qu'on s'en écarte, aussi-tost l'on se noye." But there are ever so many other ways of straying and coming to a bad end. One author, who dreads the prospect of just creeping along on the ground, goes to the other extreme and gets himself lost in the clouds—"il se perd dans la nuë" (I, 68), or drowns, as it were, in the sky. Another, like Scudéry, becomes hopelessly submerged in his own subject. Some, priding themselves on their breakneck speed, remind Boileau of

> un torrent débordé qui d'un cours orageux
> Roule plein de gravier sur un terrain fangeux.
> [I, 167–168]

Rashly the uncultivated poet, who on random occasions has been kindled by a bright natural flame, would undertake a resounding full-length epic poem:

> Sa Muse déreglée, en ses vers vagabonds
> Ne s'éleve jamais que par sauts et par bonds.
> [III, 317–320]

L'Art poétique abounds in such vignettes. In lively succession every *excès* is graphically represented, making us perpetually conscious of an incongruous contrast between this vain agita-

---

[4] Cf. Brody, *op. cit.*, p. 66.

tion, or inertia, and the motion that irresistibly carries one away and constantly reminding us that immobility and bewilderment, failures in poetic communication, leave the reader himself inert or bewildered. His plight is abundantly, richly illustrated. For example, the intolerable boredom generated by Scudéry's survey of the palace exterior and interior is farcically pictured by the motion of two forces pulling in different directions: a slow, interminable drag, to which the entrapped reader's desperate, automatic reaction is sudden and swift escape. Similarly, when a vexed rhymester, hard pressed for inspiration, throws down the flute and oboe natural to bucolic poetry and, with boorish zest, in the midst of his eclogue blows on a blaring trumpet,

> De peur de l'écoûter, Pan fuit dans les roseaux,
> Et les Nymphes d'effroi se cachent sous les eaux.
> [II, 15–16]

Comic pictures of the poet's victims in flight or in panic flash across the scene.

The problem for the victim is to break away in time, for there are lethal verses that deaden a reader's spirit before he can make good his escape, as in the works of those authors, "nez pour nous ennuyer," who drone on and on (I, 71–74), or in the cold rhetorical disputations that chill a tragedy, where all should be "passion" (III, 21–24). Sleep overtakes the reader. Perhaps that is another way out. As he takes the plunge, dropping irresistibly into oblivious slumber, all the meaningless babble and commotion suddenly comes to a dead stop for him, as for the author himself in drowning. The torpor of slumber, however, must be inoculated; there must be some measure of contact between author and victim. The dreariest picture of all is the spectacle of dead books left utterly to themselves—total inertness, within and without—vacuity which creates a spreading vacuum all around itself. There is no public left. The reader is conspicuous by his absence and complete obliteration. There is only an imperceptible stir going on in a bookseller's dark back room, where those books, stored up in piles, "Combattent tristement les vers et la poussière" (III, 331–332). In a way they are themselves steeped in absolute slumber, as they quietly rot away in obscurity, growing moldy around the edges.

This imagery of motion, sustained or arrested, is the basic language of *L'Art poétique,* reinforced by other images pertaining especially to sound and taste, and most notably to light and darkness. For example:

> Il est certains Esprits, dont les sombres pensées
> Sont d'un nuage épais toujours embarrassées.
> Le jour de la raison ne le sçauroit percer.
>
> [I, 147–149]

The captivity of a mind caught in its own clutter of thoughts is represented here by the thickness and darkness of a cloud, where the broad daylight of *raison* will not break through. Quickening illumination here would itself be a form of animation. Everything tells the story of movement and immobility. One of Boileau's most characteristic habits of style is the continual use of *aller* and other verbs of motion as auxiliary verbs. This is not a mere formality of usage. It becomes necessary that aroused passion "*aille* chercher," that it *go* and seek out the heart; Saint-Amant does not just sing the Exodus but "*s'en va . . .* chanter—*goes off* and sings," and does not just drown but "*court . . .* se noyer—*runs* and drowns himself" (I, 23–27); Ronsard does not merely hum his Gothic idyls but "*vient* encor fredonner—still *comes* humming along" (II, 21–22); hasty epic poets *go* and shout all their power away in their first lines (III, 270–272); constantly *aller, venir, courir* seem to absorb the action of other verbs, as if it were the latter that had come to serve an auxiliary function, to particularize numerous instances of motion intensively sustained or grotesquely abortive.

There is, to be sure, nothing so common in literature as the image of motion, of which various components could have reached Boileau from countless sources. But the composite is distinctively his own. For example, a very likely source, in Boileau's library, may have been Descartes, in whose works the image of the philosopher as a traveler, now pressing forward and now groping, is one of the dominant stylistic traits;[5] but it does not have this touch of satire, this dash of comedy and farce, and lays no stress on the merger of the reader's course with the author's. Boileau's own works—his *Satires* and *Epîtres* in particular—were an important training ground for *L'Art poétique* in this respect; there he had already set authors and readers on their straight or erratic courses. In none of these much briefer poems, however, had Boileau achieved the elaboration and saturation of imagery that became possible in the sizable *Art poétique*—except perhaps in the ninth *Satire,* a poem of 322 lines which offers in dense concentration pictures of the road, of *marcher* and *courir,* of forceful energy and rash ardor, of tripping, falling, crawling, and drowning, of readers asleep and of books slumbering under thick layers of dust, of frozen mind and of petrified inspiration, of flying and of molten wings.

That in embryo was *L'Art poétique*. All too often we read and interpret the latter purely as a didactic work. Undeniably, it is strewn with instructions to the would-be poet. But one of these, not sufficiently publicized, is the urgent rule to forget about rules, when necessary: the admonition to the poet that he clear his "esprit tremblant" of "scrupules" and "doutes ridicules" and learn (still in the language of the road),

> par quel transport heureux,
> Quelquefois dans sa course un esprit vigoureux
> Trop resserré par l'art, sort des règles prescrites,
> Et de l'Art mesme apprend à franchir leurs limites.
> [IV, 77–80]

Joining example to precept, Boileau here disregards, in the last line, the capital rule of the caesura, as he does elsewhere, and teaches on the spot a lesson in the free creation of rhythm attuned to the subject. His so-called Rules are misnamed. They do not constitute a body of decrees but, interspersed among images of the poet and reader on the move

---

[5] See, by the present author, "The Mixed Metaphor in Descartes," *Romanic Review,* XLI (1950), 167–178.

and couched at times in the very language of that imagery, they complement and reinforce with psychological remarks the metaphoric statement of a poetic strategy.

They are drawn up according to a rather persistent pattern of formulation, which Horace no doubt suggested but did not develop with so much emphasis. The Roman poet, for example, does not confine himself to prohibiting the showing of horrible events on the stage; he suggests, as an explanation, that such repellent spectacles create disbelief. So does Boileau: Never show, he says, anything unbelievable on the stage. That is the famous rule of *vraisemblance,* stated in the imperative. It is followed immediately, in the expository mood of the indicative, by a brief psychological elucidation or justification: an absurd marvel, he says, is for me "sans appas"; "L'esprit n'est point ému de ce qu'il ne croit pas" (III, 50). Time and again, with a shift from the imperative to the indicative, Boileau translates a rule into an observation on psychological action, stimulation, and effect. In the imperative: Discard unnecessary details. In the indicative: What is superfluously uttered is "fade et rebutant," and the mind, being cloyed, throws it up instantly—"L'esprit rassasié le rejette à l'instant" (I, 62). In recommending purity and clarity of language, he explains that if comprehension comes slowly and laboriously, "Mon esprit aussi-tost commence à se détendre," and

> prompt à se détacher,
> Ne suit point un Auteur qu'il faut toûjours chercher.
> [I, 145–146]

In requiring that the end, in a tragedy, without labor bring "le trouble toûjours croissant" to a resolution, he explains that "L'esprit ne se sent point plus vivement frappé" as when a final revelation gives everything a changed and unforeseen meaning (III, 55–60).

Boileau goes on and on in this fashion. We have grown accustomed to isolating and underscoring the imperative and hortatory in his rules, but to him a rule is essentially a commentary on what happens in *l'esprit.* A term which comes to dominate these "rule" passages, *esprit*, used more often there than *raison*, is not always easily distinguishable from the latter, but can be understood in a more general or fluctuating sense to designate the natural endowment of spirit and mind, which includes not only *raison* but other mental powers. *Esprit* is that inner world which Boileau visualizes as constantly threatened with chaos, inertness, or complete vacuity. The life of the mind, for him, hangs on its intense wakefulness, attentiveness, and concentration. This is an obsession, with him, and that is why the great epic poem, as we saw, is the one which "surprend, frappe, saisit, attache," or why even in the eclogue, for example, its sweetness must caress, stimulate, and rouse us—"Il faut que sa douceur flatte, chatoüille, éveille" (II, 9).

If these be rules, they certainly are not for all and sundry to follow. Boileau may well enjoin upon the tragic poet to warm and rouse the heart and to leave *l'esprit ému* and *frappé*. *Le secret*, he can only say, is at once (*d'abord*) *de plaire et de toucher*. With astonishing strokes unceasingly the poet must waken us—"Que de traits surprenans sans cesse il nous réveille" (III, 155). That is indeed more of a secret and a challenge than a working rule, like the recommendation that a comic poet have "un esprit profond," to penetrate the secret hearts of men (III, 361–362).

The rule of rules that every image and every proposition in *L'Art poétique* asserts or implies is that a poem communicate a live, overwhelmingly convincing experience of reality. *Coeur* and *esprit*, which Boileau also does not systematically distinguish, are both to be gripped, astounded, enthralled. The Sublime, as Boileau understood it in his reading of Longinus, is "cet extraordinaire et ce merveilleux qui frappe dans le discours" and brings it about that a work "enlève, ravit, transporte"—a sequence which depicts with rising intensity a sudden motion of carrying away. Intellect and emotion are associated; the pleasure of beauty is a pleasure of cognition, or recognition of things as they really are. Let us not expect Boileau to demonstrate; he dramatizes and metaphorizes all this. But he does state more formally, in a 1701 survey of his lifework:

L'Esprit de l'Homme est naturellement plein d'un nombre infini d'idées confuses du Vrai, que souvent il n'entrevoit qu'à demi; et rien ne lui est plus agréable que lors qu'on luy offre quelqu'une de ces idées bien éclaircie, et mise dans un beau jour.[6]

"Rien ne lui est plus agréable." Boileau had also previously stated in the ninth *Epistre*, written shortly after *L'Art poétique:* "Rien n'est beau que le Vrai. Le Vrai seul est aimable" (43). "Le Vrai," he claimed for his own works, "Par tout se montre aux yeux et va saisir le coeur" (54);

>   mon coeur toûjours conduisant mon esprit,
> Ne dit rien aux Lecteurs, qu'à soy-mesme il n'ayt dit.
>   [57–58]

Le faux in poetry, to him, breeds lassitude and revulsion precisely because, in direct contrast to *le Vrai,* it disintegrates this cognitive-emotive grasp; it is

>   toûjours fade, ennuieux, languissant,
> Mais la Nature est vraye, et d'abord [at once] on la sent.
>   [85–86]

As will be elaborated in 1701:

Puis donc qu'une pensée n'est belle qu'en ce qu'elle est vraye; et que l'effet infaillible du Vray, quand il est bien énoncé, c'est de frapper les Hommes; Il s'ensuit que ce qui ne frappe point les Hommes, n'est ni beau, ni vray, ou qu'il est mal énoncé.[7]

Obviously, by *Nature* and *le Vrai* Boileau does not mean a literal rendition of reality, which can be true but platitudinous and soporific. He means a seductive presentation of reality that makes it irresistibly present before us. Beauty is an aesthetic experience of the true.

But Boileau would not have it remain a momentary experience. He must have given thought many a time to a description of the mind included by one of his Jansenist friends,

---

[6] In the 1701 Preface to the *Satires,* Boudhors ed., p. 4.
[7] *Ibid.,* pp. 5–6.

Pierre Nicole, in his *Dissertatio de vera pulchritudine et adumbrata*:

> Naturam humanae mentis si penitus introspicere velis, et interiores in ea delectationum fontes rimari, robur quoddam in ipsa deprehendes, quadam infirmitate conjunctum, vnde magna varietas et inaequalitas oriatur. Robore enim fit ut perpetuam remissionem grevetur; infirmitate contrà, ut perpetuam contentionem pati nequeat. Hinc est quod ipsi nihil diu placet, nihil sui vndique simile.[8]

For Boileau as for Nicole, the mind is such that it delights in the exercise of its power, but a power which by its very nature cannot be lastingly excited and exercised. The wonder of great poetry, for Boileau, is that it defies this law and transcends this routine, intermittent, fitful life of the mind. Analogously to Descartes, whose great and probably impossible ambitious strategy was to connect a series of distinct and necessarily isolated intuitions into a continuous, unbroken line of deduction which might be like one extended, prolonged intuition, Boileau required above all the delight of continuity, wholeness, and oneness in poetic experience. If there are any rules as such in *L'Art poétique*, and if some turn to scattered matters of technique, versification, or formal structure, their purpose is always to keep the continuity and the oneness undisturbed and unjeopardized by the shock of displeasure, disbelief, incomprehension, or any other disruption. The secret, then, is not only "de plaire et de toucher"; the rhyme to *toucher* is *attacher*. Find magical ways, says Boileau, of holding on to me, "Inventez des ressorts qui puissent m'at-

---

[8] The *Dissertatio* was published in *Epigrammatum delectus ex omnibus tum veteribus, tum recentioribus Poëtis accurate decerptus* (Paris: C. Savreux, 1659). The pages are unnumbered; the quotation is to be found at the head of the section entitled "Interior quaedam et magis arcana verborum cum natura consensio." A French translation by L.S.G.L.A.C. (Germain de Lafaille) was published by the same press in 1689; it would seem superior to the one by Richelet published in *Nouveau Recueil des épigrammatistes françois anciens et modernes* (Amsterdam: Wetstein, 1720), II, 169–220.

tacher" (III, 26). Not only is the reader to be drawn in but he is to be "ému" and "frappé" throughout, and the poet must, in his verses, run "de merveille en merveille." In translating Longinus, Boileau inserted characteristic words of his own on the subject of the sublime in the *Iliad,* "qui marche partout d'un pas égal, sans que jamais il s'arrête ni se repose"[9]—a steady advance with never a break or a rest.

The fundamental image, around which all pictures of animation and inertia gravitate, is the ambiguous but (to Boileau) not impossible image of a road on which *raison* intently progresses toward a goal which is *raison* itself. It is on this road that *long-temps plaire, et jamais ne lasser* is crucial. *Long-temps* does not only refer to the distant future, when time and again a poem will be "encore redemandé," although this is a capital test. The prior meaning of *long-temps,* and of *jamais,* has to do with the sustained continuity of a work within the duration and extent of its own course. Paul Valéry, one of the twentieth-century minds who best understood French classicism, put it in terms that Boileau would have appreciated:

Les dieux, gracieusement, nous donnent *pour rien* tel premier vers; mais c'est à nous de façonner le second, qui doit consonner avec l'autre, et ne pas être indigne de son aîné surnaturel. Ce n'est pas trop de toutes les ressources de l'expérience et de l'esprit pour le rendre comparable au vers qui fut un don.[10]

9 See Brody, *op. cit.,* p. 58.
10 "Au sujet d'*Adonis,*" quoted from *Variété,* II (Paris: Gallimard, 1937), p. 81.

THE LITERARY ARTS OF LONGINUS
AND BOILEAU

By Hugh M. Davidson

In 1674 there appeared a volume of *Oeuvres diverses* by the Sieur Despréaux which included, among other things, his *L'Art poétique* and his translation from the Greek of what he called *Le Traité du sublime ou du merveilleux dans le discours*. The presence of these two works in the same volume is a fact in the history of criticism that is not easily interpreted. Boileau's own comment is positive but vague:

> J'ay fait originairement cette Traduction pour m'instruire, plûtost que dans le dessein de la donner au Public. Mais j'ay creu qu'on ne seroit pas fâché de la voir ici à la suite de la Poétique, avec laquelle ce Traité a quelque rapport, et où j'ai mesme inséré plusieurs préceptes qui en sont tirés.[1]

The historical fact requires one, therefore, to face here the problem of the relations, both theoretic and causal, between two elaborated positions. It invites a study of how each critic appears when seen from the point of view of the other, and it tempts one to make a guess as to what happened when these two minds met.

The relationship between the two documents may be fixed circumstantially by identifying common themes and doctrines in them, after one has given a warranted account of how Boileau came to know and to translate Longinus. Or it may

[1] The "Avis au lecteur." Cf. E. Magne, *Bibliographie générale des oeuvres de Nicolas Boileau-Despréaux et de Gilles et Jacques Boileau* (Paris: Giraud-Badin, 1929), p. 217.

be defined in the terms of periodic literary history, where the natural tendency is to trace the consequences for neoclassical values when a new element is added to the atmosphere, an element thought of, perhaps, as vivifying (since Longinus provides relief from arid formalism) or, again, as subversive (since Longinus as a crypto-Romantic furnishes the premises and tone of a new theory). One may also study the internal economies of the two positions *as positions,* as ways of making and supporting statements about literature. It is in the context suggested by this third possibility that the relationship of the two works will be taken up here, and an attempt made to say what marks the one left on the other.

It is convenient to look at two aspects of the critical scheme in each case, *objects studied* and *characteristic principles.*

The generic thing that Longinus is talking about is perfectly clear; it is language or discourse. In the opening lines of *Peri hupsous* he treats as obvious to a person of learning and culture that ἀκρότης καὶ ἐξοχή τις λόγων ἐστὶ τὰ ὕψη.[2] Boileau translates, closely enough for the present point, "Le sublime est en effet ce qui forme l'excellence et la souveraine perfection du Discours."[3] Of the many other indications that language is the underlying topic (not the specific topic, it

---

[2] I, 3. For the Greek text I have used the edition of Henri Lebègue, *Du sublime* (Paris: Les Belles Lettres, 1939). Here I should like to acknowledge my indebtedness to Elder Olson's acute essay on "The Argument of Longinus' *On the Sublime,*" in *Critics and Criticism, Ancient and Modern* (Chicago: University of Chicago Press, 1952), pp. 232–259; in general I have followed his interpretation, although I have expressed it differently. Much of the work on this study was done before I became acquainted with Jules Brody's research, but I am, nevertheless, indebted to his comprehensive *Boileau and Longinus* (Geneva: Droz, 1958); my conclusion as to the unifying principle of Boileau's critical position is similar to his, although the scope of my problem is much narrower than his, and the method I have used is different. My main effort has been to achieve a simultaneous visualization of the two texts, rather than to look forward from Longinus or to look backward from Boileau.

[3] *Oeuvres complètes,* ed. C.-H. Boudhors (Paris: Les Belles Lettres, 1942), IV, 49.

should be added, for that is a particular quality of language),
I shall mention only one: the examples cited. A very distinctive feature of the treatise is the presence of direct quotations.
The quality under study is available in short passages, a fact
that makes it possible for Longinus to bring again and again
into the body of his work the very things he is analyzing and
evaluating. These sample phrases, sentences, or paragraphs
of verse or prose show unmistakably the data with which he
is working.

Now language is not, for Longinus, as it often is in modern
criticisms, primarily the stuff of symbolic products which are
knowable as verbal images or composites of sign and meaning.
Instead, he sees it as an element in a process whereby a
speaker or writer works on an audience or reader. It follows
that discourse cannot be investigated in the Longinian mode
without considering the powers of conception, feeling, and
expression of the author, nor can it be studied without reference to the audience, whose reaction is one important sign
of the presence or absence of literary excellence. Words and
meanings are, therefore, held by Longinus in an interrela-
tionship involving two other factors. At this point it looks as
though Longinus is casting his lot with the rhetoricians, who
rely on principles drawn from the character of the speaker,
from the conditions of effective expression and from the ideas
and feelings of the audience, but he makes a distinction. The
art of the sublime is not the same as the art of oratory: οὐ
γὰρ εἰς πειθὼ τοὺς ἀκροωμένους ἀλλ 'εἰς ἔκστασιν ἄγει τὰ
ὑπερφυᾶ.[4] Sublimity of discourse moves the hearers to transport, ecstasy, not to persuasion. The difference between the
two end experiences starts us on a line of inquiry distinct
from that of Cicero or Quintilian; and, as will be seen, its
consequences are felt throughout the analysis of means that
Longinus offers. By the sublime we are taken out of ourselves
and put into a state of communication with the poet, even of
identification with him: φύσει γάρ πως ὑπὸ τἀληθοῦς
ὕψους ἐπαίρεταί τε ἡμῶν ἡ ψυχὴ, καὶ γαῦρόν τι ἀνάστημα

[4] I, 4.

λαμβάνουσα πληροῦται χαρᾶς καὶ μεγαλαυχίας, ὡς αὐτὴ γεννήσασα ὅπερ ἤκουσεν.[5] Boileau translates,

> Car tout ce qui est véritablement sublime a cela de propre quand on l'écoute, qu'il élève l'âme et lui fait concevoir une plus haute opinion d'elle-même, la remplissant de joie et de je ne sais quel noble orgueil, comme si c'était elle qui eût produit les choses qu'elle vient simplement d'entendre.[6]

If we leave aside, for the moment, further discussion of audience and author and return to the units of discourse treated by Longinus, we note that the principal and most frequently mentioned sources of sublime passages are Homer, Demosthenes, Plato, and Herodotus. Impersonally said, that means that Longinus turns for his examples to poetry, oratory, philosophy, and history; and all or nearly all of the authors mentioned in the treatise use one or another of these four forms of discourse. Longinus is not exclusively concerned with *poetic* discourse. But the real point is that these broad distinctions of kinds of discourse, which may be glimpsed through his quotations are not of technical interest to him. And *a fortiori*, he does not reason from species of these genres: it is not important for him, as it might be for another critic, that Homer is the author of epic poetry, Demosthenes of, say, forensic rhetoric, Plato of dialectical philosophy, or Herodotus of panoramic history. The units of discourse that Longinus is studying may be found, it would seem, in any type of verbal expression; and it is not surprising, therefore, that they turn out to be essentially grammatical: words, phrases, sentences, groups of lines. The longest sample consists of 17 lines of Sappho's so-called "Ode to Anactoria."[7]

This concentration of the art of the sublime on small bits of text follows from the way in which it differs from the art of rhetoric. Skill in invention (εὑρέσεως) and in disposition of

[5] VII, 2.

[6] *Op. cit.*, pp. 380–381.

[7] At the other extreme there is an instance of the sublime which consists in silence: Ajax, called up from Hades (Book XI of the *Odyssey*), is still incensed at the award of Achilles' arms to Odysseus and will not talk.

subject matter (τὴν τῶν πραγμάτων τάξιν καὶ οἰκονομίαν) are excellences which emerge from the whole fabric of the composition, while the sublime is like a flash of lightning (δίκην σκηπτοῦ) which shows the power of the speaker in an immediate and concentrated form (τὴν τοῦ ῥήτορος εὐθὺς ἀθρόαν . . . δύναμιν).[8] Nevertheless, one can see in the terms of Longinus vestiges of the traditional schematism. Rhetoric is often analyzed by classical theorists into a series of operations, beginning with invention, going on to elocution or expression, and ending in action or delivery. Additions may be made to the chain, as when arrangement is inserted after invention and memorization after elocution.[9] Each operation affects the next in the series, so that what is invented sets the standard for diction and both of those (since the process is cumulative) the standard for delivery. In the literary application of these notions, the third stage fades out, leaving two actions, invention and expression, and two correlative products, *res* and *verba*.

These pairs lead one to the center of the treatise—and to that of *L'Art poétique*, as well. Before their meanings are specified, they serve to relate the two documents, but as they take on characteristic values in each theory, they make it possible for us to distinguish the one from the other. They give us by turns a bridge and a key. For example, Longinus enumerates as follows the factors in which sublimity may reside: conception (νόησις), feeling (πάθος), figures (σχήματα), diction or expression (φράσις), and arrangement (σύνθεσις).[10] This list suggests several comments. There is first a notable variety and distinctness (if not originality) in the lexicon proposed by Longinus. There is a progression, if one thinks of a series of operations, from conception through arrangement. There is an emphasis on the soul of the poet, and of a particular poet: the origins of sublime thought and passion are found not in literary commonplaces but in the special ideas and vibrations of great souls. There is a definite break between the first two and the last three factors; Longinus be-

[8] I, 4.
[9] Cf., for example, Cicero, *De oratore*, I, xxxi, 142, and II, xix, 79.
[10] VIII, 1.

lieves that thought and passion are in great part native dispositions (αὐθιγενεῖς συστάσεις), while the others depend on art (διὰ τέχνης). This is a particularly plain indication of the value assumed by the couple *res-verba* in the thought of Longinus.

Now, if there are five aspects or elements of the sublime, is there a principle that holds them together? (The reason for the question will be better seen when we look at the position of Boileau, because it is with *L'Art poétique* in mind that one feels bound to ask it.) I mentioned earlier that one sees through the five terms chosen by Longinus a unified process stretching from conception through synthesis. But this unity is not stressed, nor does he use, other than in a general way, the classic argument for appropriateness in the fitting of style and language to content, that is, on a unity binding together the "natural" and the "artistic" sources of the sublime. Longinus seems, in fact, to prefer to leave the five sources distinct and to deal with them separately. Each of them, as an aspect of a fragment of discourse, is treated so as to bring out its effectiveness in causing the experience of the sublime. The different aspects are not made to determine or imply one another in any rigorous way. They are presented more as different means to the same end than as parts of a whole. Longinus reasons mainly, therefore, from unity of effect, not from unity of composition.

There are, without any doubt, general similarities between *L'Art poétique* and *Peri hupsous*. Boileau, like Longinus, is writing of discourse and its excellences. For him as for his predecessor the basic image is that of language passing between an author and a reader or spectator, of artistically contrived speech that is subject to the creative genius and discipline of the one and related to the character and taste of the other. A close look reveals interesting differences on both points, however. Artistic language, in Boileau's view, is offered to the reader for his pleasure; *plaire* is the great aim. It is easy to take this word too lightly and to interpret it too simply. Its meaning has depth and complexity: to impress, move, and enlighten a judicious observer who expects the poet to show in his work a knowledge of nature and a command of art. The reader or spectator is not, as in the theory of Longinus, drawn out of himself into communion with a great soul; he tends rather to be a connoisseur who tries out the work which has been made for him, who submits himself to it and then judges it. Of this there will be more to say in a later section. The important thing, for the moment, is the nature of the object or speech rather than its destination.

We know from his opening lines that Boileau's poem is about *la hauteur de l'art des vers*. His general subject matter is poetry, as opposed to prose, expression in verse (with what that implies of characteristic content) as opposed to usual and unadorned speech. As we saw, it is a matter of indifference to Longinus whether his examples occur in verse or in prose. His thinking starts from a distinction of the nonsublime from the sublime, that is, from an excellence due to the art of rhetoric on the one hand and on the other that supreme excellence due to the conditions which Longinus is trying to formulate. Boileau's unmistakable concentration on *l'art des vers* has one immediate consequence. Works of history, philosophy, and oratory become irrelevant to his poetics. The allusions to Herodotus, Plato, and Demosthenes and the quotations from them, which are appropriate in Longinus, have no place here. The very fact that Boileau writes his art in verse makes it difficult—though not impossible—for him to introduce verbatim texts from his models and victims.[11] Hence Boileau tends to be abstract and judicial where Longinus is concrete and demonstrative. Each method has its advantages.

A characteristic thing for Boileau to do—and one that is not at all so for Longinus—is to concern himself not only with passages of works but also with whole works, taken as representatives of a genre. This balance is clearly reflected in the structure of *L'Art poétique*. Chant I contains general advice about poetic qualities and textures, without reference to generic traits. Boileau seems to address himself here to a poet who will soon be writing *lines* and *groups of lines*. Such a concern is superficially like that of Longinus, but the expres-

[11] *L'Art poétique*, III, 272 and 277 ff. (in vol. II of the Boudhors edition).

sion of particular thoughts is only half of the story for Boileau. Chants II and III advise the poet on what he must do if his poem is to be an elegy or a sonnet or a tragedy or a comedy. This consciousness of poetic natures—whose specific determinations must be added to underlying general requirements if works rather than passages are to be written—is absolutely fundamental in Boileau. It gives his poetic art a dimension that is explicitly ruled out by Longinus.

In conformity with his original insight, Boileau treats poetry as discourse, i.e., as expressed thought, whether the topic of the moment happens to be fragments or whole works. In the statements and imperatives of Chant I the working of the familiar rhetorical pair, *res* and *verba*, is seen. Several different whats and hows of expression are described, and beauties or defects are assigned to them.[12] Now and again the two basic notions are related to each other, and a new set of good or bad qualities appear which result from good or bad matching of content and expression.[13] When the subject is genres, as in Chants II and III, the treatment is very similar. The same possibilities of analysis are exemplified, the difference being that the reference of the terms is not to passages or lines but to wholes. For example, the subject matter of an elegy is fixed and predictable, and there is a kind of style suitable to that matter. Sometimes Boileau's procedure leads to a balance in which both aspects are qualified about equally; at other times, and especially when he takes up the

---

[12] Sometimes, as in lines 40, 147, 151, and 204, the subject is *pensée, idée, sens;* sometimes the specific object of thought is indicated, as in lines 15–18, where we see *amoureuse flamme, exploits, Philis, bergers, bois,* or as in line 51, *palais.* On the side of expression, distinctions of style such as the following are made: *trop égal, uniforme* (71), *grave, doux, plaisant, sévère* (all in 76), *noble* (80). Examples of the treatment of versification and rhyme, two other subheadings of expression, are found in lines 104 ff. and lines 27 ff. The history of the *Parnasse françois* given in lines 113–140 is written largely in stylistic and technical terms. So is the description of the corrections made by the *sage ami* of lines 199–207 in poetry submitted to him for judgment.

[13] As in the joinings of *bon sens* and *rime* (27 ff.), of *sens* and *hémistiche* (106), of *idée* and *expression* (150–154).

larger types—tragedy, epic, and comedy—the *res* get more attention.[14]

It must now be clear that this use of the traditional pair of terms differs markedly from that of Longinus. It lacks the technical precision of an analysis based on five sources of sublimity, with two of them, thought and passion, divided from the other three, figures, diction, and σύνθεσις. In Longinus, thought and passion are events in a great soul; in Boileau, the tendency is to see this side of composition much less subjectively as the traditional or natural subjects of poetic literature. Longinus has long and rather complicated developments on figures of thought and language; Boileau treats such topics in a much more general and easily accessible way.

Enough has been said to suggest how Boileau understands the notion of artistic unity and where he looks for it. It is what you have when you have adjusted perfectly the two essential aspects of your work to each other. The emphasis tends to fall on the content term as the decisive one; it is the business of style to form itself on thought. Or, as the second possibility, unity appears in the poetic matter. It becomes a characteristic of content to be a whole of congruent parts such as character, action, and emotion;[15] and the unity of

---

[14] In Chant II note especially the descriptions of the *idylle* (style: 1–30; subject matter, 30–37), the ode (subject matter, *passim;* style and technique, 71–81), the elegy (emphasis on subject matter) and the sonnet (emphasis on technique). In Chant III Boileau refers to the *douleurs d'Oedipe* and to the *alarmes d'Oreste parricide* at the beginning of the section on tragedy, which moves from this opening explicitly concerned with the imitated object through such topics as the exposition of the *sujet,* the unity and probability of the action, the place of love, and consistency in characterization. Style appears most clearly in the development which follows the verse, "Chaque passion parle un différent langage" (133–144). For comedy, see, of course, lines 359–390, which abound in examples of *what* the comic writer studies and represents, and lines 405–428 for the noble *badinage* that should be his ideal of expression. In the case of epic, lines 160–286 speak almost exclusively of matter and lines 287–312 of technique; the remaining section (313–334), with its scornful allusions to Desmarets, combines the two topics.

[15] Such is, I believe, the underlying meaning of the insistence on

this dominant part is the source of unity in expression. The regulation of style by substance makes it possible, incidentally, for Boileau to play down all except the more obvious technicalities of poetic discourse, to concentrate instead on things like character and action which are in the area of common experience, and yet to neglect nothing essential, since technique follows from something that *is* discussed.[16]

Longinus proceeds differently. He deals seriatim with the aspects or sources of the sublime, and his manner of exposition is a sign of the fact that each source is a single and separate means to a single end. (There may, of course, be cooperation among them.) No item of the exhaustive list of topics is allowed to overshadow the others. The consequence is that the three factors of style have their turn; they are treated at considerable length and with technical exactness.

In a discussion of the *subject matter* treated in these two examples of criticism, it is advantageous to speak first of Longinus and then of Boileau, for that amounts, in a sense, to a movement from the simple to the complex. For the same reason, in a discussion of their decisive *principles* or *assumptions*, it seems better to consider them in the reverse order. There we go from elevated speech belonging to a single genre to poetic discourse subject to significant differentiation into species. Here we move from a position based on the adjustment of the work to the audience (Boileau) to a position based on the adjustment of those two terms to a third: the author (Longinus).

---

the three unities (45–46) and on smoothness of development (55–56):

> "Que le trouble, toujours croissant de scène en scène
> A son comble arrivé se débrouille sans peine."

The limits set on characterization and the use of love contribute to this unity of what is imitated in tragedy.

[16] The vagueness of Boileau's remarks about *figures,* is notable (Chant III, 287–294). They seem to stem from a recollection of Longinus. He recommends the use of figures as a source of lightness and vividness in the epic, adding, "Et je hais un sublime ennuyeux et pesant." But there is no hint of the divisions and subdivisions that Longinus brings into his treatment of the subject.

In many ways, direct and indirect, Boileau shows in *L'Art poétique* that for him the value of a poetic work is determined by the reader or spectator. Not by *le premier venu*, of course, but the principle still holds. Here are four sets of circumstances in which this evaluative scheme is embodied. (1) The *je* who speaks in the poem clearly does so not as a poet to another poet but as a judge to someone who is trying to please him.[17] (2) Poetry comes also before a collective judge: there is a liberal sprinkling of references to *lecteurs, acheteurs, public, cour*. They are always presented as arbiters. This is not to say that Boileau establishes a blank tyranny of the audience, for he can make distinctions in it. *Burlesque* is relegated to the public of the Pont-Neuf and the provinces; and Molière made the mistake of being *trop ami du peuple*. Sometimes the court is wrong, as in this very matter of the *burlesque*, where it underwent a change of heart: "Mais de ce style enfin la cour désabusée . . ."[18] Note, however, that while the court did enjoy it, *burlesque* was provided on a large scale.[19] (3) In the third place there is the often-mentioned scene where the poet tries out his work on a friend-critic whose word is law—even to the point of textual cuts, corrections, and improvements. This may be thought of, I suppose, as a test in miniature before the work is submitted to the generality of readers and spectators. And, just as the general public is subject to corruption of taste, so this friend-critic has to be watched. A long passage at the end of Chant I[20] praises the true *amis prompts à vous censurer* but goes on to make a distinction between them and flatterers. There are other variations on the theme: some stubborn poets won't listen to reason in these little tryouts; or a *sot* may find *un plus sot qui l'admire*. (4) In the fourth place, and this is scarcely more than carrying the preceding point to its limit, the figure of Louis XIV looms as the perfect judge and pa-

---

[17] See Chant I, 49–57 and 155–160; Chant II, 45–48; Chant III, 26, 29–37, and 290–294; Chant IV, 231–236.

[18] Chant I, 91.

[19] See Chant I, 69–79; Chant II, 105–110 and 176–178; Chant III, 5–14, 21–24, 145–150, 219–226, and 321–324.

[20] Lines 183–232.

tron. Artistic merit need not fear poverty or neglect in his century:

> Et que craindre en ce siècle, où toujours les beaux-arts
> D'un astre favorable éprouvent les regards,
> Où d'un prince éclairé la sage prévoyance
> Fait partout au mérite ignorer l'indigence?[21]

But we have merely pointed to the place where we must look for the decisive principles in Boileau's aesthetic theory. I use "aesthetic" in the strict sense; for, although Boileau is writing an *art poétique*, i.e., a set of factive rules, his theory depends on a psychology of art, on a notion of the way in which art impinges on the receptive powers of man. The process is most clearly indicated, perhaps, in the treatment of tragedy, which is addressed to *les yeux, l'oreille, le coeur,* and, above all, *l'esprit*. Such a poem makes its special appeals to these powers, through spectacle and language to the eye and ear, through the objects represented to the heart and mind. Each activation that results has a positive or negative exponent. The senses are agreeably stimulated or are offended; the heart responds to the affective power of the work or testifies to its *froideur;* the mind relishes its intelligibility or is embarrassed by its obscurity and confusion. When these reactions have occurred and have been noted, the critical act is over, assuming, of course, that the judge is not a person lacking in knowledge and taste. For Boileau is not saying merely that what pleases is good, but that what pleases is good and we know from precept, example, and experience that so-and-so is what pleases. It is, then, in the play of powers of sensing, feeling, and knowing that one finds the source of critical praise or blame. There is the final justification for what Boileau has to say to poets. He has put together a body of advice, loosely organized as to details though clear in outline, about ways and means to aesthetic effects.

But the poet himself is not emphasized, and this is what separates him from Longinus. The powers and acts that are clearly defined for the spectator or reader are not transferred

[21] Chant IV, 189–192.

with notable precision to the poet. We are told, it is true, that "Pour me tirer des pleurs, il faut que vous pleuriez," and we also read, "Ayez pour la cadence une oreille sévère," and

> Aimez donc la raison: que toujours vos écrits
> Empruntent d'elle seule et leur lustre et leur prix.[22]

These are obvious references to the senses, the heart, and the mind of the poet. And yet the idea of a poetic state that is first in the poet and then in the audience, the idea of a communication that becomes a communion, is lacking. Boileau regularly tends, therefore, to fix his attention on proximate rather than on ultimate causes of artistic effects, i.e., on the right choices of means rather than on original experiences of poets.

As one reads *On the Sublime* with the characterization of the audience in mind, one is struck by two points. The first is that whereas Boileau thinks of the buying, reading, and theatregoing public as French (not Italian or Spanish) or, more accurately than that, as the court and Paris, or in a real pinch as the most sensible part of *la cour et la ville*, Longinus thinks in much more general terms: his readers and audiences are defined as people of experience and judgment in literature or as people of all habits, lives, ages, and dates. In the second place, although Boileau is certainly aware of the charms of literature, he sees audiences as independent, even aggressively so; whereas Longinus insists on the helplessness of the audience in the presence of the sublime; it is carried along by the thought, emotion, and style of the author. For him, as a consequence, the reaction provoked by art is a *sign* of excellence, but not the *criterion* of it. And so his discussion leads one away from the audience to literary genius, and to questions of its nature and culture. It is there that one must look for the decisive principles of his position.

The literary gift of which Longinus speaks is not simply the basis of poetry, since orators, historians, and philosophers may have it. It is definable according to three aspects: thought, passion, and expression, each of which has a special

[22] Chant I, 37–38.

quality. First there must be thought, of a weighty and elevated kind (τὸ περὶ τὰς νοήσεις ἁδρεπήβολον); and this is
the most important (κράτιστον) of the sources of the sublime.
Then there must be emotion that is vehement and inspired
(σφοδρὸν καὶ ἐνθουσιαστικὸν). To these innate dispositions
must be added the discipline of art, whose products, in turn,
are the other sources of the sublime in the special turn of the
figures (ἥ τε ποιὰ τῶν σχημάτων πλάσις), in nobility of expression (ἡ γενναία φράσις), and in the appropriate synthesis
of all these (ἡ ἐν ἀξιώματι καὶ διάρσει σύνθεσις). Finally,
underlying both artistic and natural sources is the *sine qua
non* of a power of expression (προϋποκειμένης, ὥσπερ
ἐδάφους τινὸς κοινοῦ, ταῖς πέντε ταύταις ἰδέαις τῆς ἐν τῷ
λέγειν δυνάμεως, ἧς ὅλως χωρὶς οὐδέν). It is, therefore, in
these extraordinary natural and acquired qualities of persons
that we find at last the origins of the sublime.[23]

One's most striking impression on looking back to *L'Art
poétique* is of contrasts. There is the obvious difference in the
degree of technicality, which is nowhere more noticeable,
perhaps, than in an examination of the two critics' respective
principles. Longinus writes in an epistolary framework, but
his work is a treatise, with full awareness of method and concern for proof. There is the difference of emphasis: where
Boileau tends to reason from the work and the audience,
Longinus tends to reason from those and the writer. It must
be recognized, of course, that *L'Art poétique* is what it is
because of a particular conception of the poet's nature and
of the art engrafted there. Nevertheless, since the center of
Boileau's position lies in the audience, which is the judge of
poets and poetry, his psychological distinctions and qualities
tend to reflect the characteristics of that group. The urbane

---

[23] All of the quoted phrases are from Ch. VIII, 1. One of the
qualities, thought, is analyzed further. Acts of thought require objects; sublime thoughts are those which are directed to the superior,
the great, and the beautiful in the universe. These objects may be
attained by direct contemplation, by imitation of elevated models
and examples, and by imagination (cf. Chs. X and XXXV). The
cause of the opposite of sublimity, Longinus tells us at the end of
his inquiry, is precisely moral vice, which focuses the soul's eye on
lower objects, such as money, praise, and pleasure.

people he has in mind are certainly not average, but neither are they geniuses. And so, when notions of sense and heart and reason that are basically said of the audience are also predicated of writers, the result is a movement toward a common denominator. Longinus starts, on the other hand, with a natural disparity in favor of the writer; and it is the characteristic effect of the passages he has in mind to bring the reader or listener to some otherwise inaccessible plane. This original superiority does something to the usual rhetorical opportunities of content and style. They become attached to particular souls; they take on the ring of magnanimity; and through them as transformed we experience for a moment what the genius sees and feels.

The conclusion of the preceding analyses must be, it seems to me, that although *Peri hupsous* and *L'Art poétique* do belong to the same family of critical positions, the differences become more and more marked as one seeks to achieve an adequate grasp of each one. In neither case do the literary issues lead back to principles or theories that could be called philosophical: the nature of the questions asked is such that we are not aware of world views to which the two discussions belong either as integral parts or as methodically isolated parts. Instead both Longinus and Boileau evidently take theorizing to be interesting because of practice, and practice, in turn, means literary art more than anything else. Within this range they both think that to say something true or intelligible about literature is to exhibit its working on someone, to distinguish and then to connect the artistic and human factors involved in that working. Both see critical reasoning, therefore, as a movement back or forth along a series of causes and effects. And, finally, both start with language or discourse and its characteristics.

There the variations begin. The particular aspect of discourse which is uppermost for Longinus is its function as a means of exalted expression and communication; for Boileau that aspect is its function as a means of producing a powerful effect. The instances of communication in which Longinus is interested may be found in any kind of discourse; the effects

which are Boileau's concern arise from poetic discourse.
What is written about or versified is, for Boileau, any matter
or thought suitable for expression in a traditionally determined poetic genre; for Longinus it is the special thought
and emotion that radiate from a great soul. The particular
language of poetry, according to Boileau, follows for the most
part thought or matter; given that, style is determined as a
consequence, and there is little occasion for complicated theorizing about technique. For Longinus language is finally referred to conception and passion; but he finds it proper,
nevertheless, to include a great deal of stylistic analysis. As
I have suggested, both are making statements about sequences of causes and effects, and at significant moments
both follow these sequences into the experiences of a reader
or an audience. The differences are clear if one looks at the
results in the two cases. For Boileau the reaction of the audience ends in a verdict and a distribution of praise or blame.
For Longinus the reaction carries, certainly, an implied judgment, but its essence lies in the peculiar psychic mode of
ἔκστασις. The response is for Boileau the real first principle
of artistic theory; for Longinus it is a sign of the first principle,
i.e., of a great poetic nature.

Antithetical statements of this kind inevitably oversimplify
and prejudice things, even when they are designed to particularize and when they seek neutrality by means of terms
such as *subject matter* and *principle*. If, as I believe, they
point to realities in the texts, we are faced with the second
of our original pair of questions: What is *in fact* (rather than
in theory) the probable relation of the one to the other? It
seems plain that we must rule out large-scale influence of *On
the Sublime* on *L'Art poétique,* influence in the sense that
Boileau's manner of treatment, topics, and vocabulary are
what they are because of Longinus. Beyond a certain point
it is impossible to make Boileau say what Longinus said, or,
as an academic exercise, to translate Boileau into Longinus.
In order to state a plausible relationship between the texts,
must we not imagine Boileau's work in the process of becoming, in a middle stage of elaboration, in a phase situated between the moment at which the similarities to Longinus ob-

scure the differences and the moment at which *L'Art poétique* is finished and therefore nearly incommensurable with *Peri hupsous?* At such a stage contacts are still possible; parts of one theory can give a special twist or added momentum to related parts of the other.[24]

In concrete terms this means that the position of Longinus probably had two main effects on the position of Boileau, one on his idea of the audience, the other on his idea of literary excellence. For social and financial reasons the decisive role of the audience was a fact in the artistic life of the century, and that role was perfectly consistent with the principles of the dominant critical theory, which had its origins in a rhetorical, audience-centered tradition. What is distinctive in *L'Art poétique* is a new precision in the vocabulary that describes patrons of literature and a new intensity in the experience that they undergo. The rapture of the sublime, as described by Longinus, may well have had its part in this unusual force and exactness. And in the second place, Boileau came, as his predecessor had come, to the idea of an extraordinarily high degree of literary excellence, something far beyond the usual *beautés,* something that could be a cause adequate to the effect. But these transmitted nuances are assumed by the characteristic language of *L'Art poétique*—which is more Horatian than Longinian—and their implications are shown in Boileau's own way. For him reading or hearing poetry may be, indeed, an occasion for transport, but it is certainly an occasion for judgment, and the quality that he provides for is more the sustained perfection of an elegy or a tragedy than the lightning stroke of the sublime. This state of affairs is not necessarily to be regretted. It is not an invitation to polished mediocrity. Boileau knows quite well the value of the brilliant flash; in fact, what he often seems to be doing is to urge that poets take this supreme but momentary perfection as their constant aim, so that it may permeate whole works as well as fragments.

[24] This way of speaking has the defect of proposing to the imagination movements and collisions in space of impermeable atoms of thought. But what concerns us is an intellectual process, and therefore something immaterial and personal.

INDEX OF PERSONS

ANCHOR BOOKS

ANCHOR BOOKS

BIOGRAPHY, AUTOBIOGRAPHY AND LETTERS

LINGUISTICS AND LANGUAGE